THE WARSAW SPARKS

SINGULAR LIVES

The Iowa Series in North American Autobiography

Albert E. Stone, Series Editor

THE
WARSAW
SPARKS

G A R Y   G I L D N E R

UNIVERSITY OF IOWA PRESS

IOWA CITY

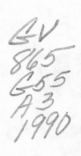

University of Iowa Press, Iowa City 52242
Copyright © 1990 by the University of Iowa
All rights reserved
Printed in the United States of America
First edition, 1990

Design by Richard Hendel

Printed on acid-free paper

Parts of this book first appeared in the *Georgia Review, Grand
Street, New Letters, Poetry, River Styx,* and *This Sporting Life.*

Library of Congress Cataloging-in-Publication Data

Gildner, Gary.
   The Warsaw Sparks/by Gary Gildner.—1st ed.
      p.   cm.—(Singular lives)
   ISBN 0-87745-270-9 (alk. paper), ISBN 0-87745-276-8 (pbk.:
alk. paper)
      1. Gildner, Gary.   2. Baseball—United States—Coaches—
Biography.   3. Authors—United States—Biography.   4. Warsaw
Sparks (Baseball team).   5. Poland—Social conditions—
1980–   .   I. Title.   II. Series.
   GV865.G55A3   1990   89-20381
   796.357'092—dc20   CIP
   [B]

This book is for

Dariusz Łuszczyna and the team

CONTENTS

INTRODUCTION

By Albert E. Stone

Gary Gildner's *The Warsaw Sparks*, the third volume in Singular Lives: The Iowa Series in North American Autobiography, fits but also evades many assumptions readers may bring to it when they learn that the title refers to a baseball team assembled in Warsaw, Poland, only two or three scant years ago and coached by the American author. We speedily learn that Gildner's Poland, an unlikely spot for the male myth of America's national sport to be reenacted, resembles only slightly the fantasy state of Iowa in W. P. Kinsella's *Field of Dreams*. To be sure, autobiographies and memoirs often share stylistic and imaginative features with fiction and the fairy tale, and when we learn that Gildner is a poet and short story writer as well as a Fulbright lecturer and passionate amateur baseball player we should be prepared for strong elements of dream and desire to be mixed into this personal history. We are not disappointed. But neither should we be surprised to read, toward the close of this zany, touching, and very personal memoir of fourteen months behind the Iron Curtain, that Gildner cannot end his story with the third-out catch by the Sparks' outfielder. This feat, producing only a routine win in Flint, Michigan, was a rare moment of team success in Chełmża, Poland. "In many ways that's where the story should end. With nineteen Polish baseball players and their founder, plus two specialists for special efforts, waiting for a dramatic catch, a catch unlike any other, involving earth and heaven. And if I were writing a piece of fiction that's where it would end."

But *The Warsaw Sparks* is neither baseball novel nor travel narrative. Though borrowing subject matter and metaphors from each, Gildner has written a bona fide memoir. The true center of these adventures of Polish (and Cuban) men learning the sport and mythos of America, their land of dreams in which Stan Musial is king, is Gildner himself. The former coach is more than chronicler of one of the stranger "seasons in the sun" on record. It is his sharp eye and pen reporting the often gritty details of life in this cheerless, courageous country whose present political drama is necessarily in the reader's mind. It is his sense of humor which matches the Poles' sense of irony as they quip and shrug their way through days and nights of collective monotony and frustration. It is his sense of the past interfusing the present which, again, brings his midwestern childhood memories to match the Poles' wryly proud historical consciousness. And, finally, these are Gildner's words in prose and verse which create a picture of himself (and his lover, Vicki, and his daughter and grandson) living an outwardly Polish life while inwardly aware always of his own complexity as poet, aficionado, teacher, athlete, coach, drinking comrade, parent, and lover.

This double focus upon the self in its worlds of past and present is a prime—many would argue *the* crucial—characteristic of autobiographical narrative. Gildner's title as well as his alternations of description and reflection testify to these dual concerns. Warsaw Sparks is not simply the name of the ragtag team of endearing klutzes Gildner coaches. Sparks igniting in Warsaw also signify the flashes of reminiscence which bring his Michigan boyhood repeatedly into present consciousness. This layering of past memory and present observation occurs in both the prose narrative and the poems which, far from mere imaginative window dressing, dot the story and compress its passing moments into permanent emotions. The title of one late poem provides a clue to the central theme of these icons of remembered feeling: "Primarily We Miss Ourselves as Children." A key to Gildner's personal history here re-created as baseball story is Grandfather Szostak. One of many touching images celebrating his beloved dead ancestor arises in the final lines about a summer day on the Michigan farm:

> In the honeyed glow of a kerosene lamp on the table
> he opened his book and we all moved away.

He lay his face on the water.
In the last light he entered the water.

Vivid prose fusions of past and present also nicely delineate the American self moving at the center of this odd foreign experience. A typically undramatic yet freighted moment occurs as Gildner walks toward the stadium in Warsaw following a successful road trip to Silesia.

And getting from Skra's main entrance to the rugby field was easy: the field lay in a far corner, maybe fifty yards from the teeming plaza, and a path beside the plaza, through a cluster of trees, let you avoid the bazaar altogether. On the way to the field I stopped beside a hemlock and unzipped my pants. Peeing, watching skis and bikes and other bright toys bob on backs among the crowd, I suddenly felt very lucky—not just about the game but about everything. About Vicki, living in Warsaw, my daughter and grandson's visit in three days, the new poems I was working on, the Sparks, Anna Mydlarska in Gdańsk (who had become my translator and introduced Vicki and me to Wałęsa), Anna's husband Jacek— a wonderful guy and fine painter—both of them our friends now, the readings around Poland I'd given, the students I'd met, my mornings free to work in a sunny room overlooking a garden, throwing and hitting baseballs every afternoon, curling up with Vicki every night. . . .

Though the sunny upbeat mood of the moment isn't entirely representative, its recaptured mixture of social observation, historical record, and private detail is characteristically counterpointed by reiterated references to games. These connect the skis and bikes in the Polish bazaar to the Sparks' baseballs and then, in the next lines, to recollections of high school athletic achievements which may or may not have happened. The trope by which everyday life is lightened if not redeemed by games may be more readily accepted by male than by female readers. Both, however, will be moved and instructed, I suspect, by Gildner's arresting descriptions of the confrontation between the Polish students and the

Milicja at Father Popiełuszko's grave, his interview with Wałęsa, and the evocation of the beautiful medieval city of Kraków showered and defaced by industrial fallout.

American baseball is thus the medium but not the message of Gildner's unusual memoir. As baseball autobiography, this story stands at an ironic distance from Ty Cobb's or Jim Bouton's memoirs of life in the big leagues. As an imaginative tale of dreams and dreary reality, *The Warsaw Sparks* shares more features with Bernard Malamud's *The Natural*, Kinsella's *Field of Dreams*, or John Krich's recent (and nonfictional) *El beisbol*. What makes this a singular life story is Gary Gildner's adroit and convincing fusion of prose and poetry to recapture a midwestern ethnic boyhood and a present-day experience of Poland seen with clarity and compassion through the lacings of a baseball glove.

THE WARSAW SPARKS

1

We were ten Juniors, sixteen Seniors, the organizer, his assistant, and me, the coach. We were one American, two Cubans, and twenty-six Poles and on a rainy, gloomy Saturday in late May, high on two victories in a row and our first road trip, we set out by bus from Warsaw for the coal mining town of Rybnik to play baseball the next day—a Juniors game at ten a.m. and the big one, against a tough, experienced team, at noon. It was 350 kilometers to Rybnik, a scheduled seven-hour trip, counting the stop for supper on the way. Dariusz, the organizer, said we should be in our hotel, in bed, by ten-thirty. "Then sleep," he said. "Then Sunday, half-past seven, sharp, stand up! Then clean, eat, bus to game, play, win. No problem." At ten-thirty on Saturday night, however, we were waiting in a dark parking lot somewhere in dark Rybnik—road-weary, sleepy, and hungry—while Dariusz went to ask the manager of a night club if he would feed us. It was our last chance for supper after eight hours on the road, and it was still raining.

The restaurant that Dariusz planned for us had been inexplicably closed. The next one we stopped at, which he went into alone, to scout, was "no good," he announced to the team. To me he said, "Very big prices, very nothing amounts. Also," he added, "horse meat only." Then we took some wrong turns. In Częstochowa, about three-quarters of the way to Rybnik, we asked a pedestrian how to get to Katowice. In soot-colored Katowice, in the heart of the coal country, we asked three pedestrians for help. "No proper signs!" Dariusz would wail. Finally we got straightened out and it was decided to push on to Rybnik—which we should reach by nine, an hour before the restaurants in Poland closed—and eat there. We arrived at nine-thirty. It took us fifteen minutes to find a parking place for the large touring coach and then to find, on foot, the one restaurant open to us. When we achieved the restaurant, the manager told us, "*Nie ma.*" You hear this expression a lot in Poland. Literally it means, "There is not." Depending on the situation, the time of day, and especially on the speaker's mood, it can also mean, "There never was," "There never will be," "He or she is not here," "I don't know what you're talking about, don't bother me." Here it seemed to mean no food, period. We walked back to the bus in the rain. Players began to count up the sandwiches and apples some of them had left from snacks they'd brought. In the rear of the bus, meanwhile, Jacek Koncki, a Seniors outfielder, was hurting: his right eye was weeping and refused to open. To his teammates who noticed it, he said it was nothing.

Dariusz returned to the bus and said the night club would feed us. A few players gave a little cheer; others said, "Let's see first." Mainly we were silent, tired, chilled. We followed Dariusz through narrow cobblestone streets in the rain. I wanted to win that game the next day—the Seniors game, the one that mattered—and began to imagine colds coming on, lethargy on the bases, dropped balls. I could see, as I had in games, a perfect throw from the shortstop popping out of Froggy's mitt. Froggy was our first baseman. He was nineteen. During practice, fooling around, he could "pick up" a ball off the ground with his feet and, in the same motion, "flip" it to someone nearby. A nifty little trick that was easy for him after years of playing soccer. But in *this* game, under pressure and having to use his hands, Froggy would sometimes freeze. Though he could hold his glove up to receive the thrown ball, he could not always react fast enough to close it. Despite a couple of errors per game by Froggy, however, plus half a dozen others, the Sparks' season record so far was 2–1. The previous season, their first, they lost all fourteen games they played—one game by the score of 42–5, other games, more typically, by 25–0 and 20–0 scores. I wanted to turn these guys into a real baseball team. Walking over the slick cobblestones, I made a mental note to wear the same yellow practice jersey I'd worn in the last two games, instead of the new peach-colored shirts we'd just been issued; then I had to laugh at myself. Walking along, I also flashed through a montage of street scenes from maybe half the foreign films I'd ever seen—its principal features all seemed to be right there in Rybnik: hunched-over, shadowy figures with their collars turned up, rain, a lonely lamp post giving gauzy light, nothing good around the corner. As we approached the night club, I heard Alejandro, the Seniors' sixteen-year-old center fielder from Cuba, mutter, "*Nie ma*, mon. *Nie ma*."

The night club looked, from the outside, like a small town IGA back home that had gone out of business, its plate-glass front painted an industrial green. We filed in like refugees. We piled our coats and hats on a counter, behind which a big-bosomed Polish woman with an Afro smiled as if she'd been waiting all day for us. And now here we were! She put on Mariusz Szpirowski's baseball cap that said "Chicago Bears" on the crown, and directed us—"*Proszę, proszę!*" ("Please, please!")—up a small flight of stairs into the main room. It was fairly large. A couple of dozen tables for four and six occupied the near half, a dance floor and band the far half. People were dancing. I couldn't tell how big the band was, though way back in the farthest reach, under very subdued purple light, there seemed to be at least a guitar and an organ. If the Rybnik night club had a name, I didn't catch it—or see anything written in neon; but someone on the planning committee, I thought, must have checked out some American Legion Halls and some Holiday Inns in places like North Dakota, and listened to a lot of three-piece combos play "Misty" into the wee hours.

The Sparks visibly brightened. This was a considerable leap from the restaurant that Dariusz had planned for them. There, the food would have been pretty ordinary—much like cafeteria fare—with sweetened tea to drink. And absolutely no atmosphere. Here, waiters in tuxedos brought jumbo bottles of Coke to our tables. Older players like Jake, the catcher, and July, the left-handed pitcher—both of whom were graduate students—had glasses of wine, as well. And Dariusz ordered double portions for everyone: a very good fillet of ocean perch, mashed potatoes, coleslaw. For atmosphere, we had the fox-trotting dancers to watch and tunes like "Blue Velvet" and "The Isle of Capri"—in mainly jumpy renditions—to listen to. When the band took a break and the dancers returned to their tables, we could check out the girls close up. There was one near me in a sleeveless white blouse and powder blue skirt who was blonde and rosy and could almost have been in the wedding party of a Brueghel picture but for her expression and manner, which seemed typical of many girls in the room—and typical of several young women I knew in Warsaw. She sat and smoked and alternately sipped from a glass of wine and a glass of Coke, and either seemed bored with the boy she was with or reluctant to make conversation because, well, it was his place to speak first. You might have thought she could take all this or leave it, it didn't matter one way or the other. You might have thought she had seen a lot of Greta Garbo and Marlene Dietrich movies. The boy, stocky as a middle linebacker, wore a longish crewcut and a white shirt open at the neck, and he sat, smoked, alternately sipped wine and Coke, and presented, roughly, the same expressions the girl did. When they made eye contact, it was brief—like a dash, or maybe a sentence fragment. They wore no wedding rings, but I guessed they would probably marry each other, and their nights out, when they could afford them, would be much like this one.

The table where I sat, with Dariusz, his assistant Henry, and the bus driver, was served first—we were simply closest to the kitchen—and when I finished eating I went to see how the Sparks were getting along. It was after midnight. We still had to find our hotel. Everyone was seriously into his food—everyone except Jacek Koncki. He sat with his face in his hands; he hadn't touched his plate. "What's wrong with Pizza Hut?" I asked. (I had given him that nickname because he was one of three Jaceks on the Seniors team but the only one who always wore a Pizza Hut T-shirt to practice. And he came to all the practices, a record most of his teammates could not match.)

"He got something in his eye," Pete, a pitcher, told me. Pete was one of five Seniors who spoke English, and I asked him now to translate for us.

"What's wrong, Pizza Hut?"

He shook his head.

"Let me see your eye," I said.

He took away his hands and let me look. In the night club's poor light I could only see that his right eye was closed to a wet slit and somewhat swollen. He put the heel of his palm up to rub it.

"Don't touch it," I said. To Pete I said, "He hasn't eaten a thing."

"I know. He was sick in the toilet," Pete said.

Jacek suddenly got up from the table and lay down on three chairs against the wall. He moaned something.

"He says he is dizzy," Pete said.

Dariusz joined us and he and Pete spoke in Polish. Then Dariusz said, "We must take Pizza Hut to hospital." We got directions to the hospital from the coat-check woman in the Afro—she still had on Mariusz' Chicago Bears hat, wished us luck, "*Powodzenie!*"—and then we all walked back to the bus. Henry helped Jacek along. It was still raining. On the way I asked Pete what had happened to Jacek's eye. He said he didn't know. "Maybe when we stopped to pee—in that forest—a tree branch hurt him. Maybe on the bus someone did this"—he opened his raincoat, pulled out his suspender strap, and snapped it against his chest. "Maybe," Pete said, "there was an accident. I don't know."

In the touring coach we made a couple of agonizingly slow, jockeying-back-and-forth turns, and soon we were heading out of Rybnik. Apparently one of our turns was wrong. Dariusz, nervous, stood by the door looking for a pedestrian to help us. The driver said something and Jake, behind me, gave a sad laugh.

"What now, Jake?" I said.

"This is some kind of comedy," he said.

"Explain it," I said.

"The driver says we are running out of gas."

It was one a.m. and very quiet on the bus. The driver made a difficult turn-around on a narrow, tree-lined road, almost slipping his front wheels into a ditch. I watched the windshield wiper on his side miss about six inches of glass—the six inches, by my reckoning, that lay in the most direct line between his eyes and the road. Jake said, "Only in Poland is this possible." I thought he meant the driver's wiper blade wearing out in the middle, and I said, "Oh no, in America that's where they go first, too. It's practically a law."

"What is?" Jake said.

"Wiper blade wear-out."

"Wiper blade wear-out?"

"Windshield wiper. That," I pointed. "That place not getting scraped."

"I'm not following you, Coach."

"It's not important. How's Jacek?"

"He's in the back, lying down. He's not rubbing his eye. But what is practically a law? I mean, if you don't mind telling me."

Like a good many young Poles who spoke English, Jake taught it, privately, for extra income. With me, he enjoyed practicing. Sometimes—to paraphrase Robert Frost, who said poetry is the stuff that gets lost in translation—Jake and I would get lost in translation. As the bus eased back into the center of Rybnik, I said to him, "You lived in the States. You know we make a kind of joke about things going wrong, or suddenly not working, exactly when we want them *not* to go wrong, don't you?"

"I was only a boy when I lived there," he said.

"Well, I might be telling some guy, for instance, that I ran out of gas while rushing my pregnant wife to the hospital, and he'd say, 'It never fails.'"

"Like us now with Jacek," Jake said.

"More or less," I said.

"In America, though, people don't really run out of gas," he said. "Or if they do, it's very easy to buy more. Not like here."

"Jake, you're giving me a hard time on this."

"But I really don't get it about wiper blades," he said.

"Same thing. You want them to work when it's raining—and just when it starts to rain, they fail."

"But they *are* working," he said.

From his point of view, he was right, of course. In Poland if the windshield wiper is moving back and forth and the rubber blade is scraping off water—never mind how much—everything is working. The real thing, like the poetry lost in a translation, is not missed. Or to put the matter plainly: in a country where many things do not work at all, what's a little blur in the middle?

The driver stopped and Dariusz called to a woman who was waiting at a taxi stand. He spoke very fast to her and she got on the bus. She would show us the way to the hospital. We got there quickly and dropped off Henry and Pizza Hut and the woman. Dariusz would return later, after checking us into the hotel.

We found the Hotel Pracowniczy (Workers' Hotel) without incident. Inside, however—it was now one-thirty, or six hours to wake-up—the clerk told Dariusz she had room for maybe half of us. He looked stunned, betrayed. He raised his voice at her, saying he had reservations. She was a small sparrow-like woman in her thirties wearing a plain brown housedress and holding a cigarette burning down to the filter. We were all gathered around her in the lobby with our backpacks, duffel bags, bats, batting helmets, and two sets of catcher's gear; several players also carried jumbo Cokes they'd bought as we left the night club. In a room off the lobby, a blue TV screen was showing an army in retreat: soldiers with their heads turbaned in bandages, or hobbling on makeshift crutches, made their dazed way behind groaning trucks. I could hear heavy gears working and somber violins and in the lobby I could smell a rag-smoke odor coming from the woman's burning filter. Dariusz raised his voice again.

She gazed at some keys in her hand as if the world had been unfair and flowerless for as long as she could remember, and here was one more day of it. She sighed. Finally, her shoulders sagging, she led us down a hallway as if to a place she knew nothing about. For a few crazy moments I felt that I was back home—in one of the old railroad hotels you can still find in America if you stay off the freeways and instead follow the two-lanes to towns like Osceola, Iowa, and Valentine, South Dakota, and pull up on Main Street. They are the hotels where engineers and brakemen and conductors used to stay—and some of them still do. A clerk waits behind the desk, or in the small lobby across the way, watching a fuzzy TV and chewing on a match; near him, a pretty girl with crimson lips and honey skin smiles out morning and night, month after month, from a herbicide calendar; the rooms smell of pine cleaner and used tobacco, of old shoes and linoleum and maybe a little of rye whiskey; and if the rough blanket on the bed smells of these things too, the sheets are fine, the peg on the door will hold your shirt and pants, the window opens, you can catch a whiff of new-cut hay, maybe see a piece of moon, and if you're tired enough and just want to sleep, your chances are pretty good.

The Hotel Pracowniczy had all of this except the moon, the rye whiskey, and new-cut hay, and the rooms the woman showed us were larger, big enough for five single beds and a central table and chairs. I could imagine a Polish family on vacation in there, gathered around a meal of kielbasa and bread, white cheese, and radishes, to save on a restaurant bill: the husband, wife, their two kids, and either his mother or hers—the *babcia*, the grandmother, the most visible and perhaps the most powerful family member of all in Poland, if not the most powerful force, pound for pound, in the whole country. I had seen *babcia*s on trams and autobuses, tough as drill sergeants, chewing out drunks; I had seen them take on store clerks practiced in the rude whine and the sulk, and I had seen the clerks change their tunes; I had seen these estimable women sweep down on possible disaster large and small—a bloody head on a playground, a run in a pretty girl's stocking—and take charge, repair. The *babcia*'s principal duty in life was to mind her grandchildren while the parents worked. Here was her real territory, where she gave to the young, so that it layered their bones, an understanding of discipline, order, patience, prayer, diet, custom, costume, manners, and fate they would receive nowhere and from no one else. In the five months that I had been coaching the Sparks, I sometimes saw myself as one of these old women in a rage for form.

How the sighing, flowerless hotel clerk was suddenly able to produce rooms for us was never explained to me, and I was too tired to ask. Passports and Polish I.D. cards were quickly collected. It was two o'clock Sunday morning. Dariusz led me and the bus driver up a flight of stairs to a two-bedroom suite that was several cuts above the quarters the players were given. In fact, it seemed in a different hotel. We had our own bath, a kitchen, a parlor with a color TV set (the driver turned it on at once), and each bedroom contained two beds covered with brilliantly white, ironed sheets and down comforters whose surprising softness I hadn't felt in a long time. I wondered if the clerk had these rooms ready for big Communist party dogs, perhaps even General Jaruzelski himself—the head of state—if they came barking in the night.

"Very nice," I said to Dariusz.

"Only one in complete hotel," he said.

"This *is* a workers' hotel, Dariusz?"

"Yes, yes, of course."

"Why is there a difference between here and downstairs?"

"Always a difference," he said, "even in Poland." Then—no time for dialectics—he said Henry and the driver would share one room, he and I the other. "Now, you sleep," he said. "Tomorrow, baseball." He left for the hospital and dog-tired I crawled under a worker's comforter. I thought—or maybe dreamt—back to my Grandpa Szostak's farm house in northern Michigan, where my own *babcia*, her frost-blooming breath smelling of apples, tucked me under a quilt full of the duck's most intimate feathers, in a room closer to the stars than any I have slept in since.

When I woke I didn't know where I was right away. Scotland? Montana? I had woken up in gray-lit, coal- and linoleum-smelling rooms in both of those places. Then I saw a jumbo Coke on the floor and remembered the night club, our game against the miners. In the other bed I saw July. What had happened to Dariusz? My watch said seven o'clock. Through the window the sky was the color of whale skin, but the rain had stopped. I got up, showered fast in cold water (there was no hot), and put on my uniform—the yellow stretch hose, powder blue knickers, my yellow practice jersey. Dariusz had got a Boston Red Sox uniform through the American Embassy and had taken it to a Polish tailor, instructing him to copy it thirty times—substituting "SKRA" for "BOSTON" on the shirts. The knickers turned out best. They were big and baggy—like the knickers you see in photos of Babe

Ruth and Ty Cobb—but instead of loops for a belt there was elastic around the waist. In case the elastic didn't keep the knickers up, there was a strip of nylon hem tape for a drawstring. As for the peach-colored shirts, the tailor skipped buttons and fashioned one-piece, one-size (large) pullovers. He also made large neck openings. On the more muscular Sparks this was no real problem, but on the slimmer, smaller players the shirts barely covered their collarbones and hung like pajama tops borrowed from a burly uncle. Our shoes were soccer shoes and our hats were anything we could find with a bill. Dariusz was very proud of our uniforms. "Polyester," he told me. "One hundred percent!"

The word "SKRA" across our shirt fronts signified our sponsor. The season I am writing about—1988—there were eight baseball teams in the Polish Baseball and Softball Association (Polskiego Związku Baseballu i Softballu—or PZBall) and each team was sponsored by, and named for, a local sports club. Officially, we were Robotniczny Klub Sportowy Skra Warsaw. *Robotniczny* means "workers." *Skra* means "spark." In English our team was "Spark—Workers' Sports Club of Warsaw."

"What kind of workers?" I once asked Dariusz, trying to make a connection between *robotniczny* and *skra*. Most of the other teams in Poland were sponsored by clubs whose names seemed to be associated with occupations. The team we were playing that Sunday, for example, was Klub Sportowy Górnik Boguszowice. *Górnik* means "miners" and Boguszowice is a section of Rybnik. Thus we were playing the coal miners of Boguszowice. Were they playing the electricians of Warsaw?

"Gary, you listen," Dariusz said. "Three levels in Communistic State: workers, farmers, thinkers. *Robotniczny* is workers—with hands."

"In our case, workers who put up electric wires?" I asked.

"I don't understand," he said.

"I am trying to find out if *Skra*, our name, means electricians. You know, light bulbs, zip-zip for trams," I said.

"*Skra* means *Skra*," he said. "A name, nothing more."

"Like the Tigers of Detroit? The Cubs of Chicago?"

"Yes, yes, I know. And the Mets of New York, my favorite. The very fine Dwight Gooden." At that point, Dariusz wanted to discuss the speed of Gooden's fastball, not linguistics.

After dressing I woke up July, then knocked on the other bedroom door. Jake came out. "Where are Dariusz and Henry?" I asked him. He said he didn't know. "The hotel clerk last night had no beds for me and July, so Dariusz brought us up here. He said we needed our strength today. Maybe he and Henry slept on the bus." While I waited for Jake and July to dress, Dariusz came in looking rumpled and puffy-eyed.

He shook my hand. "This bed was OK?" he said.

"Fine," I said. "Where did you and Henry sleep?"

He waved the question away. "Listen," he said, "we must talk. Quietly, you understand? You, me, Jake, July." Whenever Dariusz wanted to give me important information, he asked one of the players who spoke English to translate for him. Here—in Jake and July—he had two translators.

"I tell about Pizza Hut," he said. Then he delivered a burst of Polish to Jake. Jake said, "Dariusz wants you to understand the hospital in Rybnik is very good, the best maybe in Poland. The doctor who examined Pizza Hut is also very good—a specialist. Because of all the mining down here, the way of life, the government gives the workers good care."

"The best," said Dariusz.

"What about Pizza Hut?" I said.

"I know, I know," Dariusz said, and delivered another burst of Polish. Jake said, "Pizza Hut must not be moved for ten days, maybe two weeks. He must lie easy. It's a question of his central eye—this middle part—I don't know how it's called in English."

July said, "I don't know either. Where the light comes."

"His retina?" I said.

"Yes, that part," Jake said. "It might break loose."

Dariusz said something in Polish, looking sad.

Jake said, "Dariusz thinks we should not worry the others before the game. He says we should only tell them Pizza Hut is under observation and resting. Later we can tell them."

"Ask Dariusz how serious it is," I said.

"Yes, yes, I know," Dariusz said. "Maybe fifty percent OK, no problem. Maybe fifty percent operate." He spoke to Jake in Polish, and Jake said, "Dariusz wants you to understand Pizza Hut will have the best doctor in Poland."

"I understand," I said. Then we went down to wake up all the other Sparks for breakfast.

In the hotel dining room, which we had to ourselves, none of us was moving very fast. We moved as if our bones hadn't collected into their best arrangements yet. In their peach and powder blue outfits, the younger players looked even younger, the short, shorter. Many of the Sparks were still half asleep. At the far end of the dining room, we lined up at a low window with a counter; on the other side stood two women in white nylon smocks. You could not see their faces unless you bent down and leaned through the window—but you could see, very clearly, their amply filled bras and deep cleavages because the smocks were not much thicker than mist. It was like being served by two pairs of breasts.

One woman stood before a steaming tub full of sweetened black tea. She ladled the tea into mugs without handles and set them on the counter. The other woman gave us, in turn, a plate containing several slices of smoked ham, a bun, a square of butter, a wedge of tomato on a leaf of Bibb lettuce, and a big dill pickle. A bowl of strawberry jam, thick and juicy as stew, sat on the counter, along with extra buns and loaves of dark rye bread.

The dining room was long and narrow; tables filled it from end to end in four strict rows. Three rows were of tables for two, the last row, of tables for four. When you left the food line, you had a choice, as it were, of four other lines. In Poland the line and symbols of it are everywhere, present as the crucified Christ in all the Catholic churches, spiritless as a stone in a pile of stones. You line up for virtually everything: groceries, magazines, movies, baby clothes, toilet paper (when there *is* toilet paper), also to have your key copied, your watch fixed, or to have a look at a rare Chopin in the philatelist's shop. And close by, as a kind of antidote, there will hang a calendar or a poster featuring a woman's creamy breasts. Just waiting for you, day after day . . . as the herbicide girl waits on the American prairie. In the dining room of the Workers' Hotel that morning, sitting in our strict rows, we had the women in their nylon smocks.

Dariusz and I sat with the Cubans, Tony and Alejandro. At thirty and sixteen, they were the oldest and youngest players on the Seniors team. (Without Tony our average age was twenty.) Tony was our third baseman. He was also a Third Secretary in the Cuban Embassy and because of that, and because I was an American, the Warsaw press found in us good—and sometimes creative—copy. The illustrated sports magazine *Sportowiec*, for example, ran a story headlined "*Dyplomacja na bazie*" ("Diplomacy on the bases"). It was true, as the reporter said, that Tony, who had played the game half his life before coming to Poland two years ago, was our best performer. It was also true that the reporter and I had had this exchange:

"Why, when you are not being paid for it, are you coaching the Warsaw team?"

"Because I love baseball."

"Really?"

"Absolutely."

But it was not true that I was a former Detroit Tiger and in America earned $300 an hour coaching pitchers and hitters; that "news" probably came from Dariusz' enthusiasm. Dariusz too loved baseball. He was also a sports journalist. Since professional ethics prevented him from writing about us (though God knew he wanted to, in boldface and by the meter), he encouraged his colleagues to promote his passion. He told me that baseball was "the most intelligent game in history. You know this is so!" He felt that it should—and would!—replace soccer as the national sport. "Soccer is no grace, no *thinking*. I must write about this stupid game but you understand me, Gary, my heart has no feeling there." Dariusz was thirty-two. He had a flat-footed walk that reminded me of Charlie Chaplin in a hurry, but his round face was a small boy's delighted to his cheeks at being invited to tag along with the big guys. He was a member of the board of PZBall and a man who searched Warsaw for stars.

The first time I met Dariusz, he came knocking one January

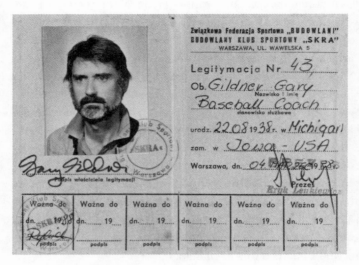

My baseball legitymacja—*or I.D.*

day on my classroom door at Warsaw University, where I was teaching a course in American literature. I was, in fact, deep into a discussion of who Ted Williams was, and what he represented to the main character of Russell Banks' novel, *Continental Drift*. I had brought to class my Detroit Tigers cap as a visual aid, and was wearing it when I answered the knock. Dariusz apologized profusely for interrupting, but he had heard at the American Embassy that I was a baseball player—and could we talk? Quickly? He had with him, to translate, a young man named Grzegorz, who was wearing, in addition to his winter coat, an old Rawlings mitt that had seen much use (and could have used, I noted, a good dose of neat's-foot oil). Caught by their visual aid, I invited them in. They said no, no, they only wanted to know if I would help the Warsaw baseball team. I said, "How? When?" They said we could discuss this tomorrow. The following afternoon they came to my apartment. Standing in the doorway, Grzegorz said, "Dariusz apologizes, but can you go with us?"

"Right now?" I said.

"Yes, if that is not inconvenient," said Grzegorz. "We are having practice tonight."

Minutes later we were pushed together on a rush-hour auto-bus, making our way across town to Gwardia gymnasium, where I would meet the Skra players at their first practice of the season. It was the middle of January, the day already dark, I could see sleet falling in the headlights of cars going past. Suddenly Dariusz began searching around in his shoulder bag, and came out with a Topps bubblegum card of Dwight Gooden. Showing it to me, he said, "Much quickness. Very great, I think, yes? We *need* this." Grzegorz said, "What Dariusz is hoping you will do for the team is make us presentable. Last year was a disaster." I'd do what I could, I said. "What position do you play?" Grzegorz asked. I had to smile. I explained to him that I'd played high school and American Legion ball and had once been scouted by the Tigers after pitching a Legion no-hitter. But that was the high-point of a short career. I developed arm trouble my last year in high school and became strictly a fan who played catch now and then. The Detroit cap in my duffel bag, I told Grzegorz, only meant that I was still crazy about the game and rooted for the Tigers.

The autobus pulled up at the Gwardia stop. As we walked in the snow to the gym, Grzegorz spoke Polish to Dariusz, and Dariusz, beaming, said to me, "You will pitch once more!" I said to Grzegorz, "Tell Dariusz I'll be very happy, and honored, to supply some coaching. But I'm forty-nine years old and I don't think I should attempt a comeback."

Grzegorz said, "A comeback?"

I said, "I'm too old to pitch."

Dariusz said, "A revelation! I am seeing much happiness. It's OK! It's OK!"

Now in Rybnik, eating breakfast with Tony and Alejandro, Dariusz looked worried. He counted the players twice. He asked Tony how he'd slept. Tony, in a sweater and warm-up jacket, said, "*Dobrze*" ("Fine"). He was a quiet, reserved, good-looking man with a mustache. Besides being our best and oldest player, he was also, at five-feet-two, our shortest . . . and the one who seemed most affected by the weather. We were most likely to see Tony at practice if the sun was shining. If it was the least bit chilly when he showed up, he wore, unless he was fielding, white cotton gloves. Dariusz then asked Alejandro how he felt, and Alejandro, already fidgeting to get going, said, *"Dobrze! Dobrze!"* Long-limbed, wiry, curly-haired Alejandro was the Sparks' talker, having played enough baseball in Cuba to know the tradition and value of chatter. When I heard him in the outfield crooning his Spanish-Polish interludes of encouragement and praise, his sputters of razz, I wished I had him in the infield, or behind the plate, to fire up his quieter teammates at close range. Out where he was, much of his song was lost on the wind. He too wanted to be closer to the action, if not everywhere at once. Often he'd suggest to me, after Froggy muffed a play at first base or a ball went through Norbert's legs at shortstop or Jake threw wild down to second, that he, Alejandro, could play first base, shortstop, catcher. "Pitch too maybe! OK?" At the beginning of practice when we warmed up our arms, he'd want me to observe his specialty, his submarine ball, which he delivered from an almost hairpin position, releasing the ball near his shoe tops. Never mind that a herky-jerky, all arms-and-legs motion (that is, a desire to fox the batter; that is, *style*) was his principal aim—which was also the case with his next specialty, the knuckler, and his next, the sinker. Never mind, he'd indicate, smiling grandly: he, Alejandro, Cuban tinker and confidence man, could pitch, *sí*, and catch (*"Fuego, amigo! Fuego!"* he'd yell from a catcher's crouch, thumping his mitt), and play anywhere else that I needed him. So far, that was center field, where he could catch any ball that was catchable, and then achieve—with speed and accuracy—home plate with his throw.

Tony and Alejandro were allowed to play on the team because PZBall had a rule that each club could take on three foreigners. The only other foreigner playing Polish baseball, as far as I knew, was a Cuban named Juan Echevarría. He was founder, coach, and first baseman of Robotniczny Klub Sportowy Stal Kutno. *Stal* means "steel" and Kutno is a town of 50,000 that makes steel; it's located 127 kilometers west of Warsaw. Echevarría, a contract worker in Poland who married a Kutno woman and decided to stay there, formed Stal Kutno in 1984. When anyone asked him about the history of Polish baseball, Dariusz would give plenty of verbal ink to Echevarría, mainly because Juan was the one who introduced him to the game. In the larger picture, Polish baseball's genealogy, Dariusz told me, went back to the old Polish game of *palant*, which went back to 1474. *Palant* had a bat (about half the size of a baseball bat), a leather ball (softer than a baseball, about twenty percent smaller), and a single base (a wooden post in the ground, placed a certain distance from where the batter stood). The batter played against a gathering of fielders. Like a tennis player serving, the batter hit the ball, then had to run to the post and back. He was "out" if a fielder either caught the ball in the air or, having fielded a grounder, hit the batter with the ball before he could get back to the starting point. According to Dariusz, *palant* was last played in Poland in 1967. "Death," he told me, "came natural in Silesia." Silesia is the coal-mining region in southern Poland where Rybnik is located; Rybnik is the town where the Polish Palant Union buried itself and then rose up as a softball team—thanks to the Czechs who taught it the rules. Klub Sportowy Silesia Rybnik became Poland's first softball team, Górnik Boguszowice became its second, and they played each other until 1982, at which time the Czechs taught them baseball. The Polish workers liked this game *bardzo, bardzo* ("very, very much"). Three more Silesian teams were quickly formed: another one in Rybnik (Kolejarz), one in Jastrzębie, and one in Rój-Zory. All five of these baseball teams were within twenty kilometers of each other. Then an outsider came in—Cyprzanów. Cyprzanów is a village of about 400 located ninety kilometers west, and a beautiful little turn south, of Rybnik. It is almost in Czechoslovakia, among rolling hills so storybook-like it seems right and proper that Cyprzanów is not even shown on the *Samochodowa Mapa Polski* (the official Polish road map). There is a church on a hill, and a red brick road winds through the village. The road leads to a creek. You cross over a bridge and come to a sheep meadow. That's where Ludowy Zespól Sportowy Cyprzanów (Folk Sports Union of Cyprzanów) plays baseball, among strict white chalk lines and clusters of sheep droppings that no one pays much attention to. Juan Echevarría's Kutno team was formed the same year as Cyprzanów's, and the next year, 1985, PZBall—with seven teams—began league play.

"Gary, you listen. I talk now about first shadows of Warsaw team." This was Dariusz' favorite part of the story, the part where he fell in love. The day he told it to me Pete was translating, but having a hard time getting *his* part in because Dariusz, using both Polish and English and snapping his fingers for words he wanted quickly, was excited all over again. The gist of the story was that in October 1985, Dariusz' paper sent him to Kutno to cover a game and interview Juan; Dariusz came home with his head full of much quickness and thinking and his heart full of passion, and he immediately began beating the capital city's bushes for baseball players. He found them mainly across the Vistula River, in the east part of Warsaw called Praga, where, if you go there, people in west Warsaw will say, you must keep your hands on your wallet and your eyes open and not stay after dark. Thieves, pimps, prostitutes, and Hungarian gypsies live in Praga, they say. Praga, they say, is working class—by which they mean that Praga has none of the cultural lights that their side of the Vistula has, like the Great Theatre, the palaces, Old Town, the university, the five-star hotels, Łazienki Park, the church where Chopin's heart is buried. Praga is also where the Russian army was camped in the summer of 1944, watching—doing nothing to help, most Poles will tell you—when the Polish home army attempted its "Uprising" against the occupying Germans and was crushed. Praga was where, in the fall of 1986, you could buy black market Russian caviar, the best, for twenty dollars a kilo, and where Dariusz found the first shadows of his baseball team.

He found Adam Ziółkowski (called "Blackie" by his teammates because of his black hair and black mustache and perhaps because of his black temper too), who declared himself the first baseman—he liked the idea that a runner could go nowhere without getting past *him*. Dariusz found Mariusz Szpirowski, a muscular high school student whose rugged good looks made him seem older, to play second base, and he found jumpy little Norbert Gajduk, also a student, to play shortstop. Norbert's right arm, of which he was justly proud, was a real baseball arm; his throws to first base or home plate were on-a-line stingers, absolute honeys to witness, and part of a problem that would come up later.

Dariusz found pitcher-infielder Piotr (Pete) Załęcki who, when tempers flared, stepped in as peace-maker. Pete too was in high school that year, and wondering where his life was going. Dariusz found outfielder Paweł Płatek, who ground lenses for glasses and who, like Alejandro, could catch anything. Where Dariusz, walking, made me think of Chaplin, curly-haired Paweł, smiling, made me think of Harpo Marx. Unlike all the other Sparks, Paweł was totally unflappable, which was why they voted him team captain. Dariusz found outfielder Grzegorz (Greg) Stabeusz, who was his translator the first time we met. Greg was a university student majoring in business; he'd spent his junior high years in New York City, hence his English and the Rawlings glove. Dariusz found catcher Cezary Komorowicz (called "Komo"), who, whenever he had to reach high or to the side to catch a baseball, would perform a somersault. He could also speak Japanese. Komo preferred to meditate to loosen up, rather than stretch or run laps. He wore wire-rimmed spectacles and looked like a humorless revolutionist, but when he went to catch or throw a baseball he seemed to want to imitate a moth above a candle flame. He was twenty-three and married when Dariusz found him, and he did not last long as a Spark. Dariusz found three more players that fall of 1986: a pitcher named Mark Gierasimowicz, 16, a big, hard-throwing kid with a pompadour of hair so blond it was almost white; a pitcher named Jacek Małecki, 19, who was dark and bony and threw very hard too, and who became our first loss; and slow, steady Pizza Hut, 17, who often appeared to be ready for a nap because of his hound-like brown eyes. All of these ten original Sparks were among the Seniors getting up now from their breakfast in Rybnik—except Greg, who was home studying for an exam; Komo, who had become an umpire and was working the game in Kutno (the strange is not so strange in Poland); Jacek Małecki, who cut some tendons in the wrist of his pitching arm by falling in a pile of junk glass; and Pizza Hut. Dariusz counted the players again as they left the dining room.

"Ten Juniors, only *fifteen* Seniors," he said to me.

"*Spokojnie*, Dariusz," I said. *Spokojnie* means "calm down" and is a word we all used often.

"OK, OK," he said. He lit one of his foul-smelling Polish cigarettes. "But you listen, Gary, I think about Jacek, about Norbert, about Paweł, and now Pizza Hut." He was counting on his fingers our injuries so far—indicating a streak of very bad luck. Jacek Małecki's injury occurred a month before the season began; most likely he was lost for the year. The day before our opener, Norbert twisted his ankle running down some steps and was lost for two games. Then Paweł twisted his ankle kicking a soccer ball around with some little kids; he missed our last game and was doubtful for today's. Now gone was Pizza Hut, a dependable reserve outfielder, whose injury troubled Dariusz the most. "I don't know how we must behave!" he said. We walked out to the bus, and he counted everyone again.

Górnik Boguszowice played its home games just outside Rybnik, about a fifteen-minute ride from our hotel. Leaving the mainly soot-colored town—the twin towers of a brick church looking more black than red, more like towers where grief's story, not joy's, rose from the worshipers' lips—leaving this town where coal and its acid odors and an ancient faith in "black gold" held the Poles in a grip there seemed to be no getting out of—not for a long time—I was surprised to see, suddenly, so much green rolling ahead. It was the morning-after-an-all-night-rain green, a green that made you feel everything was not lost, at least not for today. It was a green that said, "You are forgiven. Breathe." We passed meadows bearing bright dandelions, little orchards whose slick-limbed cherry trees grew among tall grasses. We passed a milk cow chewing her cud in belly-high timothy beside the narrow road, and farther out, man-size scarecrows made from rags and straw were guarding a field of something young, something with brave shoots. We passed houses of brick and houses of cement block (in many upper windows, pillows and blankets were piled to take the air), and we passed people walking to church on the road's shoulders in their Sunday best: willowy blonde girls under white hats, broad-hipped women in dresses printed with flowers, old men all buttoned up in dark suitcoats, *babcia*s arm in arm with each other, with a younger woman, or alone with a cane. The whale skin–colored sky was behind us and going away, going down behind distant smoke stacks. Up ahead, the sky was blue and white and the sun, just where we wanted it, was breaking through.

At a fork in the road offering two equally attractive tree-shaded lanes, Dariusz hesitated, then told the driver which one to take. After a kilometer or so, it seemed to be the wrong one. We weren't finding the crossroads that Dariusz remembered from his visit out here last year. He stood at the door looking for a pedestrian, becoming visibly more nervous. I tried to calm him down with a joke. I said to Jake, "Tell Dariusz it's very simple: next time we go anywhere we should bring along an American Indian." Jake translated this, but Dariusz remained frozen to his mission. Finally he spotted a boy on a bike. The boy straightened us out. When we got to Klub Sportowy Górnik Boguszowice and were leaving the bus, Dariusz said to me, "Gary, I promise you something—next time to Rybnik, no improvisation! No night club. I make reservation for *all* meals and complete hotel. Please, no American Indian."

He was so apologetic I felt ashamed. "I get lost a lot myself, Dariusz," I said.

"But I tell you, no more improvisation!"

"Right. Let's play baseball."

Most baseball diamonds in Poland were laid out on soccer fields, which usually resulted in a deep left field, an even deeper straight-away center field, and a short right field. Since almost all the players threw and batted right-handed and tended to hit the ball to left and center, that layout worked fairly well. (The occasional ball hit to deep right, and into the stands that were often there, was a ground-rule double.) What did not work well, however—and thank God it was dying out as the Poles came to understand baseball better—was their fussy practice of laying down canvas carpet on the pitcher's mound, at home plate, and along the base paths, to save the grass. When the field at Skra was being prepared for our first game that season, I told the Klub manager we were going to play baseball, not conduct a wedding, and I took the carpet away. The Górnik diamond did not have carpet; in fact, the base paths were dirt (or dirt and cinders—these guys were tough indeed) and the pitcher threw from a true mound. Right field was short—about 175 feet, ending in a thick stand of oak trees—but otherwise here was a real ball field. It was also very soggy from all the rain. Third base, in the worst shape, was a small pond. Tony found a shovel and, wearing his white cotton gloves, dug a hole about twelve feet away from the base—in foul territory—and then scooped out a canal leading from the pond to the hole. It was a wonderful piece of engineering: the water flowed.

The Junior Sparks did not flow. Neither did the Górnik Juniors, for that matter. They played a five-inning game (the limit for Juniors unless one team was ahead by ten runs after three innings; then a "knock down" was declared and the team behind spared further humiliation). They played a game in which two groups of adolescents slipped and rolled over in the wet grass a goodly number of times, made an occasional catch, an occasional put-out at first base, hit the ball maybe six times, walked a lot because they were small or afraid to swing the bat, struck out a lot because they were eager to swing at anything (especially when the pitch came in hat-high), and in short demonstrated that they had spent the important part of their youth bouncing soccer balls off their foreheads and feet instead of throwing and catching and hitting baseballs. The Junior Sparks were all seventeen and eighteen years old (eighteen was the cut-off for Juniors; there were no age restrictions for Seniors) and, except for one player, had never held a baseball until six months ago. (The exception was our center fielder, Paweł Tymiński, who had lived briefly in New York City.) I didn't know about the Górnik Juniors' experience, but they did not seem to possess any more skill or savvy than we did. That surprised me, in view of the fact that Boguszowice had been playing the game five years longer than Warsaw. It also surprised me that our Juniors were physically much bigger than theirs—I had expected to see size and muscle on *all* the players in Silesia. Our catcher, Mariusz ("Whale") Tumulski, a good eater who made his mother and grandmother happy over the years, was not an outrageously big kid for a Pole (six feet, 190 pounds), but he looked almost freakish next to those local boys. In any case, it was a sloppy game that Górnik won by a score of 14–12. The young

Sparks were not overly disappointed. They knew they were learning a difficult sport and found consolation in the handful of decent plays they'd made. They also knew that the next game was the one that counted.

PZBall rules declared that a Seniors pitcher could pitch only seven innings. (The limit was three for a Junior.) When I asked Dariusz why, he said, "Is necessary." He explained that prior to the rule a team would pitch—exclusively—the player who could perform that function the best. Thus few, if any, new pitchers were being developed. There was another way to look at the situation: an outstanding pitcher in the Polish league—like an outstanding pitcher in Little League in America—could win a game practically all by himself. All he had to do was throw hard and throw strikes. If he had a good curveball too, the only help he needed on the field, for most games, was a catcher. Silesia Rybnik had such a pitcher—Jan Cnota. Storybook Cyprzanów, of the sheep meadow, had a pitcher almost in Cnota's class named Janusz Rzytki. In the first year of PZBall, 1985, Silesia Rybnik won the championship, Cyprzanów finished runner-up. Silesia Rybnik successfully defended its title in 1986 and 1987. I didn't doubt that the abilities of Cnota and Rzytki did a lot to encourage the seven-inning rule—especially since games were scheduled only on Sunday, which gave a pitcher all week to rest up. We would meet these two strong arms in our sixth and seventh games, both on their turf. And in our fifth game we'd go against Juan Echevarría's steelworkers, who had faced Cnota in their season's opener and lost only 7–5, a real baseball score—a score that did not indicate a minefield full of errors and walks. Meantime—today—we had Boguszowice's coal miners, who were fighting mad, we heard, because they'd lost their first three games (to Cyprzanów, Kolejarz, and Kutno) and wanted our fancy big city hides. I hoped that the sight of July, wearing aviator shades and plugged into his Walkman when he stepped off the bus, made them see stars.

July's full name was Arkadiusz Lipiec (Arcady July), and though he was hardly a summer rustic of the Peloponnesus gazing contentedly upon fleecy sheep, he *was* the guy reclining on one elbow in the sunshine, not thinking about too much at the moment, oh maybe a little bit about his girlfriend Agnieszka, and maybe a little bit about his girlfriend Renata, and how he might discover, maybe, which one was his real love. July was twenty-four. He drove a fast royal blue Ford Sierra (bought by his engineer father in West Germany, with dollars earned in Libya), and he combed his thinning blond hair forward, like Caesar, but in almost every other way July was laid back. He was also a rare item in Polish baseball, a left-hander, and because of that and his snaky motion, he spooked the hell out of most batters. Never mind that a right-hand hitter ought to fare better against a southpaw, it was the fact that July threw from over *there*, and fast, that gave the jumpy hitters visions of their kissers crushed. That was what the Sparks who faced July in batting practice told me (reminding me of the myth I believed years before, in Midget League, that all lefties were wild and could kill you), and for that reason and because he could throw strikes but mainly because he was laid back, July was my starting pitcher. I hoped to get at least two innings out of him, then bring in our ace, high-kicking Mark Gierasimowicz, to pitch the next seven. If July—who did not have his baseball legs yet—could go three innings, all the better; then I'd still have Mark in case the game went an extra inning. In reserve, I had two more pitchers: Pete and a young bull named Adam Jaworski who, before he turned to baseball, threw the javelin for the national track team. Pete had good control but not a lot of speed. Adam had speed; frightening speed. His problem— which most of the Sparks shared—was that until he played an inning or two and could get calmed down, his beating, thumping heart was raging to escape his chest. In each of our first three games—all at home and all started by Mark—we walked at least two batters, committed at least two errors, and spotted the opposition at least three runs before we even came up to hit. Today we were up first. I hoped we could get rid of our jitters right away at the plate. But if not, I hoped that laid-back July, when we took the field, would help us be cool for a change out there. We wouldn't have Paweł's cool too, unfortunately; during our warm-up he still couldn't run full speed on that ankle.

The chief umpire was the president of PZBall, Jan Liszka. He called for the two captains (Mariusz was our acting captain in place of Paweł) and explained some rules: if one team was ahead by ten runs after five innings, the game was over; if a ball was hit into the oak trees in right field, it was a double; if a ball was hit beyond the yellow flags in left or center—and no one caught it—it was a home run; if either team had a complaint during the game, the umpire would discuss it only with the captain; if a player on the field swore, he would be ejected.

After the umpire finished his instructions, I quickly gathered the Sparks in a huddle to review our signs.

I held up my palm.

"No swing!" they said. "Take."

I pulled at my chin.

"Steal!"

I pulled at my earlobe.

"Bunt!"

I made as if to tie my shoelace—our sign for the squeeze play.

"Must bunt!"

I brushed my arms.

"Erase! Change sign!"

Then I told them the batting order. It went like this:

> Jerzy (George) Biń, rf
> Norbert Gajduk, ss
> Tony Valcarcel, 3b
> Mariusz Szpirowski, 2b
> Alejandro Tellez, cf
> Marek Sobkowicz, lf
> Adam (Blackie) Ziółkowski, dh
> —hitting for Jacek (Jake) Kalinowski, c
> Tomasz (Froggy) Małkowski, 1b
> Arkadiusz (July) Lipiec, p

Although the Sparks knew ahead of time pretty much what the line-up would be, they didn't want to know the batting order any sooner than necessary: having that knowledge to carry around would only add juice to their beating hearts. We touched hands at center-huddle, then broke away with a yell—"OK!" The Sparks lined up along first base, Górnik lined up along third (they were big fellows, unlike their Juniors), and the two opposing players closest to home plate slapped hands in greeting, followed by the next two moving up to the plate, and so on. The umpire then yelled, "*Pałka!*" ("Bat!") and we were ready to go. I trotted down to the coach's box at first base.

The Górnik pitcher, a guy with a five o'clock shadow heavy as Richard Nixon's, walked George on four pitches. He walked Norbert on five pitches, and then he lost Tony on a 3 and 2 count. We had the bases full. Mariusz, our clean-up batter, could hit the ball a kilometer, but was himself hit—in the ribs. Like many Poles who are hit by pitches, Mariusz' initial reaction was rage. He threw down the bat. But seconds later he flashed a sweet smile at the pitcher—"It's nothing, forget it"—and raced happily to first base, scoring George. Alejandro struck out, swinging from his heels for Cuba (at high pitches!). Marek, playing left field in place of Paweł, walked, forcing in Norbert. Like Pizza Hut, Marek came to practice faithfully and, like Dariusz, was passionate about this game. When he arrived at first base, he said, "Coach, I am nervous. Let me steal to calm down." I said, "Marek, the bases are loaded." He looked mortified. "I'm sorry, Coach."

Blackie came up. Blackie was on probation. In our season's opener, playing first base, he made a nice catch of a high throw from Norbert at shortstop and the batter was out. Blackie was so pleased that he thrust a triumphant fist into the air and performed a little parade in front of the happy local crowd that took him and his euphoria into short right field. Meanwhile, a runner on second base, taking advantage of Blackie's celebration, ran to third and, seeing that Blackie was still full of himself, continued on toward home. Blackie woke up just as the runner crossed the plate, and *then* he threw the ball to Jake—who all this time had been shouting for it, but Blackie heard nothing except the cheers from the stands for his wonderful catch at first. Between innings I spoke to him about this error. He hung his head and said he would make amends. When he came up to bat, he hit a triple. He stood on third base with his fist held high. From the coach's box across the diamond at first, I returned his salute. Then I signaled for him to take a lead. He could take a big one because not only was the pitcher ignoring him and winding up but the third baseman was playing a good dozen feet from the bag. Blackie could easily have taken six steps toward home. Instead, he continued to stand on the base, like a Polish prince who had just recaptured his rightful land, telling me (I could see the word issuing from his mouth, could almost hear above my own shouting its self-assured, completely-in-control tone), "Moment, moment." Blackie was at that moment a Polish prince indeed—not a factory worker, not a twenty-two-year-old guy who still lived at home with his parents and grand-mother in a two-room apartment because that was the way it was in Poland unless you had dollars, or joined the hated Milicja (the State Police) and right away got a nice apartment and a nice salary, or had some uncommon luck, which was mainly a myth. Yes, at that moment Blackie was in charge and he wanted to savor his territory, his victory, and again he thrust his fist to the heav-ens. Meantime, the pitcher delivered his pitch and the batter hit it toward the third baseman. At *that* moment Blackie decided to conquer home plate. The third baseman fielded the ball, juggled it, fired to his catcher. They got Blackie by a step. Later, when I explained that had he taken even a dinky two-step lead he'd have been safe, Blackie hung his head like a man who had miserably failed everyone, including his mother and grandmother and the great nineteenth-century national poet Adam Mickiewicz, whose fiercely patriotic verses and plays gave the people hope when Prussia, Russia, and Austria partitioned their country and for-mally it did not exist, and for whom Adam "Blackie" Ziółkowski was named.

He came to bat now against Górnik with the bases loaded. He was our designated hitter and, Lord, I wanted him to hit one. The first pitch was low, in the dirt. The second was high. "If it's in there, Blackie," I yelled, "whack it to Moscow!" He dug his soccer cleats in the mud; he swung the bat a few times to get loose; he was ready. The pitch came and bounced off his batting helmet. Blackie's fury was so great he couldn't move right away. I reached him just as he raised his fist to the sky—just as a long wailing note declaring filthy injustice left his throat. The umpire pointed to first base and I took Blackie there, telling him if he made one more noise he was on the bench.

Tony trotted in from third base with our third run. The bases were still loaded. Froggy came up and walked on four pitches, forcing in Mariusz, and the Górnik coach had had enough of Five O'Clock Shadow on the mound. The new pitcher—I did a double-take—was a southpaw. And the first batter he faced was July. Lefty against lefty, a very rare sight in Polish baseball. He got two quick strikes on July and I thought, Oh no, the spook. Then a beautiful thing happened. July smacked a sharp single to right field—the first hit of the game—and in raced Marek (who I hoped was no longer nervous) and Blackie (the fist high) with our fifth and sixth runs. And still only one out. I looked over at Dariusz who sat at a small table beyond third base (he and his counterpart from Górnik were keeping score together) and he beamed a big smile at me, as if to say, "What did I tell you? No problem!" George came up again and bounced to the shortstop, who flipped nicely to second base to force July out. Norbert fanned—on high pitches!

In Górnik's half of the first inning, the leadoff batter struck out. July looked slick as snake skin hitting Jake's target three out of four times with his sidearm fastball. I kept my pitchers off the curveball as much as possible. For one thing, they were erratic with it (only big Mark could throw it reasonably well) and for another thing, they didn't need tricks in this league. A good fastball and control, and occasionally a change-up, would win games. Thus, Jake's signs to the pitchers were mainly for fastballs, in these locations: the inside corner of the strike zone, high and low; the outside corner, high and low; and straight down the middle. July walked the next batter on four pitches. He was still basking in that first strike out. He was a good pitcher, but like Blackie, like most of his teammates, and like Stephen Crane's Henry Fleming who was shocked to see the Rebels attacking again after they'd been repulsed once, July did not quite understand yet that one little victory did not automatically assure a second little victory.

Now he was distracted because the runner had stolen second base and Norbert and Mariusz were going through a Cuban number that Tony had taught them, with pencil and paper, on our interminable bus ride the day before. In effect, Norbert and Mariusz were describing a delayed figure 8, with second base the midpoint. Just as July went into his stretch, Norbert took off for a quick circuit around the bag, then Mariusz made a circuit. The idea was to fox the runner into watching Norbert return to his shortstop position—thereby enticing him to take a big lead—at which time Mariusz would be approaching the bag and, theoretically, a throw from July. They'd have the runner dead. The only hitch in all this choreography was that the runner wasn't being foxed, and stayed close to the base. Did this discourage Norbert? No, he continued to make his half of the figure 8, leaving a big hole at shortstop just when July had to decide whether to pitch the ball or attempt a pick-off that was clearly pointless. But Norbert, like Marek who wanted to steal second when the bases were loaded, was nervous, and this was his way of calming down. Finally July threw a very wide pitch to the batter. I yelled at Norbert to forget the runner, damn it, and play shortstop. I yelled at July to throw strikes. He threw two, then the batter flied out to George in right field.

OK, two down. We might get through a first inning yet without mayhem. Górnik's clean-up hitter stepped in. He looked like Mickey Mantle—blond, boyish, good shoulders—and he got hold of July's first pitch just a little late and drove it—foul—over the stand of oak trees behind George. At least three Górnik Juniors raced to search for the ball. (The supply of game balls was a precious two—provided by the home team.) July rubbed up the new ball. I yelled at Jake, "Keep it low, inside. Make him hit it on the ground." July followed through. He jammed this big-shouldered blond perfectly, and the guy hit a routine grounder to shortstop— only it went through Norbert's legs into left field, scoring the runner from second. Norbert made his two usual mistakes on the play: he turned his head and he didn't get his glove down far enough. Since January, beginning in the Gwardia gym, I must have hit a thousand grounders to Norbert, and he almost always turned his head, taking his eye off the ball. But because he was quick, he was successful—in practice—about eighty percent of the time. And because of his superior arm, he looked spectacular when he was successful. In our first three games, however— under pressure—his success rate on grounders dropped to about fifty percent—dismal for any fielder but disastrous at a position where so many balls are hit. When I experimented with Norbert at third base and Tony at shortstop, Norbert performed even worse. And he brooded over there—never mind what I said about his arm being more useful at third—he interpreted the experiment as demotion, defeat, shame. Another Polish prince being deprived of his territory. Yes, yes, he understood about errors, about a team needing to be strong up the middle of the diamond, but *he*, his anguished eyes said, was the shortstop. He and his good arm! From Norbert's point of view, I knew, a spectacular put-out somehow erased the error or errors that preceded it. In fact, one really good play a game, or one good hit, could make the whole game worthwhile to a player, even if the final result was a loss. No one said any of this of course, but in a country where mounted cavalry had ridden out with their sabres to meet Germans with tanks, where an electrician from the shipyards of Gdańsk had stood up to the Communist party and won, briefly, a taste of freedom, no one needed to say it.

The next Górnik batter was the deposed Five O'Clock Shadow, who was still in the game, playing center field. He too hit a grounder that Norbert missed. Norbert raised his hands and face to the sky to argue with an unfair Power, instead of retrieving the ball, and while he argued (and while the ball, resting ten feet behind him in the wet grass, was being chased down by Tony, Marek, and Mariusz), the runner on first went all the way to third and Five O'Clock Shadow reached second. If I'd hit a thousand grounders to Norbert, I'd also told him fifty times that when he took a personal time out to grieve and wail, *the game was still going on*. I yelled that to him now and he pounded his glove, resolved to rise from his ashes.

Tony brought the ball to July, telling all the infielders, softly, "*Spokojnie, spokojnie*, OK?" He patted July on the back and returned to his position. I said, "Two outs, July. Forget the runners. Go after the batter." July nodded and threw a strike. "Do it again!" I said. He did. "All right, baby, one more!" I said. The Górnik batter, their shortstop, ducked from a pitch at his head. Then he ducked from another. "Easy, easy, go easy, July," I said. The batter fouled off one, and then—unbelievably—he fouled off the next five. July threw a ball. The count was 3 and 2. Then July lost him to load the bases. I called time and went out to the mound.

"How do you feel?" I said.

"Maybe I am unhappy," July said.

"You're not sick?"

"No, no, I'm OK that way," he said.

"Is the ball too wet?"

"It's wet. But not too wet."

"You're not tired?"

"No, I'm OK," he said.

"You feel good?"

"I feel good."

"OK," I said, "let's get this next guy."

The next guy, their catcher, was six-feet-three and weighed at least 230 pounds. He stepped into the batter's box and took a few warm-up cuts like a man intent upon making permanent and ugly injury. He looked like Bluto, only bigger. July walked him on four pitches, forcing in Górnik's second run. The bases were still loaded. I looked over to where Mark was warming up. I didn't want to bring him in yet, nor did I want this first inning to get out of hand. I yelled at Pete to get loose, then I yelled at July to bear down, throw strikes. "You can do it, July!"

Górnik's next batter, on a 3 and 2 count, also walked, forcing in their third run. Were we jinxed? Doomed to give up three unearned runs every time we started a game? And things could get worse, I knew. A year ago in Warsaw this same Górnik team defeated the fledgling Sparks 34–3, in a game mercifully stopped after five innings by the knock down rule.

The ninth man in the batting order came up. Surely he was their weakest hitter. I decided to let July pitch to him. "He wants a walk," I said. "Don't give it to him." "OK," July said, but he just stood on the mound looking toward the plate as if he were unsure what to do. "Come on, let's go!" I finally yelled. July looked slowly around at first, second, third—all the runners were standing pat. Then July glanced at Norbert, who seemed to be posing as someone suddenly moved to religious devotion, a brand-new ascetic whose face was saying, "I am not here . . . I have renounced all worldly concerns . . . pay me no mind." I knew that look and I knew what was up—the god damn hidden-ball trick, which the Poles loved as children love candy. If I had let them, the Sparks would have tried to pull it on every runner who reached first base, but I'd made a speech after our first game (in which we had been successful once with the hidden-ball trick, but had also committed nine errors): none of that Little League stuff, I said, until we can throw, catch, and field the ball. At that point, I said, we won't need tricks. Still, it was a habit difficult for some Sparks—like Norbert—to break. I yelled at him now, "Give the ball to July, damn it, and let's play baseball!" Sheepishly he brought the ball to July, and July struck out Górnik's ninth batter on four pitches. We led, 6–3.

In the top of the second inning, Tony led off with a booming triple down the left field line. Mariusz struck out, Alejandro struck out. Tony scored on a wild pitch. Marek flied out to left. In Górnik's half of the inning, July tossed out the first batter on a bouncer back to the mound. He walked the next two batters and I almost pulled him. I was glad I didn't because he struck out their cleanup hitter, and then Tony fielded a sharp smash and threw to Froggy to end the threat. We led, 7–3.

We got another run in the third inning. Blackie singled, stole second, advanced on a fielder's choice, and came home on a wild pitch. (A runner on third base can give a Polish pitcher melancholia.) In their half of the inning—Mark was now on the mound for us—the coal miners sent ten men to the plate. They got two bloop singles to right field and three walks, and two men reached base via errors by Mariusz and Froggy. Górnik had four runs across and had the bases loaded, with only one out, when Mark struck out the last two batters. We now led by one run, 8–7. Dariusz came over from the scorer's table, walking like Chaplin in a hurry, and said to me, "Gary, you listen, no problem. We will win!"

In the fourth inning Mariusz walked and stole second. Alejandro walked. Mariusz stole third, a decision of his own and a foolish one, because Górnik's catcher, Bluto, had a powerful arm; but Mariusz was on his charger. Marek then walked to load the bases. Blackie hit a single to left, scoring Mariusz, but Alejandro, who took time between second and third to whoop it up, was thrown out at the plate. I had to remind myself that he was sixteen and that all of his glands were turned on all the way, *olé*. Marek went to third on the play. Froggy bounced to the shortstop, who tried for a double play but only got Blackie at second. Marek scored. Mark went down swinging for the third out.

Bluto came up to start Górnik's half of the fourth and hit a towering blow to deep center. The ball kept going and going and then there was Alejandro, beyond the yellow flag, robbing the man of a homer. Mark struck out the next batter, and I thought—especially with the number nine man in the batting order coming up—that maybe we'd pull off a rare thing, a three-up, three-down inning. Mark got two quick strikes on the guy, rocking back, kicking his leg out in that wonderfully smooth, big-league motion he had when he got in his groove. Mark stood six-feet-two, weighed 180 pounds, and was only eighteen. He was going to be a real pitcher; already he moved around the mound like one, threw the ball hard, and understood how to use the strike zone, how to go for the corners. All he needed was experience—and to learn *spokojnie*. When he got excited, his big white-blond pompadour seemed to puff out from under his hat like a soufflé. His third pitch to the Górnik batter was very close to a strike, so was the next one. He looked over at me and shook his head in disgust at the umpire's judgment. I said, "This guy can't hit, Mark. Go get him." Mark gave him a fat one down the middle and the guy, swinging late, blooped it to right for a single. Angry at himself, Mark walked the next two batters to load the bases. I called time and went out to visit.

"Umpire is no good," Mark said.

"Take it easy," I said. His cheeks were flaming.

"I throw strikes, he says low, he says high."

"Just settle down," I said.

"I am OK. *He* is not OK."

"It was a cheap hit that guy got," I said.

"Cheap?"

"Worth about ten *złotys*. About what you'd pay to use the toilet in a restaurant."

"What are you saying?"

"I'm saying go get this next guy—forget the umpire."

"I must! He is blind!"

Górnik's number three batter stepped to the plate and, on a 3 and 2 count, blooped yet another single to right, driving in two runs. But their clean-up batter, the guy who looked like Mantle, hit a line drive straight back to Mark to end the inning. We led 10–9. Dariusz again came over. "It's OK! It's OK!" he said. "We will win!"

In the top of the fifth, George walked and went to second on a wild pitch. Norbert struck out and left the batter's box talking to all of his ancestors in heaven, asking them, "*Dlaczego? Dlaczego?*" ("Why? Why?"). Tony fouled out. Mariusz got his first hit, a single to center, scoring George. I said to Mariusz, who was standing on first base burning to run, "*Spokojnie*, OK? Watch me. *Wait* for the steal sign." Not listening, not waiting, on the first pitch delivered by Górnik's southpaw, Mariusz stole second. Talking with Mariusz now was like trying to reason with a man caught up in the flash and flame of battle. Lefty then hit Alejandro on the leg. Lefty was a short, heavy man with a crank-like motion, and his shoulders were sagging. Marek came to bat. I showed him my palm—the take sign—and then I yelled at Mariusz to stay on second base, damn it. Marek had a good eye at the plate; he'd walked twice already and I figured—hoped—with Lefty apparently running out of gas he'd walk again. Then we'd have Blackie up with the bases loaded—and Blackie was hot. Lefty threw high to Marek, then even higher. His third pitch was almost over Bluto's head. Everything was going perfectly for us—and then Mariusz, who could no longer contain his fire, tried to steal third. Bluto threw him out to retire the side.

When Mariusz came running to the bench for his glove, I grabbed him by the shirtfront, up at his neck, and said, "*Dlaczego? Dlaczego?*" His eyes had a shocked glaze over them—he was confused, then angry. I continued to hold him by the shirt. He wouldn't look at me and wouldn't answer. I said, "Damn it, Mariusz, there was no point to stealing third!" I let him go. He found his glove and raced over to Dariusz. He yelled at Dariusz, threw his glove on the ground, shook his head violently. I didn't know what he was saying, but I could guess he was unhappy. I was unhappy too. We'd just blown a good opportunity to score some runs. Worse, we were now commencing to fight among ourselves—so many Polish princes and only so much land. Mariusz finally ran out to his position at second base and Górnik came up for their half of the fifth.

We had the lead, 11–9, but that soon changed. Their first batter walked, and then Alejandro, waiting for a routine fly ball, dropped it. A funereal gloom passed over the Sparks, gray as the Rybnik sky we had slept under. Out in center field Alejandro flapped his arms at his sides like a maimed bird. When the next batter, Bluto, smashed a one-hopper at Norbert and the little Praga tough scooped it up and made one of his spectacular throws to Froggy for the out, the team revived. But then the next batter poked one into the oak trees behind George for a double, driving in two runs; and then Tony, of all people, made an error. He picked up a grounder and fired it over Froggy's head, letting another run come in. Mark threw out the next batter and Norbert caught an infield fly to end the inning, but Górnik now had the lead, 12–11. Dariusz came over, his face looking sunburned, and said, "It is no problem, believe me!"

Well, I wasn't so sure. In our half of the sixth—facing a new pitcher, a right-hander—we got the bases loaded on two walks and a hit batter, with only one out, but then Norbert was called out on three straight strikes and Tony, going after the first pitch, popped up. The Sparks returned to the field like men who were sore in body and spirit.

Leading off the Górnik sixth, the blond clean-up batter laid into Mark's fastball and sent it so high and deep to center that I thought, Here's where the roof falls in. But Alejandro caught it over his shoulder, robbing the miners of their second home run. He jumped up and down—no longer a maimed bird—and constructed a string of Spanish syllables that Bizet could have spread around Carmen at her feistiest. OK! The next batter hit a bouncer back to Mark. He dropped the ball, then couldn't find the handle because he kept looking at the runner. He was furious with himself. He tried to pick the runner off first base and threw the ball over Froggy's head. I yelled at him to forget the runner, who now stood on second base. Mark didn't hear me—couldn't hear me for his fury— and tried to pick the guy off second! This throw ended up in center field, the runner advancing to third. "Now will you forget about him!" I said. "OK, OK," Mark said. But his concentration was a mess. He threw two fat pitches to the next batter, who fouled off the first and sliced the second into right-center for a triple, scoring the guy on third. Then Bluto blooped one out toward George that George couldn't quite reach. Another run in. I yelled at Jake to go out and settle Mark down. I told Pete and Adam to warm up. I yelled at Mark to *forget* about Bluto and get the batter. None of us thought the big catcher would try to steal anyway, but he did; on Mark's first pitch he lumbered over to second like a beach bully hugging an inner tube around his middle. We simply watched him. Then the batter bounced to Norbert. Froggy, moving to cover first base, slipped in the wet grass and fell down. Suddenly there was Mariusz, still on fire, sprinting to first to take Norbert's throw. They got the runner on a close, spectacular play, their favorite kind. Two outs, the Sparks were flying. Never mind Bluto moving to third and raising his fist à la Blackie. Well, we weren't quite flying yet. Mark walked the next batter, who stole second and then scored behind Bluto on a single. Finally Mark retired the side on a strike out. Górnik led, 16–11.

Once again Dariusz came over. "I have much happiness," he said, "because I know we will win!"

In the seventh inning neither team scored. The Sparks made a very promising start: back-to-back singles by Mariusz and Alejandro. But then Mariusz, *still* needing to prove something, took a suicidal lead off second base, daring the pitcher to pick him off, and the pitcher did. This was opera, not baseball. If Alejandro, earlier, called up Bizet, Mariusz now, storming back to the bench, was Lieutenant Don José, fuming to get revenge in the last act. Marek then popped up and Blackie struck out. In Górnik's turn at bat, they went down one, two, three: a strike out, a fly to Alejandro, and a line-drive to Mariusz—who, after he caught the ball, slammed it into the wet grass at his feet. Dariusz came over.

Before he could speak, I said, "Do you still have much happiness?"

"Of course!" he said.

"We've only got two more innings, Dariusz."

"All we need!"

Froggy walked to start the eighth. Mark struck out. Górnik's pitcher, smelling victory, was now getting too eager. He walked George and Norbert to load the bases. He was aiming his pitches, trying too hard. I called a quick huddle and said, "Listen—nobody swings the bat unless I say so, OK?" I looked at Mariusz, brooding on the periphery. "OK, Mariusz?" I said. He said, "OK." Tony stepped to the plate then and walked, forcing in Froggy. That made the score 16–12. Mariusz came up. He followed my take sign until the count was 2 and 2. "If it's in there now, Mariusz, hit it," I said. A home run would tie the game, and he was our home run hitter—and overdue. But what he did was hit a feeble fly to the shortstop, and then walk back to the bench like a man who was completely no good. Two outs. Alejandro came up. Taking all the way, he had a 3 and 2 count on him when Tony—dancing a little too energetically off first base, trying to rattle the pitcher—slipped to one knee. Bluto, who had the ball, fired it to first and Tony was dead. We'd had the bases loaded, only one out, our power at the plate, and we got only one run.

To make matters considerably worse, Górnik came up and, slam-bang, got a single, a double, a walk, and a triple. Three quick runs, nobody out, and a runner on third base. They led, 19–12. Here goes your old ball game, I thought. Three more runs and they'll get us on the knock down rule. But then the Sparks, instead of tossing their sabres in a heap, put on a sharp little show to end the inning: George raced in to catch a blooper to right field, Jake fielded a bunt in front of the plate and threw the batter out, and Mark fanned the clean-up hitter on three straight pitches. Still, we were seven runs behind. As Dariusz made his flat-footed way over from the scorer's table, he did not look like a man who contained much happiness.

"Did you come to tell me we're going to win?" I said.

"Maybe we can!" he said. "Maybe we can!" His voice sounded awfully punished by all the Polish smokes he was going through. Then—desperate—he said, "Maybe George is no good today in right. Maybe Paweł is now OK?"

I said, "It's the ninth inning, Dariusz. We need base runners."

Our first man up should have been Alejandro, I thought, because he hadn't had a chance to complete his turn at bat the previous inning. But the umpire said no, Marek was up. I didn't want to get involved in a discussion that might lead to heat and distraction (when you're behind it doesn't take much, and Blackie, among others, was always primed to join a fray), so I let the matter go. I was sorry I did because Marek promptly fanned. The Górnik players, shouting, raised a finger at the sky. One out! Blackie came up. I hoped he could contain himself and follow my take sign. He did, and walked on four pitches. The Górnik pitcher was aiming the ball again. He walked Froggy on five pitches and lost Mark on a full count. The bases were loaded for George.

George was the smallest and youngest Polish player on the team. He was five-feet-four, weighed 120 pounds, and would celebrate his eighteenth birthday in two days. He wore one of those baseball caps you can buy in the States that are half plastic mesh and have a strap in the back to adjust the size. His strap was on the first hole and still the cap—a New York Mets model— was too big for him. To prevent it from flopping in his eyes, he stuffed some cloth under the sweat band. Like Greg and Jake, he had lived for a while in New York when his father, a chemistry professor, was on a Fulbright grant. George's junior high American classmates gave him the baseball bug, and he still had it. The first time we met—that January at Gwardia—he said to me, "I am Jerzy, Coach, the catcher. Call me George, like George Herman Babe Ruth." On almost every Friday afternoon after that meeting I would run into George at the American Embassy. I was there to collect my mail, he was there for the latest *Sports Illustrated* and any other magazine in the Embassy Library that carried baseball news. "Aren't you supposed to be in school now, George?" "Ah," he would say, "school is dull today." Or, "My teachers are all in a bad mood—I don't like to see it." Or, "Hey, Gary, the Mets will start spring training soon!" The Sparks' very early spring practice at Gwardia—which began January 13 and ended March 30—was every Wednesday, Saturday, and Sunday and George never missed. He wanted to be the first-string catcher. He worked hard at it, but Jake, who was six inches taller and weighed fifty more pounds, and had a stronger arm, got the job. George was the back-up catcher. I played him in right field or made him the designated hitter. He was our lead-off batter because he could get on base. He had his own bat—an aluminum model, with red tape on the handle, that he'd bought in Queens—and every time he stepped up to home plate, he would whisper to this bat. "What do you say to it, George?" "I tell it to be good." He stepped up now against the Górnik pitcher who was two outs away from victory.

George had walked five times that day, and I wanted him to walk again. The pitcher threw high. "OK, George, he'll do it again!" I said. But the pitcher didn't do it again—he fired two quick strikes across—and now George had to swing if the pitch was close. On the bus ride back to Warsaw, I would remember the next few moments of the game more than any other. George stepped out of the batter's box and gave his bat two kisses, both in the same place—presumably the spot where he planned to hit the ball. Then he did hit the ball, down the left field line, for a double. Blackie and Froggy came in to score. It was now 19–14, with two runners on and Norbert up.

Lord, I thought, let Norbert crouch down low like a monk with abundant humility on his mind and let him stay there; let him not be tempted by the high pitch of pride or the wide pitch of ambition; let him be cool. Cool was mainly what I hoped for, giving him the take sign. The pitcher threw a strike, and then he threw another strike. Then trying very hard to finish off this cocky Praga tough—who between pitches swung his bat as if he intended to make big trouble—the Górnik right-hander threw four consecutive balls. We had the bases loaded again, and Tony at bat. The veteran. The Spark, could I have chosen any of them then, I would have chosen. The Górnik coach called time and went out to settle down his pitcher, a guy with thick legs and a boxer's thick neck and a motion a butcher might use to chop meat. I think the coach wanted a new pitcher, but he had no more; and Polish rules forbade him to re-use a pitcher, even if the pitcher were still in the game. Once a pitcher was removed from the mound and sent, say, to play third base, he could not return to the mound. The umpire called, "*Pałka!*"

Tony took two balls. Then he watched a slow, fat pitch float across for a strike. It was like a dollop of ice cream, easy and sweet, but our desperate strategy continued: not to swing unless the pitcher got two strikes on us. The pitcher laid another fat one across. OK, Tony! It's up to you!" I yelled. The pitcher threw wide, making the count 3 and 2. He delivered another fat one. Tony swung. The ball rose about five stories straight up. When it came down, Bluto had it for the second out. The Górnik players went momentarily nuts, waving two-fingered salutes at each other as if they'd just discovered that number.

Now it was Mariusz' turn. I gave him the take sign, but I was not confident his passion would allow him to obey it. He pulled his Chicago Bears cap down tight and took a slow, measured warm-up cut that said he wanted to *do* something—he'd had too many bad moments that day to live with! The feeble pop-up last inning, getting picked off second base, that humiliating incident following his attempt to steal third! The expression on his dark, handsome face said that he was suffering. If he could sing, he would have made a very good Don José indeed. The pitcher delivered, and Mariusz watched the baseball go past—it was ice cream and pie and the look in his eyes said that he was starving. I gave a cheer. Starving or no, he was playing baseball. And the pitcher walked him, forcing in Mark. The score was 19–15, the bases were still loaded.

If I had Mariusz' passion to worry about, I now had Alejandro's youth. Holding my palm up, I said, "Do you see this?" Alejandro nodded, wiggling around in the batter's box hoping to unnerve just a little bit more the already plenty nervous pitcher. And while he threw his hips and elbows around, the pitcher threw wide, he threw low, then he almost threw the ball in the dirt. Bluto was furious. Alejandro was beside himself with joy. All the Sparks were. One more bad pitch and he was on base. The pitch came up—it came straight for his smiling face—and Alejandro bunted the ball. I believe my heart stopped. To bunt at all was madness. To bunt on a 3 and 0 count—and at a bad pitch—well, there was no word for it. The ball was rolling down the third base line. Alejandro, shocked, stood where he was and watched it, jabbering he didn't *mean* to do that. The Górnik pitcher was also shocked, but he soon found his wits and ran for the ball. All he had to do was pick it up, walk about six steps, touch the still-stunned Alejandro or touch home plate—the choice was glorious—and then he could go have a beer. But the ball rolled foul, inches from the pitcher's hand. Alejandro made the Sign of the Cross. The pitcher walked back to the mound, his shoulders slumped, and delivered a fourth ball. Alejandro *ran* to first base and George came in from third, making the score 19–16. On the bus much later, Dariusz would be drinking a beer and saying to me, "*Chrząszcz brzmi w trzcinie w Szczebrzeszynie.*" Jake would be translating: "'There is a beetle making sounds in the willow in Szczebrzeszyn.'" Dariusz would then say, "Yes, and I hear this tiny animal, believe me, when Alejandro tries to make his bunt. I hear no thing in my head, or down where I have my heart, only this tiny animal."

Marek, who began the inning by striking out, came up again and walked on four pitches, scoring Norbert. We trailed by two runs now, 19–17, with Blackie stepping to the plate, the bases still loaded. There was a lot of shouting and cheering from the

Sparks' bench for Blackie, and Blackie shot a fist to the sky, shouting with them. This caused Bluto to shout something. Blackie then thrust his bat at the sky like a sword, and the umpire—a man who would brook no displays—rushed out from behind Bluto and made an angry speech directed at both catcher and batter. I ran over and grabbed Blackie's arm (he was so tense his arm felt like wood) and told him in a burble of wisdom that if he didn't play baseball, he wouldn't be playing baseball. Then I assured the umpire everything was OK. He yelled, *"Pałka!"* We all returned to our places. I gave Blackie the take sign. He nodded, fiercely, and then glared at the pitcher. The pitcher, whose thick neck seemed to have gotten thicker—in fact it seemed painful for him to turn his head to look at the runners—met Blackie's glare and raised him. Blackie's head stood up like a rooster's; he took practice cuts that declared manslaughter was on his mind. All I could do was send him a stream of encouraging chatter—"Good eye, baby, good eye, easy does it, *easy* does it"—and hope it would soothe him, hope he would not swing the bat, even though, in my gut, I wanted him to knock one past a yellow flag.

Blackie walked on four pitches, sending in Mariusz, to make the score 19–18. It was the eighth walk of the inning and I was convinced, as Froggy came up, that the law of averages had to turn now in the Górnik hurler's favor. Moreover, Froggy stood very still at the plate; he presented no rattling theatre. All the pitcher had to do was throw two easy strikes, and then all the pressure would be on Froggy. And every Spark knew how chancy Froggy was under pressure.

The pitcher threw two easy strikes, and Bluto was making sounds like a bear who'd finally found the honey hole. Blackie, standing on first base, was quiet. So were his teammates. This was it. Froggy swung at the next pitch and missed. I turned my head, I saw the Sparks on the bench slump like puppets when the master drops all the strings, and then I heard the umpire cry, "Foul!" The Poles had adopted a few terms from American baseball, and this one, at that moment, was the prettiest. Froggy fouled off another pitch, and then, one by one—and they were the most painful and the sweetest pitches I believe I have ever witnessed—he watched four balls go by. Alejandro came in from third with the tying run, hooting Spanish, Polish, and English. Every Spark was jumping up and down except Froggy. He stood on first base like a man who had just given his blood—all of it—at the blood bank.

The Górnik pitcher also looked drained. He'd started this inning with a seven-run lead and now it was gone. And the bases were still loaded. Full of disgust, Bluto walked out to the mound and slammed the ball in the pitcher's mitt. (Bluto had to be plenty mad at himself too: if he'd held onto Froggy's first foul—a foul tip—the game would be over.) Now the pitcher, throwing to Mark, hit him in the ribs. Mark was delighted, the Sparks delirious. Marek came in to give us the lead, 20–19. While the Sparks celebrated his arrival at the plate, the miners of Boguszowice, their heads bowed, walked in little circles at their respective positions like men who had just been told their girlfriends married better prospects. Finally the umpire wanted a batter and George stepped in. George worked the pitcher to a 3 and 2 count, kissed his bat, and then walked, sending Blackie home. Blackie crossed the plate in a handstand, grinning like a kid wearing a false mustache. We'd gone from the opera to the circus. Norbert, our fifteenth batter that inning, stepped in. He too worked the pitcher to a 3 and 2 count, but fanned for the third out. In a way I was grateful for the out. To be seven runs behind in the ninth inning, and then to score nine runs on one hit, one hit batter, and ten walks—and requiring more than an hour to do it—makes for a lot of wear and tear on a guy's personal ebb and flow.

Well, the game wasn't over. The Sparks were up high, but if Górnik got runners on base and we started making errors, started arguing among ourselves, it would be a long, flat ride home. (Going into the eighth inning of our season's opener, we led, 17–14, but lost our cool and lost the game, 28–17.) Górnik held a meeting, which ended with many arms raised to the sky, and then Five O'Clock Shadow stepped to the plate. He worked Mark to a full count. Mark kicked out his leg, fired, and the umpire called, "Strike!" Another very nice borrowing from American lingo. The next Górnik batter swung at the first pitch and popped it up. Mark caught it for the second out. The Sparks in the field were slapping their mitts and the Sparks on the bench were slapping each other. Bluto stepped in, fuming. I yelled, "He's dead, Mark! He's finished! He's too mad to see straight! Blow it past him!" Bluto swung at the first pitch, hit a one-hopper back to Mark, who grabbed it and made a beautiful throw to Froggy. Froggy dropped the ball. Bluto stood safely on first base pounding a fist in his palm, showing *me* who was dead. I yelled out at Mark, "Forget the runner! He's not going anywhere! He means nothing to us!" Mark went into his stretch, threw to the batter, and Bluto took off for second base. I couldn't believe it. Jake had the ball and was cocking his arm to throw down to Mariusz, and I was yelling, "Why! Why!" On the bus later, Jake said, "Coach, when I heard you yelling 'Why!' I almost didn't throw to Mariusz. But I said to myself, 'That catcher is slow and crazy—mainly slow'—and I remembered the last time he stole second on us, and I thought, 'He shouldn't be allowed to do it again.'" Dariusz, who had just given me the sentence about the beetle in the willow in Szczebrzeszyn, now gave me another:

"*Drabina z powyłamywanymi szczeblami.*"

"Jake, what does that mean?" I said.

"It means 'A ladder with broken-out steps,'" Jake said.

Dariusz laughed. Then he said, "*W czasie suszy szosa sucha.*"

"That sounds like you've got a mouthful of bees," I said.

"No, no, I have *piwo* in my mouth," Dariusz said.

"Give me one of those beers," I told him. Then to Jake I said, "What did Dariusz' mouthful of bees mean?"

"I think he is saying 'A drought makes the road dry,'" Jake said. "But I don't know what he's getting at. Maybe he is just giving you Polish tongue-twisters, for fun."

"That was one hell of a throw, Jake," I said.

"It was easy," he said.

2

Every Wednesday from mid-January until the end of March, I waited on Krakowskie Przedmieście Street for the 175 autobus to Gwardia. Across the street stood the story-high black iron gates of the university—where I had just come from—and above the gates, brazen in gilt, stood the Polish Royal Eagle, a symbol officially banned by the government everywhere in the country, but obviously not up there. (The Royal Eagle wore a crown.) It would be around four-thirty—in January the day already dark and cold—and then my students, almost all of them women (who had taken a moment to freshen up), would be rushing under the eagle for this bus stop or that along the street. They were fourth- and fifth-year students in their middle twenties, and out here they looked even more beautiful than they did in our little garret-like classroom. Standing before a dimly lit shop window, against the relentless gray of the buildings, they shone. They were blonde and dark and had red hair the color of cognac, their skin was very fair, and they all wore high heels; and in a way that Royal Eagle—representing a time long ago and glories gone for good—was their muse. They seemed lonely and romantic, apart, and because they always spoke to me in proper English— accented English—they sometimes seemed like the lovely and lost Sashas and Natashas and Nadyas I had read about in my youth, come dreamily to life. Many would be smoking cigarettes, one or two holding an apple they might take a small bite from, their coats never completely buttoned up, their scarves loosely wound about slim necks, and their lips bright with fresh lipstick. They dressed as if they were meeting someone for a drink at the Europejski Hotel around the corner, or for a piano recital at the

Palace in Old Town. Indeed, Kasia and Agnieszka, giving goodbye embraces to their friends now and walking up the street, probably did have such rendezvous. Most, however, had students waiting for them, private students—children, mainly, of the professional class wanting to learn English—and they must hurry. "I am always this way, one appointment or another, and always late," Agata might say. "Yes, this is how it is," Ewa would echo, sighing, "we never have a moment to ourselves. It's a pity."

Sometimes Magda would join me on the 175, to ride as far as Nowy Świat Street, to meet her grandmother, to pick up something in one of the little shops there, or just to escape the cold for a moment, she would say. Magda smelled like Paris at night in the spring. Like her fellow students she was sophisticated, intelligent, and not exactly spoiled or coddled but close to it. To be in the university—not easy to achieve—meant you were special. It meant you were closer to things much larger, and nicer, than the present; it meant you could get permission more easily than most to leave Poland for visits to the West; it meant—for the time being, anyway—that you did not have to work at a job you hated and go home at night knowing the next day would be the same forever. You could sleep in, if you were a student, because you had been up late studying, or drinking wine with your friends, discussing ideas, music, writers, having hope, making delirious plans, or just dancing and getting beautifully drunk.

When the bus stopped on cozy Nowy Świat, I gave Magda the three kisses she had assured me were necessary for a proper good-bye in Poland—on one cheek, the other, and back to the first. Then she slipped out the door, leaving behind a scent I savored for quite a while.

Turning off Nowy Świat, the bus entered wide, traffic-thick Jerozolimskie Avenue. It passed the five-star Forum Hotel on the corner of Jerozolimskie and Marszałkowska, and the huge, gray, Gothic Palace of Culture on the opposite corner. At the hotel you could buy from the waiters blackmarket *złotys* (their rate was three times better than the official rate) and you could buy, as the Arabs did—always, I was told—a beautiful blonde for the night. At the Palace of Culture you could see *Citizen Kane* and a lot of escapist fare featuring car chases—approved by the censor—and you could see Hamlet grieve in Polish on the stage; you could hear jazz, watch folk dancers, buy luxurious art books showing holdings in the Hermitage, eat garlic chicken in the Russian restaurant, visit an exhibit of children's watercolors, swim, watch sleek women take off most of their clothes in the basement disco, and you could ride an elevator to the thirtieth floor, the top of the Palace of Culture, the highest point in the capital, and look all around. It was the best place to see Warsaw from—went a popular joke—because then you didn't have to look at the Palace of Culture. The Palace was a gift from the Soviets and most Poles ridiculed it, said they hated it, as they hated the system, the poverty, the dirt in the streets, and the Arabs who came to buy their beautiful blondes.

The 175 autobus then passed the main train station, Centralna, which looked from a distance like a mausoleum with wings, like a box that might fly, a strange, huge, uninviting blocky bird- or bee-thing, but always busy inside, a gray, eerily quiet hive, long lines at the ticket windows, the travelers dressed in their best colors hurrying down three levels to the platforms underground, boarding the blue and green Kraków Ekspres, boarding other trains, fast and slow, for Budapest, Berlin, Gdańsk, Rybnik, or coming back from their journeys red-eyed and rumpled, hauling up the stairs big cartons and bulging suitcases tied with ropes, greeted by old women wearing aprons over their rough coats who were selling roses and tiny bunches of wildflowers laid out on newspapers spread on the floor.

At the corner of Raszyńska and Wawelska the 175 passed Skra Stadium, where the baseball team would move in April (and where, at the intersection, atop a thirty-foot monument honoring Polish aviation, a figure in goggles embraced a propeller), and then the bus headed for the suburbs. Gray, boxy apartment buildings waited out there for my fellow passengers going home from work, all of the apartments the same cramped quarters despaired of by those who had them and desired by those who didn't. At Racławicka Street, at the edge of the suburbs, I got off. Gwardia was a ten-minute walk. I turned my thoughts away from Magda

and her plum-colored lips, away from the stony faces pressed
close to each other on the bus, and toward the gym.

A CIRCLE

First day out we form a circle—
in a Mets cap, smiling wide,
this guy says, "I am Jerzy, Coach,
the catcher. Call me George. I will
translate." He is bat boy–size,
eager from his cheeks to Christmas,
the youngest of the bunch.
On his feet he wears the kind of
sneaks I wore in elementary school.
I say, "You slay dragons, George?"
"Please," he says, "Piotr . . . Tomasz . . . Adam
. . . Paweł . . . Mariusz . . . Norbert . . ."
One by one his friends step forward,
bow like monkey-suitless diplomats
and shake my hand. My joke's been jammed
by consonants, formality. I snap out,
"Choke the bat, the squeeze is on,
play shallow, hit the cut-off man!"
All these sober Poles look
puzzled. "George, how long
you guys been at this baseball?"
"Coach," he says, "one summer now.
Every game we lose. Sometimes twenty-five,
sometimes more to nothing—
tell us what we need to do."
They're standing in my circle—
I am in the middle, in the place
my eighth grade coach would hitch
his pants up, spit,
and tell us, "Gentlemen, the world
is dog eat dog. It's dig and sweat
and pray you don't stink up

your underwear. That's it.
That's everything—let's go!"
Beyond the gym's dim windows now
snow is falling on a city still
pulling bricks and books
and other fragments of its history
out of holes. And I am saying,
"George, we need to bark
and fetch. Tell these guys to
grab their feet and stretch."

At five o'clock in the afternoon in January, the Gwardia gym
was lit by yellowish-white ceiling lights which gave the players a
sickly glow as they stood in two lines, facing each other, and
threw baseballs back and forth. Some of them had never held a
baseball until a week ago, and they were having trouble—they
couldn't quite get it about stepping out with their left foot and following through with their arm as they released the ball. They
threw, George said, like girls. George was feeling a little cocky
because he had his own glove, a Greg Luzinski Rawlings, and a
season under his belt of playing junior high ball in the school-
yards of Queens. He knew how to step out and follow through. *He*
knew what "steal" and "slide" and "hit-and-run" meant, and he
could name all the major league teams, name their stars, and
he could discuss with me—insider to insider, guy to guy—the
most recent World Series. Greg and Jake, the only other players
who had been to America and had thrown and batted baseballs
there, did not possess George's fine knowledge of the game; they
hadn't kept up; but they were older now, graduate students in
business and economics, and they had their futures to worry about.
They showed up at Gwardia mainly to help out Dariusz, they let
me know. Of course they'd like to play, they said, but I had to
understand that life in Poland was difficult, and some things were
more necessary than others.

Altogether there were thirty-three names on the roster that
Dariusz gave me, and for the first few weeks most of these hope-

fuls came to practice. We had a lot to learn before our first game on April 17 against Jastrzębie, and we had to learn it, for the most part, on a basketball court. When I pointed out to Dariusz that there were only so many things we could do in there, he said—with great confidence—"No problem! April second we go outside, to Skra!" As if two weeks outdoors was all the time we needed to do what we couldn't do in a gym.

What we did at the start was run laps and wind-sprints, play catch, field grounders. Pitchers threw to catchers, learning control, the strike zone. I also taught them "pepper," an exercise in which three or four players, standing a few feet apart, take turns tossing the ball a short distance to a batter; he hits the ball, not very hard, back to them. It's a drill to sharpen your eye, your reflexes. And those guys, who grew up on soccer and would often stop a low throw with a foot instead of bending down for it, needed *bardzo* sharpening. Sometimes I felt I was watching a bunch of guys who were trying to catch up on something they didn't even know they'd missed, and then I'd drift back to all those springs and summers I had had, those long days of stepping out and following through, of firing over and over under the sun, into my buddy Eddie Hill's oiled mitt, and never wanting to quit this thing, this motion, this smooth overhand wave taking in Newhouser and Kaline and Mays, taking in, as darkness came on, all the stars and taking them home: night after night the perfect plays wrapped in my glove strapped to my bike's handlebars, or tucked in a rear pocket like glorious cash that couldn't be given for anything ordinary: night after night of keeping my tail down and scooping up dream grounders, tossing the fleetest runners out by half a step, by inches, by those whiskers that wouldn't appear for years yet, and maybe—fixed to that time and place, it seemed, forever—never.

But there in Gwardia, in January, in a cold gym, I had thirty-three guys who were already shaving, most of them, and throwing—too many of them—as if they were about to fall over.

After a month or so I figured we ought to try batting practice. In the gym were four big, dark green mats, about a foot thick, filled with foam rubber; gymnasts must have used them to fall on. We put one behind the catcher and the others down at the far end of the floor, against the wall (behind which a man, who more or less kept track of things around there, sat in his office and smoked cigarettes and watched television). A dozen fielders spread out in front of the mats; I stationed a couple in the balcony above the mats, among the wooden seats. Their job was to throw back balls hit up there, though if they could catch the balls before they struck the seats—and prevent a racket—all the better. To the right of the batter, out where first base would be, were tall windows protected by iron grillwork, so we didn't worry about those. In the balcony to the batter's left, however, was a row of smaller, unprotected windows running the length of the place. To guard those would have required more hands than we had, so we ignored them and hoped for the best. As it turned out, only George broke glass up there—twice—and surprisingly the chain-smoking *robotnik* never heard it or complained to us. He did come bursting into the gym, though, steaming, when a line drive got past a fielder *and* a mat (the mat had sagged out of position) and went booming against the wooden partition that separated him from us. He collared the first person he saw—a Junior—and was firing a blast of consonants in the kid's face. Everything stopped while this porky clerk, who looked like Nikita Khrushchev with a crew-cut, got louder and redder. If you shouted in Poland it usually meant you had power, a position of authority. I walked over to the guy from mid-court, where I'd been watching the pitcher throw, and told him he was messing up my practice; I told him he was an ill-mannered, bad-smelling pig-fucker. He didn't understand my language, but he did recognize my volume and backed off.

We also broke a couple of light bulbs in the ceiling. The two windows that George broke, and then the light bulbs, brought greater and greater cheers from the players, as if we were doing a lot more than breaking glass. And indeed we were: Gwardia had been built for the Milicja. When the players told me this, I wanted to try for more lights and windows by having outfield practice; but the ones we'd broken had not been replaced, and the gym was already dark and cold enough as it was.

One day Froggy got beaned by Pete.

Yesterday at batting practice
Froggy got a mouse—
he watched, dead still,
as one of Piotr's fastballs came
and caught him in the cheek.
A straight, no fooling thud.
                              At once
Piotr ran and kissed him
where the mouse would be, crooning Polish.
Froggy is a car mechanic, his big
meaty hands are nicked all over,
half the nails are blue.
He put an arm around Piotr,
crooning back. The pitcher
gave him three or four more kisses,
loud smacks across the knuckles,
then they laughed.
                              I tried to picture
something like this in the States.
Maybe at a nursery school you'd see it,
where people have good manners, love,
and other things to teach—
but not on any fields that I knew of.

Around this same time something struck me as hard, in a way,
as a baseball in the face. Almost from the beginning I had felt that
something was missing, an element as close to the game as the
smack of a ball when it's caught exactly in the glove's pocket.
I'm talking about talk: chatter. Those Polish guys were quiet as
mourners unless we broke something. And after the glass was
swept up, they went right back to their near-silence. (Alejandro,
the voluble Cuban, wasn't with us yet.) Maybe I hadn't noticed
the absence of chatter because there was an absence of so many
other sounds you hear around baseball: the crack of a fungo bat
hitting flies, fielders rhythmically pounding the pockets of their
mitts with a fist, the *fisk-fisk* of a batted ball cutting over the in-

field grass, the *smack . . . smack* two guys playing catch will make. Though not often enough, the Skra hopefuls did catch the ball in the pocket, but because they didn't oil their gloves (there wasn't any glove oil) and therefore have a slick nesting place for the ball, the sound they produced was muted, dull. Also, most of them were using Cuban-made gloves, which, compared to American or Japanese gloves, were like the stiffened, leathery carcasses of some desert animal that possessed five spiny appendages. You can't make a lot of music out of something stiff. In any case, it hit me one day that we were a very quiet bunch of guys, and I made a speech to George.

RAVENS

We do wind-sprints, we play catch
and pepper, but we do not chatter—
it's so quiet we could be in church
when I shut up, or on the street
like all those silent Poles in line
for lemons, leeks, and toilet paper.
"George, baseball players *talk*.
They razz and praise each other,
they're like ravens, man, they haw
and quack and keep their heads up—
listen, your guy's pitching
you say come on baby blow it
past this ugly cripple he can't hit
kielbasa come on baby smoke it
hum it Jacek humbabe humbabe
swing batter *swing*, and if
he does and misses give the needle
to him, Georgie, croon like you just got a
kiss off Miss Polonia in her underwear—"
"Coach, I think I couldn't think
on baseball." "Right, Georgie, pay
attention, your guy's up to bat now
you say good eye Andrzej good eye
baby pick the cherry pick the plum—

hey pitcher this one's coming back
between your jollies buddy
this one's on the grits it's all she wrote
hey pitcher pitcher this one's
going going this one's going—
where's it going, George?"
"It's going over the fence, Coach."
"Hell, George, give it a ride, baby,
pound it over the tallest joint in town."
"It's going over the Palace of Culture, Coach."
"All *right*, all the way to Moscow boom boom
and landing on Lenin's tomb."

Riding the bus to Gwardia, I noticed another kind of poem—a kind of movable, found poem—on the license plates of cars registered in Warsaw. Each license plate consisted of three letters followed by three numbers. To read the poem you simply took the letters off any car going past, then added them to the next car's letters, and so on.

WAP
WUP
WIP
WUY
WAR
WAR
WAR

Milicja vans carried the letters MOP. Cars driven by the Ministry of Information said PAP. There was a message here, intended or not. In a rigged country where apartments could be bugged, phones tapped, and where enough citizens to worry about were paid to spy on other citizens, you generally kept your lip zipped, your act as clean and simpleminded as possible. If you spoke out at the wrong time or in the wrong place, you would be corrected.

There were comic and not so comic extremes. In April when we took the field against Jastrzębie and Jake, catching, chanted to the batter, as the pitch came up, that his shoes were on the wrong feet, wrong feet, wrong feet, the umpire stopped the game and gave Jake a lecture. Jake could talk, yes, but not to an opposing player like *that*. At the university, several demonstrations expressing student support for Solidarity were held—usually disguised as something else—and the Milicja stayed out. The Milicja was not far away, though, and on one occasion, around Christmas—when the season's songs were really songs asking for free speech—the goons did not hesitate to crack a few heads when some demonstrators attempted to carry their fervor beyond the university's walled-in grounds to a church next door.

The locker rooms at Gwardia were assigned to the various teams that practiced there by the chain-smoking *robotnik*. (I should call them dressing rooms with showers, for there were no lockers.) When we arrived at the gym, one of the players would go to the man's office window and request a key for a room. The man would survey all the keys hanging on his wall and frown. Often he would murmur, "*Nie ma, nie ma* . . ." If we got a *nie ma*, a few moments later another player would go to the window, request a key, and this time the *robotnik* would give us one. In the beginning, I couldn't understand it. The man knew we were coming: Skra in fact had a contract with Gwardia for our use of the place.

"What in hell is this '*nie ma*' nonsense?" I said to Pete. "Why do we have to ask the man twice?"

"Maybe he is lonely," Pete said.

The floor of the dressing room we'd get was invariably covered with clumps of mud brought in by soccer players who had stomped their feet to clean their shoes. Sometimes we had to find a broom—not easy—to sweep the room before we could use it. Even then, we all stood on the benches to change our clothes; what the room really needed was mopping. More than once we also had to sweep the gym floor.

The showers, three to a dressing room, were separate stalls with hoses. No spray; just a thick rush of water. Sometimes the water was hot, more often lukewarm or cold. The players never seriously complained. If the water was cold, the player who discovered that fact announced it as if it were the tag line of a joke, and the others laughed or shrugged.

"Polish life, Coach."

SPEAKING IN TONGUES

In a light just right
for Boris Karloff's grin,
my guys are still too tight—
they throw like stiffs
the boogieman concocted out of
nuts and bolts and spider guts.
Balls are falling everywhere.
"George, I have a speech to make.
Tell these men the ball is
part of them, their arms, their souls—
it should travel true and beautiful.
They're moving like the devil's
got their peckers packed in ice."
He blushes. "Coach, that's complicated."
"OK, Georgie, tell them God
is hunkered on the bench behind us,
watching with His perfect squint,
a wad of Red Man bitter in His cheek.
Casey, Leo, Sparky, Yogi, John McGraw—
they're all around Him, close
but not too close: they hate it
when He dribbles chew across their cleats.
He hates it when a piece of soul is
muffed or thrown away.
Make it simple, Georgie. Listen:
God is hungry for a Warsaw win.
His stomach rumbles and He
mumbles to Himself, ' . . . made a pocket
. . . made, like Michelangelo, two hands . . .
whenever both of these reach out
to help the pocket gobble up the ball
I am real glad . . .'"

In this frigid gym whose light's a cross
between Muscatel and hell, a shade
not even God can get the Polish
Boris Karloff bureaucrats to brighten,
George is talking turkey now,
passing on the word . . .
and my guys are trying hard to catch
the lingo and the rhythm.

Jacek Małecki (who would later cut his pitching wrist) came to me after practice one day and said, "Coach, I speak for Norbert. He needs favor." Then to make sure I understood him, Jacek asked George to translate. George said, "Norbert wonders if you will help him deposit some U.S. dollars in the Polish bank." I understood and said sure. Norbert had forty dollars that he bought on the black market for *złotys*. Since the dollars were illegal, he couldn't officially claim them; he needed an American, or any foreigner, to say at the bank that the foreigner was giving the dollars to him, presenting him with a gift. All the foreigner needed was proof—a Currency Statement—that he'd brought dollars into the country.

So Norbert and Jacek came to my apartment the next day in Jacek's tiny car, a brindle-colored Polish Fiat that had no muffler, coughed a blue, sputtering exhaust, and called for a special tool—which Jacek had rigged up out of wire and a stick—to open the doors. Introducing his car to me, Jacek said, "Polish mule—small but strong." It was like that cartoon circus car twenty clowns crawl out of. In we squeezed and found a bank.

Norbert spoke to a teller, then to me:

"Bank says no, is full."

"Full?"

"Polish life," he said. "Next bank."

In the mule again we coughed and hurtled several blocks up Marszałkowska Avenue, the Palace of Culture looming ahead.

"Coach," Jacek said, "a joke to tell."

He told the joke about the best place to see Warsaw from, and we all laughed, and then doubled back to a bank right next door to the one we'd left. Were my boys pulling a diversionary tactic? Did they think we had a tail to shake? Uncoiling from the back-breaking mule, we went in. Again Norbert spoke to a teller and again we were turned away.

"Still full," he said. "Next bank."

"Let's walk. Walking is good," I said.

"Not possible. You are guest!"

"Norbert—question," I said. "Why are you called Norbert? That's not a Polish name, is it?"

"Ah," he said, "my mother one time went to France. Many years ago."

Back inside the mule we passed two Milicja.

"Polish *kupa*," Jacek said. He held his nose and, grinning, moved a foot up and down, to let me know he was always quick enough to miss stepping in *kupa*, which means "shit." We passed the main police station. Jacek gripped his right biceps, and said, "My friend can make, one throw, a stone go over that."

"That building?" I said. It was four stories high.

"Small stone," he said. "Nothing famous."

Suddenly the mule slowed down and coasted to a stop in the middle of traffic. Jacek worked the starter, but the engine only growled.

Norbert cracked, "Mule is crazy poodle."

We scrambled out and pushed the car up on the sidewalk. Fiddling in the engine, Jacek disconnected the rubber gas line and sucked it. "Ah hah! Drink is necessary," he said. "Now we hope, OK?" He opened the trunk and pawed among the stuff in there—a shoe, a hat, rags, a muzzle for a dog he used to have ("Nice dog, it died, it tried to chew some Polish *kupa*"), and finally, at the bottom, he found a can of petrol. "OK!"

Another bank. Inside it was smoky as a throat-hacking last-stop old men's hotel lobby by the tracks in Omaha. The signs all around saying PALENIE ZABRONIONE (SMOKING PROHIBITED) obviously did not, however, govern the tellers: six or seven young women with Day-Glo polished nails and slender, inky fingers who were enjoying their cigarettes and tending, in no great rush, six or seven lines so many Poles deep it was exhausting just to look at them. Norbert inquired about depositing his forty dollars, and a blonde teller, whose lush, curlicuing locks copied Shirley Temple's, snapped, "*Tak! Tak!*" ("Yes! Yes!"). And handed him three papers he and I needed to tell six times, front and back, our intention on, and sign. We did that and then joined a line, which wound around a post. Jacek laughed, "Polish snake. Now we wait, like mice."

Waiting, I noticed that a lot of foreign currency was being deposited; one well-fed gent in leather, for example—accompanied by a stylish lady with nice legs—pulled out a stack of hundred dollar bills thick enough to choke a capitalist *and* his horse. I also noticed that it was very quiet in there, the quiet you hear when people come in the presence of their redoubtable god. But Norbert, Jacek, and I were talking, and we attracted a white-haired man who had something, please, would I look? He gave me a letter from the Royal Air Force. It was a response to a letter he (or someone writing for him) had sent the RAF, asking, "Where was his brother Andrzej? Where was his coat? His hat?" The RAF replied that Andrzej had died in 1942, near France . . . "his body washed ashore." He was flying with the Polish Air Force under RAF command. The letter said the RAF gave Andrzej "medals and awards" and if the brother wished further information he should write the RAF again. With Jacek and Norbert helping, I explained all this. The old man nodded. Then I noticed what I was holding—slick, almost buttery from handling—was dated nine years ago. Was that possible? Nine years to find words, an explanation, for a brother's absence? The man's watery eyes fixed hard on the paper I continued to hold, as if it might turn into—what?—a brilliant sky? the missing hat and coat? a voice calling out: hello, hello? At length a low, rough, guarded bunch of sounds issued from his throat.

"What's he saying?" I said.

"Begs to know," Jacek said, "can he catch any moneys from the RAF?"

The man's mouth was tight. He rubbed a nicked, old fist across it—a drinker's gesture—then he nodded as if God damn it he meant business now.

"Tell him I don't know. Tell him write a letter and inquire."

The man took his paper and left. We waited in our Polish snake, mice with dollars to deposit. Norbert said, "Coach, shake," and slipped them to me.

In August of 1987, when I arrived in Poland, a beginning nurse earned fifteen thousand *złotys*, a month, a beginning medical doctor twenty thousand. The chairman of my department at the university—an associate professor—earned forty-five thousand. Autobus drivers in Warsaw and coal miners in Silesia made about what I made: ninety thousand. Ninety thousand *złotys*, at that time, was the equivalent of about $270. If you took $270 to an official Exchange, ninety thousand *złotys* is what you'd get.

However, if you had dollars to begin with, and wanted to buy *złotys*, you wouldn't be in Poland very long before learning that you did not go to an Exchange; you went to the Forum Hotel for lunch. You told the waiter you needed, say, $270 worth, and when he brought your bill in a little leather notebook, inside would be almost 300,000 *złotys*. There were other places of course to buy black market *złotys* but the Forum was always safe. Unlike many money dealers on the street, the waiters would not use sleight of hand to cheat you. The Forum was also pleasant. Roast duck, venison, broiled salmon, wild boar—all of these were delicious. Lunch for two, with wine, might be five thousand *złotys*, or about $5 at the black market rate. And everyone knew what the rate was, daily, because it was published in the newspapers. Normally it was three times higher than the official rate; during the labor strikes the following summer it was six times higher.

One day Pete and I were waiting for a bus after practice, talking. A man nearby pointed at me and said, "From U.S.A., *tak*?"

I said, "*Tak.*"

He nodded, swaying, feeling no pain. Then, "If he has ten thousand dollar, he live like king!"

Pete said to me, "He means if *he* had ten thousand dollars, I think."

"*Tak*," the man said. "Ten thousand dollar, here, is ten millions of *złotys*, *tak*? I live like king." Then he spoke to Pete in Polish and Pete, hesitant, finally said, "He says he wants to work in States and earn ten thousand dollars. He asks can you help him with visa."

"What kind of work does he do?" I said.

"Anything," Pete said. "Dig ditches, sweep floors."

The man, who was maybe thirty, then said something in Polish about Miss Polonia and laughed. His front teeth were yellow and black and small, like kernels on a cob of corn stricken by blight.

"He says he will come back with his ten thousand dollars and marry Miss Polonia and live like king," Pete laughed.

"*Tak*," the man laughed again.

When the bus came, the man shook our hands and wished us good luck, and waved till we were out of sight.

Imagine that you are an American in Warsaw shopping with black market *złotys*. Buying a loaf of delicious rye bread you pay, in effect, three cents. A kilo of potatoes costs a nickel. For about two dollars (2,000 *złotys*), you can buy a beautiful head of Bibb lettuce, a kilo of sun-ripened tomatoes pretty as those in the glossy pages of *Gourmet* magazine, a fresh chicken that had hunted and pecked freely under the sky, and a bottle of vodka.

Now imagine the average Pole who earns 15,000 *złotys* a month. Out shopping, he—or more likely she—doesn't buy chicken very often. A chicken is a day's pay. She buys baloney—lots of baloney—and white cheese and radishes. And most days she stands in line for twenty minutes to an hour per item.

First, though—if this is at a supermarket—she stands in line to get into the store. She can't simply walk in and begin taking cans off the shelf. She needs a basket, one of the store's baskets, and since there are only so many baskets because only so many people are allowed in the store at one time, she must wait in the basket line. This might take half an hour.

Finally she has her basket and is shopping, going up and down the aisles. But there's some cheese she wants (and a line for that) and some meat (and separate lines for beef, pork, and chicken).

It doesn't take long to understand why it's very quiet in Polish stores. Talking takes energy.

But at the head of a line, of course, there is usually some speech. The customer needs to say how much she wants. And sometimes there is additional speech. A customer in the pork line, for example, with a little extra to spend, might point at a particular piece, and the clerk might pull off the hook a different piece.

The customer might say: "No—the other one."

The clerk might say: "They are all the same."

The customer: "Maybe you are mistaken."

The clerk: "I am not."

There might be stronger speech. There might be a loud stand-off. Several minutes might go by. Drag by. The others in line—their shoulders aching from holding their potatoes, their jars and cans—might feel this discussion will go on forever; or they might find, vicariously, new energy in the confrontation, relief from the tedium of waiting, maybe even feel something like a thrill. What will happen?

Finally, if the customer is strong enough, the clerk might fetch that other piece of pork off the hook, slap it on her chopping board, and bring down her cleaver with murderous blows against the meat.

The customer, despite a few cat-calls from the audience, has won. Like an athlete's after stiff competition, her face is serene.

Now, if she is all finished shopping, she joins the line where you pay.

At the Pewex shops it is much easier to buy things. Pewexes are all over Poland, though principally in the larger cities and towns, and they have almost everything: Danish hams, Colgate toothpaste, Swiss chocolate, German coffee, Italian washing machines, U.S. tires, Rolex watches, Camel cigarettes, Wilkinson razor blades, Lego blocks, Opium parfum by Saint Laurent, Dr. Schieffer's Biovital vitamin drink with the big red heart on the bottle, Scotch whiskey, Heineken, wool yarn, Dole pineapple slices, Parker pens, bananas, you name it, it's likely in one Pewex or another, but only for dollars, Deutsche marks, pounds. Hard currency.

You stand in line here too, of course, but somehow you don't mind it so much. First you line up to tell the clerk what you want, and the clerk fills out a form listing your items. Then you take the form to the cashier and stand in line to pay. Then you take your receipt to the line where the items you've paid for are handed over.

Polish vodka is also on sale in Pewex.

"You know how the black market price for dollars is fixed?" July, my left-handed pitcher, said to me.

"How?"

"By the price for Polish vodka in Pewex," he said. "I will explain."

It worked like this: if a bottle of vodka cost 1,200 *złotys* in the Polish shops and $1 in Pewex, a Pole would buy a dollar from you for 1,100 *złotys*, take that dollar to Pewex for his vodka, and profit 100 *złotys*.

Pewex advertised on television (using models with good cleavage), so you were encouraged to want dollars.

Television and Pewex too, of course, were run by the government.

And of course buying dollars on the black market was illegal and you could go to jail for it.

Lingering outside the Pewex in my neighborhood were half a dozen money changers. They were there every weekday, from nine to five, from time to time taking out their wads of bills and counting them, smoking Marlboros, dressed in Levis or Lucky jeans and wearing little tweed porkpie hats pulled low over their eyes and pointy shoes you associate with pimps.

My friend Alicja, who lived around the corner, would usually visit one of these men in the morning. "That one with the nice face—you know him? I am a very good judge. We can trust him. The others I am not so sure." With the man whose face she liked, Alicja would trade a few dollars from the supply her father regularly sent from Canada.

Her father had gone to Canada "five or six years ago" on a tourist visa and was still there.

"Hasn't his visa expired?"

"Maybe he is a citizen now. I don't know."

In the meantime, Alicja's mother continued to live in Kraków. Alicja had gone to the university in Kraków and studied Spanish but did not take her degree. She married Andrzej, a young film director, six years ago and moved with him to Warsaw. They had two apartments (one was his studio) and an Afghan hound. They had two apartments—and many nice things in them—because they had dollars and because Andrzej's first film, a short called *The Rat-Catcher*, won several national awards and was nominated for an Academy Award. The Polish prizes made him laugh because *The Rat-Catcher* is a bitter criticism of the government which the censor completely missed. Not a second of the film was cut. When the film arrived in California, however, the American distributor deleted the first five minutes—where the theme, in a laboratory, is painstakingly established in cool scientific talk. The distributor said the talk was "too slow." All he wanted was the rat-catcher cozying up to the rats, feeding them, getting them to follow him like sheep, and then the slap-and-wap of the kill.

"Sometimes I wonder what my life is like if Andrzej and I do not marry." Alicja was a pretty woman, slim and blonde. She felt very frustrated, she said, because she wanted to work but Andrzej was against it. She said he wanted her home and food on the stove when he got there. He was ten years older than she was, a man who smoked a pipe and spent much of his time alone, thinking about his next film. "Very jealous is Andrzej," she said. "One time my last boyfriend telephoned and Andrzej does not speak to me for one month, can you imagine? Come," she laughed, "I will introduce you to my banker. Then we must go by taxi to Mokotów for oranges. That shop there—do you know it?—it has them. It caters to foreigners. And I have suddenly much desire for this fruit."

We found the man whose face Alicja liked and trusted (he was blond, about thirty, her age) and they exchanged smiles and money. On his left hand, he wore two rings with big amber stones in them, and on his right hand, a ring with an ivory horse head.

In the taxi, Alicja said, "He asked me to go with him to London."

"That man?"

"Which man?"

"Your banker?"

"No, no," she laughed. "My last boyfriend. But that was a long time ago. Maybe, though, I will think about it myself. I need to improve my English. Oh, Andrzej would be very angry!"

I lived in Żoliborz, a woodsy district in north Warsaw. The director Andrzej Wajda, Alicja's husband's hero, also lived there. So did the popular pro-Solidarity priest, Jerzy Popiełuszko, until he was murdered by the Polish secret police in 1984. I lived on Staffa Street, named for the poet Leopold Staff. I had the second floor of a two-story house: three large rooms and a kitchen you could have a party in. Luxury by Polish standards. Heaven. The living room and dining room, side by side, faced a garden, faced the sun coming up and the moon at night. Light filled these rooms because the walls facing the garden were all glass. Mornings that autumn I could step through sliding glass doors and pick sweet purple grapes off the lush vines hugging the balcony. I could not reach far enough for an apple or a pear off the trees that were also loaded with fruit, but I could, when she arrived from the States to join me, dance with Vicki out there.

And very early in the morning, in our bedroom, we could smell the breads and rolls and other good things being made in the best bakery in Warsaw, a block away.

The line for this *piekarnia* was always long. Vicki took a book along when she went for our bread.

The longest line in Warsaw, bar none, was at the American Embassy. Poles hoping for tourist visas would arrive there by five a.m., sometimes earlier. Three hundred hopefuls a day, waiting eight, nine, ten hours in line.

Students were generally successful, especially if they had a letter from an American inviting them to spend their vacation in Des Moines or Queens or Oregon City. Or if they had a scholarship to an American university. Or could run one hundred meters in world class time.

*Babcia*s were hard to turn down—especially if they had relatives in Chicago, Milwaukee, L.A., Hamtramck, and they almost always did.

Professors got visas. Their biggest problem was getting the Polish government to let them go.

Taxi drivers never got visas. Unless they had papers saying they were brain surgeons and could manage to fool the interviewer.

Poles with property were likely to come back, so they got visas.

Poles with money, who traveled a lot, got visas.

Poles with not much going for them—the majority—did not get visas.

Embassy interviewers referred to their assignment as "being on the line." They were not fond of it. Every two minutes or so another nervous hopeful.

"You know what sweat and garlic smell like together?"

"Try sweat and garlic and Opium."

"I'm getting mine down to a minute and a half, no bullshit."

"This woman came in yesterday with two little kids. I turned her down, all three of them. She tried to ream me out. Said I was heartless, a pig. Their daddy was in the States and *I* wouldn't let them go see him. 'How long has their daddy been there?' I said. 'Two years,' she said. 'Listen, lady, it's not *me* who's heartless. Nobody's forcing him to stay there.'"

"He's probably driving a cab in Queens."

"Sending back big bucks."

"That's all they're after."

"They hit the States and start pumping gas."

"I hate this crap."

Embassy people often had accents with a little bit of Florida in them, a little bit of Virginia, accents hard to place.

"I'm not *from* anywhere. I grew up all over. My old man was in the Service."

"Hey, Lucy, where you going on your vacation?"

"Spain. Can't wait. I hear they got a Wendy's in Malaga."

"I'm buying a condo there—up the coast."

"Not me. They're cheaper in South Africa."

"Jesus, I didn't hear that."

"Who needs another beer?"

"What time's chow?"

"They're serving now."

"Thanksgiving in Poland. That's a contradiction in terms."

At this point I think of my grandfather, whose name was Stefan Szostak. And of Joseph Conrad, and of my mother. And of all that they have in common, including the art of fiction. To my mother, for example, weather, physical description, a good line, are more interesting than strict historical chronology, getting names or dates right. "Sometimes," she will say, "I did not go to school because I had no shoes." When was that? "One winter—it was so cold the potatoes in the cellar were hard as rocks." But how old were you? "I was a *girl*, a skinny thing—but my hair, no one had such pretty hair. It was the same color as Jean Harlow's." My mother's hair, for years the color of wheat, would be gray now if she did not dye it. My grandfather's hair was black and thick, like his mustache, his eyes. In the *American Heritage Dictionary* there is a picture of Joseph Conrad ("Original name, Teodor Jósef Konrad Korzeniowski. 1857–1924. Polish-born English novelist and short-story writer") that shakes me. Cut the gray beard from his chin and take off the tie and tailored coat, and you have my grandfather looking off toward the woods where the bull ran one morning, his nostrils flared and his black eyes glaring—my mother said—"bloody murder."

"The bull was glaring bloody murder?" I said.

"They both were!" she said. "They were both alike!"

What I know of my grandfather comes from the summers and holidays I spent on his farm in northern Michigan when I was a boy. And from my mother's stories. He was a man who kept mainly to himself, who bore pink, flower-like scars on his shoulders and back from the hot Detroit steel that had splashed him. A man who, like his team of plow horses, could lay his face in the creek, mouth first, and collect small, sparkling drops of water on his mustache, just as Nelly and Prince collected such sun-filled drops on their own fine muzzle hairs. I knew he came from Poland and did not speak—or care to speak—English. And I knew something else. He read books. He was the only member of my family I ever saw read books.

The summers I was sent to his farm from the city, to learn a few things, I watched him put his stool beside Sophie, beside Jola, Angel, and Daisy—press his ear just above their udders, as if listening to their bellies—and squeeze, the bubbles in the pail between his knees rising. When he offered me dippers of this milk I always drank it, but what I preferred was the cream that came thick and sweet from the separator. I watched him fork manure, fill the barn with hay, and make his own sausage. If something broke—something made of steel—he fired up the forge in his blacksmith shop and fixed it, his face above the flames the color of rhubarb. Wearing the reins over a shoulder, he walked behind his plow murmuring to Prince or Nelly a simple song I could figure out, about staying in line. In the late sunlight he carried a bar of Ivory soap down to the creek where minnows and silver suckers slithered through, and bathed his bright shoulders. At night after supper he said his rosary in the kitchen, kneeling beside the table. Afterwards, he got out his bottle of whiskey, and in the glow of a kerosene lamp read a book. Grandma would take me into another room then, saying, "Leave him be."

He read, I learned later, whatever he could get, and always in Polish. Joseph Conrad was his favorite. When he died—in the hollyhocks one morning—a book by Conrad was found in his hands. My grandmother, who was not a reader of anything except her Daily Missal, put that last book in his coffin before it was closed. She couldn't tell me, when I was old enough to want to know, what it was called; but I have always believed it was *Heart of Darkness*.

I loved my grandfather mainly, I think, because he was a mystery to me. A man who did not speak the words I spoke, who flew into rages and for days kept his distance from everyone, spending hours alone in the apple orchard, in the far pasture—but who once, in the midst of his silence, picked me up in a stubbled field and sat me between his legs on the hay cutter, and gave me the reins, shouting "Gee!" and "Haw!" as we charged ahead, and turned, and charged back. All of his sons and daughters were a little afraid of him; he was a mystery to them too. "What would Pa say?" was a phrase I heard often. These were grown men and women, my uncles and aunts, who spoke softly in his presence. He sired eleven children; two died in infancy. After he finished his whiskey, he picked up his lamp and went upstairs, taking with him long, dangerous, thrilling shadows. He slept by himself in a corner, under the rafters, and when I went up to bed later I passed by his corner quickly and quietly, not wanting to disturb anything. He slept completely covered, as if in a cave.

Years later—drinking my own whiskey, reading about a man alone in the jungle—I sometimes saw my grandfather holding his lamp and casting shadows in the low, earth-smelling cellar, his breath also a shadow, while everyone else was gathered in the parlor opening presents. Reading about a storm at sea, I sometimes saw him, soaking wet, gazing out the barn door at lightning—his face streaked with it—and the wind whipping his beans down. And sometimes I'd see my mother, her face flushed with memory, telling me about the weddings he gave his daughters in the orchard—a platform built for three days of dancing, tables rich with hams he'd cured, beef he'd slaughtered, and that wonderful sausage packed with garlic and pepper. Helen's wedding, Nettie's, my mother's own, and Rita's. "Oh!" my mother would clap her hands.

"But what about Aunt Mary's wedding?"

"Oh," my mother would sigh, and turn the story back, back to when they all lived in Detroit—back to the time before Grandpa was burned in the foundry, before they had to move up north—and how it was *she*, my mother, who got to return the library books. The books he'd read that week. And how proudly she handed over to the librarian the list of new ones he wanted.

"I had to go all the way to Woodward Avenue!"

But drinking whiskey and reading, remembering, I knew what had happened to Aunt Mary, the eldest child, knew that her wedding was never mentioned because there hadn't been one; knew that she'd met a man somewhere, and produced a son, my cousin Donny, and then lived a long time—long after my grandfather's death—in a hospital that my mother and father and I took my grandmother to in the car, bringing along the fresh tomatoes my aunt loved so much, which she ate sitting on a bench in the sun beside my mother and grandmother, while my father and I walked in the woods nearby. Some things I understood then: I understood it was important for my father and me to leave Aunt Mary alone for a while with Grandma and my mother, and I understood that my cousin, who was sixteen and lived on the farm, was not happy pulling beans and forking manure because when he came in late from setting pins at the bowling alley in town on Saturday nights and woke me up to give me a Baby Ruth, he would make a fist and shake it out the door toward the dark corner where Grandpa slept, and tell me that next year, *next* year, Grandma would sign the papers letting him join the Navy and not tell *him*. But I did not understand everything, my cousin said, because I was a boy. Much later when I thought I understood everything, my grandfather and grandmother were dead, my father was dead, Aunt Mary was dead, and Donny was dead. Cleaning his deer rifle, my mother said.

"What does Joseph Conrad mean to the Poles?" I asked a professor at the Jagiellonian University in Kraków.

"He is not a Polish writer," the professor said.

"But he was born here."

"He did not write about Polish matters."

"The spirit in turmoil? Survival? Salvation? These aren't Polish matters?"

"He left. He turned his back on Poland. He wrote in English. Mickiewicz, Sienkiewicz, Miłosz—these are Polish writers. Not Korzeniowski."

If Conrad was not a Polish writer, I thought, then what was my grandfather not?

On Sunday, April 17, Vicki and I got up early and ate oatmeal in our sunny dining room. I was in my uniform, she had on her running shorts and a T-shirt with a fish leaping between her breasts. We'd met exactly ten months before, in June, at the top of

Lake Michigan. She was in the audience I was reading my poems to, her hair hugging her cheeks and filled with streaks of silver, like minnows slipping through. We spent three days together, then I had to fly to California for eight weeks, to study Polish in one of those intensive courses where you do almost nothing else except memorize vocabulary and talk back to tapes and repeat little conversations that Ewa and Andrzej are having in your text-book about going to the cinema or the zoo and was the film inter-esting? no, it was boring, and what animals they'd seen. There were also daily lectures by a professor who had, for example, in-teresting parallels to draw between certain archaic Russian end-ings and certain archaic Polish endings, "for the Russianists in the class." I spoke to Vicki in English two or three nights a week on the telephone. I asked her to come to Poland with me. She said she first had to quit her job and sell her house and pack or give away "a whole lot of accumulation," but she thought she could do it. As soon as we got together again, in August, we flew to Lon-don. A week later I would continue on to Warsaw; she would re-turn to the States to complete the sale of her house, see her eldest daughter off to college, attend a going-away party, then meet me in ten days. I remember eating a pretty good curried lamb dish in London, but mainly I remember waking up and walking nowhere in particular and going easily to sleep with this woman I had been with, until then, less than a week. She was forty-six, though that was hard to believe. She could run seven miles in an hour. She could bake in our Polish oven any kind of pie, from scratch. She was five-feet-four and fit curled against me at night like a good dream come back. At the going-to-Poland party, twenty-seven of her girlfriends gave her twenty-seven pairs of panties so she would not be caught short behind the Iron Curtain.

After we finished our oatmeal, she sent me off to the stadium—and to our season's opener against Jastrzębie—with a good luck slap on my tail. She'd catch a taxi for the stadium later, after her run, and bring along young Wojciech, a neighbor boy she gave English lessons to. He wanted to see what this baseball was all about.

When I got to Skra, I was astounded. Inside the main gate the entire, and very considerable, walking-around area was thick with people, perhaps twenty-five thousand. But they weren't baseball fans. They were buyers and sellers of merchandise, of Western goods, mainly, smuggled into the country in the cars and suit-cases and on the backs of Poles trying to get ahead. Every Sunday from eight a.m. to two p.m., Skra was a bazaar. A big one. To make your way from the main gate to the stadium—past the tennis courts, past the outdoor basketball court, and across the sprawling central plaza where the heart of the bazaar lay—took almost half an hour, if you were aggressive, whereas on normal days you could make the trip in a couple of minutes. No one, not Dariusz, not George or Pete, had warned me about the bazaar. I suppose they assumed I knew, as they assumed I knew many other things I came to find out on my own.

You paid two hundred *złotys* to get in. What you saw, after the great mob, were rows and rows—as tidy and almost as close to-gether as rows of potatoes or pickles in a farmer's field—of things; and orderly as always, the people walked shoulder to shoulder, slower than pilgrims, among these rows. Looking. They looked at jeans, video cassettes, shoes, comic books, bicycles, tricycles, can openers, stereos, tents, sixpacks of Certs, threepacks of Jockey shorts, toilet seats, ice cube makers. Each "shop" was as large or as small as the blanket laid on the ground for the items it offered. On one blanket I saw a child's wagon, a long-play record by the Beatles, a pair of shoelaces, and three bright telephones. Next door was a complete set of salmon-colored Samsonite luggage. Next door to that a pair of red high heels, several bras, two brooms, and a bowl of wax peaches. Blanket after blanket, a still life for sale. At the ends of many rows, you could buy orange soda, cotton candy, kielbasa in a bun, or a piece of bread spread with melted cheese and tomato sauce, called *zapiekanki*. I thought of the jar of cool spring water waiting in the hedgerow on my grandfather's farm, at the end of a row of beans, where a pheasant sometimes exploded into flight.

Uttering "*Przepraszam*" ("Excuse me"), I jumped across blan-kets and ducked under unfurled sails being examined; I squeezed past men bent over by TVs on their spines, past women pressing nylon slips and blouses to their bosoms, measuring for size; I got caught behind a man with a cigarette in his mouth and a twelve-volt battery balanced on his head: one arm held the battery in place, the other carried, over his shoulder, a pair of fishing rods with threatening barbed tackle—spoons and pop-eyed frogs— dangling in his wake. Over a loudspeaker someone was saying that at ten o'clock and at noon, inside the stadium, Skra would be play-ing baseball games. Everyone was invited. At that moment I had made it about halfway across the plaza. It was nine-thirty. I needed to urinate. I spotted a space between two blankets where I could escape the barbed spoons and pop-eyed frogs. I leaped over—into the leathery embrace of a girl wrapped in a flight jacket. Her eyes were closed, her expression bored. "*Przepraszam*," I said. She opened her eyes. I was not the right man. She turned, found the right man, and modeled the jacket for him.

I leaped over another row. I saw a big woman holding up a pair of pink panties and remembered a scene I had witnessed the pre-vious October: a warm, dreamy, Indian summer day, a perfect day for walking in Łazienki Park under the blazing red and yellow leaves—and I was heading there, on the bus, to meet Vicki. The bus was crowded and hot. It stopped for a light. On the sidewalk beside us a large woman in a housedress was talking with another woman. Suddenly the large woman reached under her dress, re-moved her underpants, and stuffed them in her purse. I glanced around the bus, expecting to see a few smiles, but I saw only the usual passive, stony expressions. I saw them now at Skra, almost everywhere under the sunny sky, even on the faces of those loaded down with purchases. Perhaps on their faces most of all. Nothing really, they seemed to say, will make us happy. (Several months later, Irena, a prostitute in the Victoria Hotel, would show me that look better than anyone.)

The stadium, like the country, was in poor shape. I got a hint of that the first time I tried to get in, two weeks before. Facing the plaza were seven gates, marked N, O, P, R, S, T, and Z, but only S was in fact a gate; the others were boarded up. I didn't know that. Going from sealed gate to sealed gate, I got the feeling I was very late; and I could smell, as I had smelled outside the Colosseum in Rome, that odor of old stone become flaky. Finally at S, easing past iron grillwork fuzzy with years of rust, I saw a green field. I saw a man vaulting himself through the air on a pole.

Inside the stadium, which was horseshoe shaped, the field was lovely that early April when I first saw it, but everywhere else the place was rough. Seating—for maybe twenty thousand—was simply an arrangement of long concrete steps. Every thirty yards or so, shorter, less steep steps let you walk up or down. Here and there the concrete was pebbly from age and neglect, and across the field part of a section had long ago collapsed; the rubble, still there, lay like boulders and stones and chunks of bridge in a dry riverbed. Down on the lush, freshly mowed field, however, men and women in bright red warm-ups were stretching their hamstrings, throwing javelins, running around the pink all-weather track circling the grass. And a quartet of pole vaulters, one after the other, with no success, kept trying to fly over a bar.

Two weeks later on that bazaar Sunday of our first game, inside the stadium at last, I had no trouble finding Dariusz because the stadium, all ours today, was practically empty and he was barking—instructing some Junior players how to measure a baseball diamond and line it with lime. It was almost ten o'clock, game time. I said, "Dariusz, these guys should be warming up. Can't someone else help you line the field?" He held an unlit cigarette and the spool of a steel tape measure, not hearing me, barking out his instructions to half a dozen players gathered at the tape's other end, down around first base; neither he nor the players seemed able to agree on exactly where to lay the tape for the truest line between first base and home plate. Meantime, other Junior Sparks sat on the grass changing into their uniforms, or were hauling cases of mineral water into the stadium, or dragging big carpets onto the field.

"What are those for?" I said.

The carpet-haulers shrugged and looked over at Dariusz.

I found Paweł Tymiński, a Junior who spoke English, and asked him. He said, "These must be put down to protect the grass." I pointed to a corner out of the way. "Put them there," I said. I spotted George arriving, told him to help Dariusz line the field, and then one by one I collected the Junior Sparks. Using Paweł to translate, I said, "Your game is supposed to start in five minutes. Get loose."

"Coach," Paweł said, "the game can't start in five minutes."

"I can see that. The field isn't even lined." I looked around. "And where's Jastrzębie?"

"I don't know," Paweł said.

"Anyway, get loose. Two laps around the track, then start throwing," I said. I saw Pete and Pizza Hut and a couple of other Seniors coming onto the field. I put them to work hauling two long benches from way down at the other end of the stadium, over to where the Skra and Jastrzębie "dugouts" would be. Then I did what the Sparks did when they had to urinate: I went into one of the gate tunnels sealed at the other end.

When I came out, the Juniors had stopped running; some were hauling the carpets back onto the field, some were milling around third base, the rest were gathered behind Dariusz, who stood on home plate sighting down his arm toward left field like a general about to order an attack. I went over to him.

"Damn it, Dariusz," I said, "these guys need to get loose."

"Lines very difficult," he said, as if we had been discussing this for some time now. He continued to sight down his arm, moving it slowly toward third base.

"Where's George? I told George to help you."

"George?" he said. "I don't know where is George."

"And where is Jastrzębie?" I said.

"Moment, moment," he said. He instructed someone in the group at third base to move the base slightly to the left. Satisfied, he turned to Robert, who stood by with the lime spreader, and told him to lay down the line to third. Then he found a match for his cigarette.

"Very difficult job," he said.

"I guess so, judging by the size of your crew," I said.

"My crew?"

"I want to warm up the Juniors, Dariusz. They can't just start playing."

"I know, I know. We must wait for Jastrzębie."

"What I'm talking about is getting *ready* to play," I said. "They can't get ready standing around watching Robert make lines. Or dragging rugs on the field."

"It's OK, Gary."

"It's not OK. And those damn rugs have to go—they're dangerous."

At that point we were joined by Mr. Richard, the Klub manager, a scholarly looking man who always wore a suit and tie. He expressed concern about the grass. I expressed concern about tripping, broken bones, and overall ugliness. He and Dariusz went back and forth in Polish on the subject, and finally—but not happily—Mr. Richard ordered the rugs removed.

"Now what about Jastrzębie?" I said. "Where are they?"

"I tell now about Jastrzębie," Dariusz said. "They phone to me about travel to Warsaw. This day," he pointed at the ground, "you understand? Not before. They travel from Silesia maybe four, five hours ago. Maybe here late."

"How late?"

"How late? I don't know. Maybe eleven o'clock."

"When did you know this?"

"I know it for sure," he said, as if I doubted the information. "Now I tell you. No problem."

Jastrzębie arrived at noon. Dariusz, who had gone out to greet them and assist them through the bazaar, seemed happy to tell me the coal miners looked sleepy. He wanted very much to beat them, not so much because a year ago Jastrzębie whipped Skra 33–3 and 25–5, but because they were Silesians. I was learning that Warsaw and Silesia were not close. I had even heard some Sparks say that the people in Silesia were more German than Polish. Certainly there was a strong German influence in that part of Poland; you could see it in the architecture, the food. Certainly, too, the Polish government favored the coal miners and their families with better wages, better medical care, more—and easier to get—consumer goods than Poles elsewhere got. And long-standing soccer rivalries between Warsaw and the Silesian clubs helped maintain a clear and steady "us and them." But Dariusz' feelings about Silesia were shaped by baseball: Silesia was where the power was (i.e., PZBall's headquarters) and where Dariusz had to go, hat in hand (and seven hours each way on the train), whenever he needed balls, gloves, bats, etc., from the cache of equipment—including more than $20,000 worth given to PZBall by U.S. companies—that was down there. More than once, Dariusz described what these visits were like: "I sit, you understand, and listen. Mr. Liszka, president of Polish baseball federation, he says to me everything. I say nothing. This takes much time. After all this talk, he gives to me twelve new base-balls. Mr. Liszka does not go like this"—Dariusz patted me on the head as if I were a little boy—"because this is not necessary."

PZBall often seemed like a territory consisting of eight duchies, with all of the requisite intrigue, envy, and brandishing. That six of the eight teams were located in Silesia did not make the Duke of Warsaw easy in his bed, or anywhere else.

     The Juniors' game got started about twelve-thirty, the Se-niors' game at two-thirty. The latter lasted four hours. Through-out the entire afternoon and early evening, Dariusz sat by himself in the press box at the topmost level of the stadium and explained over a loudspeaker what was going on. He looked very small and lonesome up there. His audience was a couple of dozen friends and relatives of the Sparks and maybe a hundred shoppers who had drifted in from the bazaar, some of them simply to take a load off their feet and eat a kielbasa and drift out again. His commen-tary was steady and detailed—more detailed than necessary, it sounded like to me. Most of the time, involved in the games, I tuned him out, but when I listened he sounded like a professor who had been long at the lectern. Though I'm sure he was trying his best to maintain an impartial, professional tone, his volume rose and his consonants banged into each other when Mariusz hit a home run for us. And when the Senior Sparks took a 17–14 lead in the bottom of the seventh inning, I could hear him breathing like an obscene phone-caller, all hot and bothered. But in the eighth and ninth innings, when the Sparks lost their cool, the

*Before our first game, in Skra Stadium. The U.S. Embassy
orchestrated the picture, largely, it seems, to get the man in the
necktie in it. He is Deputy Chief of Mission Darryl Johnson, whom
I never saw before that day or afterwards. Kneeling (l–r): George,
Norbert (partially hidden), Pete, Chuck Powers, Capt. Paweł,
Alejandro, Greg, and Andrzej Majchrowski, whose medical school
studies soon forced him to quit the team. Standing (l–r): Pizza Hut,
Blackie, Jake the catcher, Mark, July (behind Mark in sunglasses),
Adam, Tony, Marek, Chris Płatek, Jackson Diehl of the* Washington
Post, *Mariusz, me, Froggy, Johnson, Henry, Tomasz Konarzewski
(who quit the team after a few games), and Komo. We're wearing
our practice clothes; our new uniforms were not ready yet. Dariusz
is not here because he was up in the press box.*

lead, and finally the game, committing one error after another, the voice up there was that of a man on his deathbed. He might have been asking for water, water, or for a priest.

So we lost our first game, 28–17. (The Juniors also lost.) That we had put on a pretty good show, though, and might even have won—a possibility the Sparks the previous season could never seriously entertain—was enough reason to enjoy a few beers back at my place. Vicki warmed up a big Virginia ham she bought at the Embassy commissary, made a pot of potato salad, a bunch of brownies, and rather liked being (she told me later) the only woman at a party for men.

"What did you like most?"

"I liked how they kissed my hand. And were so polite. And ate everything."

In the middle of the night she woke me up. She said, "Did you hear me?"

"No. What did you say?"

"I said, 'Between a rock and another rock.'"

"What does that mean?"

"You were talking in your sleep, I guess. You said, 'Vic, I have a question: if Conrad is not a Polish writer because he went West, where do you put all those Poles wearing Levis and Opium and eager for visas and dollars?'"

"Did I say anything else?"

"You said you didn't care if our apartment *was* bugged."

About eight kilometers south of Warsaw, in a sweet, gently rolling pine forest, lay a settlement of handsomely done-up dachas that could have been set down in any good woodsy neighborhood in the States without lowering property values one penny. The dachas were big and smart and had lush lawns and were very inviting but for the serious fences protecting them. Some fences had barbed wire strung along their tops and some, the brick fences, had shards of glass fixed up there. Many yards also had German shepherds strolling among the roses.

Vicki and I were riding in this neighborhood with Dariusz and

Mr. and Mrs. Richard, in the Skra manager's tiny Polish Fiat, looking for the American Embassy's dacha. A party was being given. I don't remember what the occasion was, if there was one, but spring had arrived—maybe that was the occasion—and the baseball fans in the Embassy had invited some locals involved in PZBall. Besides Dariusz and Mr. Richard, Kutno's Juan Echevarría and Waldemar Szymański were coming. Szymański occupied the same position at Kutno that Dariusz did at Skra, and these two organizers, I came to find out, kept a very careful eye on each other, as good dukes should.

Mr. Richard was having trouble finding the American dacha. The streets were tire ruts in the sod, single-lane trails; here and there a house number was nailed to a tree. We had a map and were looking for a yellow roof. The late afternoon sun cut through the timber, and you could smell pine resin and sandy loam and roses.

"Who lives in these houses?" I asked Dariusz. He was in the back seat between Vicki and Mrs. Richard with his knees high as his shoulders. Packed in, but cheerful about it, was how they sat.

"I don't know," he said.

Then we came up behind a Warsaw taxi.

Dariusz said, "Ah hah, Juan Echevarría and Walter Szymański. With their womens."

We followed the taxi over the ruts. In Polish, Dariusz and Richard exchanged quick comments about Walter Szymański. Dariusz laughed at his own comment. "I tell about Mr. Szymański," Dariusz said to me.

"What did you tell?"

Dariusz laughed again, but didn't say what he told.

The taxi came to a corner, turned around, and waited for us to go past so it could return down the same street. When we passed the taxi, Dariusz waved. A man with a black mustache, smoking a cigarette, waved back.

"Juan Echevarría," Dariusz said.

We turned around and followed the taxi.

"How are you doing?" I asked Vicki.

"I'm glad I didn't wear a hoop skirt," she said.

The taxi went up and down the street again and we stayed behind it, looking for a yellow roof. My back was killing me. Finally I suggested that Dariusz and I get out and go up to a house and ask for help. When we stopped, the taxi stopped too, and Echevarría and Szymański and their women got out. The taxi drove off. The two couples walked toward us, the men leading. The women wore what looked like hoop skirts, and they had trouble walking in the sandy tire ruts in their high heels. I heard Vicki say, "Well, well."

Dariusz made introductions. Then Walter Szymański, looking around, wanted to know which house was the Embassy dacha. Dariusz said he thought we were a little lost. "But we will ask," he said. Szymański did not seem happy about that, nor about giving up his taxi. He was a man with all of his buttons buttoned and his coat hankie puffed like a rooster's comb.

Echevarría, the Cuban steelworker, was about five-feet-nine, very thin, and very dark. I had expected someone bigger. His jacket, in sharp contrast to Szymański's, seemed not to belong to him—or perhaps came from a time when he was heavier. He was happy to hear Skra had a coach, he told me, and patted me on the back. He was looking forward to playing us. He spoke a mixture of Polish and English and I liked him right away. I wanted to ask his opinion of the other teams in Poland, but Szymański, impatient, wanted to find the Embassy dacha. Dariusz went up to a gate and pushed a button. A woman came across the lawn carrying a trowel, wiping sweat off her brow. "*Tak, tak*"—she seemed to know, before Dariusz even spoke, what we needed; apparently other lost party-goers had stopped there. She promptly got in the car beside Richard and directed him to the dacha. He deposited Vicki and his wife, then returned to shuttle the rest of us. Dariusz and I said we'd walk. I was hoping Juan would walk with us, but he didn't.

"You really don't know who lives in these houses?" I asked Dariusz.

"Who you think?"

"People with money," I said.

"Sure. And party members," he said.

"Good times."

"Good times, sure."

"Judging from the dogs and barbed wire, they don't seem real comfortable."

Dariusz grunted.

"Is Szymański a party member?" I asked him.

"I don't know. Is all bull *shit*," he said, cutting the last word in half. "Big ears, big listen, you understand?"

Dariusz was quiet for a while. I was too. He seemed a little upset—perhaps because Juan, whom he greatly admired, had elected to ride on ahead with Szymański. We walked along in the piney evening and for the first time in eight months I began to feel homesick. We might have been walking in northern Michigan. Even the occasional caw and shriek of a nightbird overhead sounded sweet. Then Dariusz waved his hand in disgust. "They come to me," he said. "What I know? What? What? I tell them baseball. They go away, come back. I say to them baseball." He shook his head. "Bull *shit*, you understand? For me, only baseball. Only. No big ears, no big listen. Now they stand over there. But *I* know how they do. Watch. You understand?"

I almost told him about the funny buzzes and clicks Vicki and I heard when talking on our telephone, and about other odd noises in the apartment—and about the same strange men on the street we seemed to have seen more than a couple of times before. None of which bothered us. We laughed at it, especially the time when she and I were in bed, playing around, and the phone started to whine, the water heater popped its lid, and the faucets in both the bathroom and kitchen began to flow: all together in a crazy, slam-bang concert. "Sounds like the boys at the other end are getting excited," Vic said. But I didn't tell Dariusz any of this because the big ears for him were not funny at all.

At last we came to the yellow roof, a handsome spread. I saw that it too was surrounded by a serious fence, but one that stopped short of barbed wire or broken glass at the top.

Inside we found the beer—iced tubs of Heineken—and then the corner where the baseball talk was in progress. I was glad to see Chuck Powers back in town. Chuck was the *Los Angeles*

Times correspondent in Warsaw and just as nutty as I was about baseball. (He had on his Red Sox cap.) Though often away on assignment for weeks at a time—to the other eastern European capitals, to Gdańsk during the strikes—he came to the Sparks' practices and games whenever he could and helped out. (As did Jackson Diehl, of the *Washington Post*, for a while.) Chuck had played high school ball in Missouri and a year at the university in Columbia and had arrived in Poland about the same time I did. He and Juan were talking when Dariusz and I came over.

"Echevarría here," Chuck said to me, "thinks Kutno is going to whip Warsaw again this year. He doesn't know Warsaw has learned to throw and catch."

"Throw and catch?" Juan smiled. "This is good. Better for us. How is Norbert?"

"Much progress," Dariusz said.

"Very big arm," Juan said.

"Watch out," Chuck told him, "we've got two Cubans on the team."

"Tony!" Juan laughed. "I know. And Alejandro. Very good!"

"*Much* progress," Dariusz said. He was beaming, a baseball man among equals.

"I heard someone say progress." This was Cameron Munter, from the Embassy's political section. He had worked for Peter Ueberroth during the 1984 Olympics and was eager to help the Polish baseball program. It was Cameron who sent Dariusz to me back in January. He turned from Walter Szymański, with whom he had been talking, and put his arm around Dariusz. "Are these guys"—he meant Chuck and me—"any help?"

"Very much progress," Dariusz said, glancing at Szymański. Szymański was listening, but pretending not to.

"Whatever you guys need," Cameron said to me, "let me know. We'll try to get it."

I said we needed balls and gloves and neat's-foot oil and that real baseball caps would be nice. He winked.

Szymański then said something in Polish to Cameron and the two of them stepped aside to discuss whatever it was Szymański had on his mind. Dariusz, smiling, said to me, "Walter Szymański makes now special efforts. Is very funny."

"We're all making special efforts," I said, "and it's making me hungry." I went out on the deck for a hamburger. Vicki was there.

"Oddest thing," she said. "The Richards came in, took one look around, and left. Try the hotdogs, honey. This Marine knows what he's doing."

"Fresh off the plane from Oscar Mayer," said the Marine working the grill. He was a big boy with a brush cut.

"I tried recruiting him for the team," Vicki said. "But he tells me he can't fraternize. Not since that flap in Moscow."

"Lonestar," I said.

"Close enough," said the Marine. "Lonetree. But that's right, he took us all with him."

"No Polish sports of any kind," Vicki said. "What a shame."

"I'm not hurting too bad," said the Marine. "I'm flying my girl over next week for my birthday."

"Get your iron," Vicki said.

"Yes, ma'am," he said.

The Sunday following our loss to Jastrzębie, we hosted another Silesian team, Rój-Zory, whose name means "hive." "Like with bees," Pete told me. It was April 24, cold and overcast, and by the second inning of the Seniors game snowflakes were flying around. I counted six fans in the stands when it was over—Mariusz' girlfriend, Mark's girlfriend, Froggy's father and sister, Pizza Hut's father, and Vicki. We gave up three runs in the first inning—errors and walks—but then we started catching the ball and hitting it everywhere. In the bottom of the third, when we took a 15–3 lead, a Junior player—Paweł Tymiński—came running over to me and said, "Coach, Dariusz has a message for you. He thinks we can win by a knock down."

I looked up at Dariusz manning his microphone in the press box, cigarette smoke swirling around his head, and heard him explaining to the tiny audience that there was no Polish word for "homer." (Mariusz had just hit one.) I said to Paweł, "Maybe we can. But go tell Dariusz I'd rather not win by a knock down. We need the playing time. Tell Dariusz I'm thinking of making a lot of substitutions."

A tall, thin, altar boy–looking kid, Paweł hustled up the stadium steps to the press box. In a couple of minutes he was back, breathing hard. "Coach," he said, "I'm sorry to interrupt, but Dariusz wants me to say a knock down is no problem."

"Go tell Dariusz I'm going to start calling him George Steinbrenner," I said.

"I don't understand," Paweł said.

"Tell him *spokojnie*."

"He says it is cold today."

"Tell him I know."

Paweł took off. Rój-Zory came up to bat and Mark, on the mound, walked the first two hitters. Then Dariusz was standing beside me, trying to look very casual. I yelled out to Mark to throw strikes.

Dariusz said, "Very cold this day."

The batter lined out to Froggy, who stepped on first for a double play.

"Did you see that, Dariusz? Hell, we should pray for snow all summer," I said.

"I see, yes, but—" Dariusz lit a cigarette. "Gary, what you think about knock down? Theoretic only. *Only* theoretic. What you think?"

"I don't like that rule," I said. "It's Little League."

Mark struck out the next batter and when the Sparks came in I told Adam, Pete, and July to warm up. Dariusz looked alarmed. He said, "They will pitch?"

"Maybe," I said.

"But why?"

"We're twelve runs ahead. They could use the practice."

"But Gary, Gary, Adam is maybe big nervous today. Maybe Pete, maybe July—all no good."

"How will they get better, Dariusz?"

"I know, I know, but—"

Adam, Pete, and July had plenty of time to get warm because we sent ten men to the plate that inning, scoring five more runs. Everyone was having fun, whooping it up. Mark borrowed a scarf from his girlfriend and wore it when he went up to hit. He smacked a double. Then everyone else borrowed scarves—from Froggy's sister, Vicki, Mariusz' girlfriend, from each other. Chuck Powers offered his parka to Tony, who already had on—beside the white gloves—two jackets and a hooded sweatshirt. We were all having fun in the swirling snowflakes except Dariusz, who was smoking and rolling up his Scoremaster as if he might try to smoke that too. "Must win. Must. Very important."

In the top of the fifth—we led, 20–3—I put Adam on the mound. I figured to let him get the first out, July the second, Pete the third. Rój-Zory had to score eight runs that inning to keep the game going.

Adam's first pitch bounced off home plate. His second pitch sailed over Jake's head—and the umpire's—into the stands. His third pitch almost hit the batter. I called time and went out to the mound. I put my arm around Adam's steaming shoulders. I could feel his heart pounding to escape. Jake joined us. "Jake, tell Adam to ease up on his fastball and just play catch with you, like in practice. Tell him nice and easy into your glove."

When play resumed, Adam threw a strike. He looked amazed that he could do such a thing. He threw another easy one—for strike two—and then raised his pitching arm in a salute, grinning as if the world might be an OK place after all. These were the first strikes he'd ever thrown in a game. Against Jastrzębie he threw eight consecutive balls to the only two batters he faced. If this big, strong, former javelin champion could pick up some confidence on the mound, we'd have a hell of a pitcher. He delivered again and the batter blooped a single just over Froggy's head. I told Jake to tell Adam that was OK, the pitch was in the strike zone. But I could see it was not OK with Dariusz, who paced back and forth behind our bench like a man in prison.

The next batter bounced a very slow roller to Tony that Tony wisely held onto—no chance to get anybody. "Adam's doing fine," I said to Jake. "Tell him to throw just a little harder." Adam walked the next batter—on a 3 and 2 count—and Dariusz, seeing the bases loaded, seemed to have stopped breathing. His face was plum-blue. Rój-Zory's next batter hit a big-hopper straight back to Adam; he caught the ball and threw it cleanly to first. He got his out. He was bursting. When I brought in July, Adam raced from the mound like a kid who had something good to tell his mother, and all the guys on the bench held up their palms for him to slap.

July gave up a walk to load the bases again, but fanned the next batter. When I called time to bring in Pete, I saw that Dariusz was now sitting on the bench with his face in his hands. We had a 20–4 lead and he couldn't bear to watch. Pete, who had the best control among all our pitchers, delivered two quick strikes and Dariusz was peeking through his fingers. The next pitch slipped out of Pete's hand and skittered past Jake. The runner on third scored. I didn't look at Dariusz; he might have been bleeding; for sure he was thinking that if Rój-Zory put on a rally, we had no more pitchers. But the batter popped up to Tony, and the umpire stood on home plate and declared a knock down. Dariusz rose from the bench like one who had come from a long and terrible journey. "History, history," I heard him rasp.

It was the Sparks' first victory ever, breaking a fifteen-game losing streak that began the previous year. Dariusz brought over a man whom he introduced to Chuck and me as "chief of Skra." In all the excitement I never caught his name, if it was given, and never saw him again. He was short, bushy about the eyebrows like Brezhnev, and all bundled up. A bulldog-looking gent. Dariusz hung on the man's grunts as if they were poetry.

In the happy shower room later, I said to him, "Did the chief want a knock down?"

"Chief of Skra? No."

"Why was it so important?"

"Knock down not important."

"Dariusz, you were very eager to win by a knock down. Do not give me bullshit." Then I yelled to Pete, who was enjoying a warm shower, "Hey, shoot that hose over here." I held Dariusz so he couldn't escape the spray.

"Win. Only win is important," Dariusz sputtered.

"We *were* winning. Big," I said, holding him in the spray.

"Gary, you listen," he said, water falling on his serious expression. "This is Poland. Win is never sure."

We didn't play the next Sunday because it was May Day and only public events of an official (i.e., party) nature could be held. Well, this was Poland, where out of a population of thirty-four million, almost thirty-three million did not belong to the party.

Vic and I took a bus to Plac Komuny, five minutes from our apartment. Just off the Plac was St. Stanisław Kostka, the church where Father Popiełuszko served when he was murdered. We stood in the parking lot behind the church looking up at the priest who was celebrating Mass for us on the balcony. There must have been a thousand of us. It was very bright and hot that morning and after a while I had to put on my baseball cap to keep the sun out of my eyes. Banners proclaiming SOLIDARNOŚĆ were everywhere. The priest on the balcony asked the crowd not to demonstrate in the streets after Mass but rather to hold "a meeting" in the parking lot. The crowd roared with laughter. Then hymns were sung to conclude the service.

Everyone sang. Everyone held up his right arm, the first two fingers forming a V, throughout all the hymns. Some people held up small crosses. The singing lasted perhaps twenty minutes. Then the "meeting" began. Speakers took turns using a portable microphone. All of the speeches were applauded hugely, and between speeches chants for Solidarity went up. A recording of Father Popiełuszko's voice was played and right after it, after great applause, someone took the microphone and urged the crowd to march. From the church's loudspeakers came a counter-sound—music—to remind us of the priest's request not to demonstrate in the streets. Vic and I were standing near some young people dressed in olive drab jackets and berets; they were all smoking, alert, ready to go. They began to move very slowly toward the street under a banner that said WARSAW UNIVERSITY—SOLIDAR-NOŚĆ. Vic and I moved with them.

A student I recognized eased over to us. "You remember me?

I am Magda's friend, Piotr," he said. I said, "Of course." He said the Milicja would likely intercept the march and if things got rough we could run into the churchyard. "The Milicja will not go there," he said.

We came to the edge of the parking lot, next to the churchyard fence, and Piotr said we should wait there a moment and let some other people go first. I couldn't see what was happening ahead of us, if anything yet; there were just heads and banners out there. The churchyard fence beside us was brick for half its height, about four feet, then iron bars ending in spear points. Through these bars I could see all the fresh flowers around Father Popiełuszko's grave—a garden of them, bouquets great and modest—and I could see the parish men—steelworkers—guarding the grave. (It was guarded day and night, always.) About two dozen men were on duty, more than usual, and a chain had been put up to keep people out of that part of the churchyard today. Beyond the grave and through the fence at the far end of the churchyard, I could see a gathering of uniformed Milicja. They were spilling out of vans and trucks, preparing to meet the demonstrators.

Suddenly inside the churchyard several steelworkers were racing to the fence at the far end. A young man over there had just jumped down from the spear points. Now he was running toward Father Popiełuszko's grave. The steelworkers jumped up on the fence's brick part; they were trying to stop some men from climbing over the spear points. Four or five men managed to get over, and past the steelworkers, and now were pursuing the young man.

"Stool pigeons," Piotr said.

That was what the Poles called plainclothes cops. Uniformed Milicja would not enter the churchyard, but stool pigeons would. They were easy to spot—anywhere. Their eyes were hard and busy and their hair was cut in the best hotels to look like the models in ads for hair cream. They chased this young man, this kid, across the churchyard and out the main gate, into the crowd that hadn't reached the street yet. We couldn't see if they'd caught him, but Piotr seemed to think they would.

"He must be a lesson," Piotr said.

"What did he do?" Vic said.

"I don't know," Piotr said. "Maybe he provoked them."

I wanted to move. I took Vic's hand.

"Ready?"

"Maybe," she said. "Don't let go."

Piotr came with us, directing us to stay close to the sidewalk.

"How about we actually use the sidewalk," Vic said.

"Even better," Piotr said.

The sidewalk, not crowded, allowed us to move up the street a ways and have a good view of everything. It was as if we had front row seats. Vic's hand was sweating.

Calmly, Piotr pointed at the formation of Milicja. "You see there the Smurfs," he said.

They stood shoulder to shoulder in six or eight lines the width of the street. They all looked about twenty years old. They wore heavy black boots and white helmets and carried white rubber clubs. Marching very slowly, as if one, they moved toward those demonstrators from the parking lot who had achieved the street. The demonstrators stood there and watched the Milicja come closer. "Oh, Christ," Vic whispered. When the Milicja were ten yards from the demonstrators, they stopped. The two groups stared at each other.

Piotr said, "We must keep moving."

Just then, ahead of us, a uniformed cop stepped on the sidewalk and began pushing a tall, white-haired man, because the man wasn't moving along.

Another old man, watching this, yelled in Polish at the formation of Milicja, "You are primitives, Communists, and you beat women for money!"

Piotr said to us, "Three terrible things all in one sentence. Come," he added, "we must not stop."

Slowly we continued up the sidewalk past the Milicja, away from the demonstrators. It appeared to be a stand-off back there. Of course the demonstrators had absolutely no chance of advancing anywhere. Farther up the street the Milicja had a second formation in reserve; and behind that were vans and trucks filled with even more of them.

Vic and Piotr and I continued to walk. We met a young woman pushing a baby in a stroller. She looked at the cops as someone looks at a big hole in the ground; a not very interesting hole, just a hole. We met others on the sidewalk who looked at them with similar expressions. Big dead nothings in the road.

"Why would anyone want to do that?" Vic said.

"Do what?" I said.

"Be in the Milicja."

After a moment, Piotr said, "They are paid quite well. They are given apartments. Sometimes in Poland people wait all their lives for an apartment."

We passed several vans with cops packed into them. Behind windows covered by steel mesh, they looked like prisoners. We passed huge brown water trucks dripping water: ammunition for high-powered hoses. We passed Milicja mounted on horses and waiting, all in a row, under some trees where it was cool.

Coming to Plac Komuny (which before the war was called Plac Wilsona—for Woodrow Wilson) we saw a Milicja van on the sidewalk surrounded by a small crowd: four or five cops had got hold of a young man in a brown jacket and were trying to put him in the van. A woman was screaming at the cops and they were pushing her away and trying to put the man in the van. Others on the sidewalk watching this were yelling how brave the Milicja was. Suddenly a stool pigeon jumped out of the van with a can of Mace or tear gas and, pointing it at the crowd, ran in a circle around the van, yelling, "If you come any closer, you'll get this!"

The cops pushed the man inside the van and closed the door. Then they seemed to be waiting for the stool pigeon, who was still threatening the crowd. Now the van's side door slid open and out leaped the man. He ran a few steps into the crowd and stopped; he was grabbed again. The three cops who held him swung their white rubber billy clubs at his legs. Why hadn't he run when he had the chance? The woman continued to scream at the cops. They put the man back in the van and in a few seconds he leaped out again. And again he did not try very hard to get away. Was he only trying to show how inept the cops were? It was not really funny and yet it was. The Milicja were nervous, angry, frustrated, and behaving much like cartoon characters, like the Smurfs on Saturday morning television the Poles liked to laugh at.

But underneath all this nothing was funny. The man was captured again, put in the van, and this time the van began to ease away from the sidewalk. Then it had to stop and wait for an autobus that had pulled up and blocked its path. A few passengers in the bus, who had witnessed the capture, yelled out the windows.

"How brave these men are!"

"How like animals!"

Some of them came out and joined the small crowd, which was now blocking the bus.

The woman who was screaming—whose eyes were sunken, purple with grief—directed her fury at the officer who seemed to be in charge. "How can you sleep!" she screamed. He was a fat man with a toothbrush mustache. Pushing her along, he said he was proud of his position.

The crowd mocked him, saying, "He is proud! He is proud!"

He was trying to move everyone across the street so the bus could move so the van could move. He looked like a traffic cop who was not very good at his job. He was now surrounded by mockers, and yelling back at them. The crowd seemed to be moving *him* into the street.

His fellow cops stayed where they were, close to the van, as if they did not want to get involved.

When we were all out in the street far enough, the bus pulled away, followed by the van. Vic and Piotr and I continued on across. Then, suddenly, the crowd abandoned the cop—as if he were too disgusting, finally, to be near. They came across the street and he was left alone in the middle. Cars—which had stopped and were waiting—now passed him on either side, in two steady streams. He was trapped there, momentarily, to the crowd's great delight. They hooted. He had been found out! He was nothing but a fool, of course! I hooted with them. Almost at once I felt sad. It was such a tiny victory.

Vic and I walked slowly around Plac Komuny with Piotr. At the corner farthest from St. Stanisław Kostka, the day seemed normal. Couples sat on benches under trees, dressed in their Sunday best. Young boys rode past on their bikes. Children stood in line at an ice cream shop for cones. It was warm, dreamy weather here. The sycamores put out fuzzy new buds. Inside Milicja vans parked here and there away from the action—waiting in reserve—the young cops were drinking soda, smoking. I saw one, by an open door, whose jacket was unbuttoned and whose helmet lay upside down in his lap. He had pimples and a short military haircut and inside his helmet, surreptitiously, he held a book.

The Sunday after May Day the Sparks again did not play—nor did any of the other teams. Why, I don't know. Dariusz could only shrug, the schedule was not up to him, and Pete could only say, "Polish life." So after playing two games, we had a two-week break. That was nothing: come mid-June, after the eight teams had all played each other once, there would be a ten-week break. The season wouldn't resume until September, at which time the teams would begin a second round of seven games. Thus the 1988 PZBall season, stretching from April 17 to October 16— a span of six months—would see each team playing only fourteen games.

I could understand the Sunday format, what with the players having job and school obligations, but why that big hole in June, July, and August?

"People need vacation," Dariusz said.

"But those are the best months to play baseball," I said.

"Vacations very important to Polish people," he said.

"So these guys who are just starting to get the hang of the game suddenly stop and go lie on the beach?"

"Beach traditional," he said. "Also mountains."

"So no baseball in Poland for ten weeks."

"No, no. Big tournaments."

"Tournaments?"

"Very big tournament in Kutno. July two and three. Italy, Holland, Sweden, Czechoslovakia, Austria—all come to Kutno. Maybe more tournaments."

"Why am I only hearing about this now?" I said.

"I tell you now," he said.

"And these Polish guys on the beach pop over to play?"

"Pop over?"

"Who is going to play these teams from Italy and Holland?"

"Also Sweden, Czechoslovakia, and Austria," he said.

"Right. But will Poland have a team in the tournament?"

"Of course. Polish national team."

"I see. What about practice?" I said.

"Training camp maybe for two, three days in Kutno."

"Dariusz, listen to me: baseball players in America play almost every day during the season. They play all summer long. They don't play once in a while, and they don't go lie on the beach for ten weeks. *Nobody* goes to the beach for ten weeks in America, for Christ's sake, except maybe some spoiled brats and beautiful people."

"Gary, Gary, I don't understand."

"Hell, you've got it better here than you think. Ten-week vacations. Jesus."

"I have no ten-weeks vacations. Bull *shit!*"

"Dariusz, listen. Baseball players, like musicians, like doctors, need to practice. And they need to play games. This once-a-week stuff is bad enough. But a ten-week break is terrible."

"Gary, you listen, please. Polish people all year work, work, and think how much they do not like all things. You understand? Big hate. Big no good feeling. *Must* go away in summer, they think. Must. I explain only for them. For me, no go away. No big beach. No mountains. I know we need practice. Believe me."

We were sitting in the Skra *kawiarnia* (coffee shop), waiting for the players to assemble for practice that second Sunday in May. A few were already there: Pete, George, Froggy, Pizza Hut, Jake the catcher.

"George," I said, "do you go lie on the beach for ten weeks every summer?"

"Ten weeks? I would like that."

"Only if his girlfriend is there," Jake said.

George blushed.

"What about you, Pete?" I said.

"I don't have a girlfriend. I am too poor," he said.

The others hooted.

"I mean do you flop on your back for ten weeks every summer?"

"No," Pete said, "I don't have the strength for it."

"Does Froggy? Does Pizza Hut? Do you, Jake?"

"It's complicated," Jake said. "Some guys go away with their families. Or with their friends. Maybe with both, at different times. Some people go abroad to work for a while. It's a chance to make some money. So we are here and there."

"Like gypsies," Pete laughed.

It was almost two-thirty, time for practice. Dariusz said, "Gary, we can maybe discuss summer later. No get all excited now." We picked up our gear and went outside. The bazaar was over and out on the plaza a work crew was cleaning up. They were young men in their late teens and early twenties, wearing gray uniforms and black boots and looking a lot like Milicja, except for their brooms. They had formed a single line at one end of the plaza, and now in a grand, neat sweep were pushing a long worm of dirt and refuse across to the other end. Their brooms were like the brooms you see witches ride past the moon on in children's books—a bunch of straw tied to a stick. When they saw us coming they stopped. We walked past them, stepping over their line of dirt, on our way to the stadium.

We played our third game on May 15, hosting Kolejarz Rybnik. Kolejarz, which means "train workers," got three runs in the first inning and four in the second, but so did the Sparks. For six innings, in fact, the two teams traded runs even-Stephen, making a kind of clickety-clack/spark metaphor down the line score:

Kolejarz	3	4	1	1	1	1
Warsaw	3	4	1	1	1	1

Then in the top of the seventh, Mark's last inning on the mound, the train workers got a goose egg. We came up and scored four runs, to lead 15–11. In the top of the eighth, July replaced Mark. Kolejarz loaded the bases on an error and two walks, and then July struck out the side. He ran off the field with his pitching arm raised high. The Sparks were charging now, wrecking the metaphor: they were leaping over the moat and climbing the castle walls. They scored six runs in the bottom of the eighth to win by a knock down, 21–11.

In the dressing room, George and Pete and July, manning the hoses, created a three-part fountain, and Dariusz, a soggy cigarette in his mouth, was carried under it and rocked like a baby. Our win against Rój-Zory may have been historical, but this one meant the Sparks were for real. Naked, all soaped up, Mark strutted around the room, flexing his muscles, flicking soap like confetti. His eye caught Marek, quiet in a corner, bent over untying his shoes—the only Spark not whooping it up. This was Marek's style: after the game—any game—he could relax. He was the outfielder who in our next game, against Górnik, would be standing nervously on first with the bases loaded and asking me to let him steal second to calm down. Now, Mark eased over to him and with his hand on his soapy penis, said, "Marek!" When Marek looked up, Mark gave his penis a few quick strokes, collected a gob of soap in his hand as if it were jizzum, and flicked it in Marek's lap. Mark roared. Everyone roared. Warsaw—forgive us all—had come alive.

And the next Sunday, down in Silesia, when we trailed Górnik by seven runs in the top of the ninth and battled back to win, 21–19—and found ourselves tied with Jastrzębie for second place and breathing down Silesia Rybnik's neck for first—there was a feeling among the Sparks that no one could ever beat them again. Bring on Rybnik!

3

On the Sparks' chartered bus after that big victory over Górnik, Dariusz told the players what the doctors had said about Pizza Hut's eye. He also told them that Pizza Hut must stay in Rybnik for maybe two weeks, for observation. Dariusz didn't ask any questions about the accident, and no one else did either. His report was short. We were all quiet for a while after hearing it. I thought about the high mood we had set out in, on Saturday afternoon, and about the boisterous ceremony that Dariusz called "like what is done for a new baby in church." He meant of course baptism. This took place at the back of the bus in the last row of seats: two players held a player between them—a player making his first road trip—and the rest of us lined up to give him a whack on the ass. For each rookie that meant almost thirty spanks. Pizza Hut, who had traveled with the team the previous season, escaped. In the quiet bus riding back to Warsaw, night falling, I drank another Polish beer and saw Bluto shake his fist at me. I saw George kiss his bat. I heard Tony and Alejandro murmuring Spanish, as if offstage, as if they had gotten in the wrong play and were discussing what to do now. "Choo-choo . . . choo-choo"— that's what the word to pee sounded like. It was whispered in the aisle as if by children put to bed hours ago and now prowling the stairs. The driver stopped and we filed outside under the stars in the middle of nowhere, one by one issuing up to the road as if up to a trough . . . a maneuver spontaneous, unspoken . . . twenty-eight figures pissing in a row . . . twenty-eight glistening, personal rivulets. And then we were moving again, back to our *piwo*, our dozing, our schoolbooks and novels illumined by flashlights. The sparrow-like clerk of the Workers' Hotel came to me, wringing her hands, saying she had no room . . . and then the rhyme about the old woman who lived in a shoe came to me, except that I had her giving her children forty whacks, and I knew forty whacks—with an axe—belonged to somebody else but I couldn't remember who, and there was nobody I could ask. I woke up just as the bus passed Skra. I saw the granite aviator holding his propeller, the red beacon atop the Palace of Culture. A few minutes later, at Centralna, where we could catch city night buses and taxis to our respective neighborhoods, we all got out and stood in the ghostly light of the station. We were stretching and yawning and looking a little lost—and no doubt looking a little strange too, with our bats and batting helmets: a couple of patrolling Milicja kept their eyes on us. Then July, plugged into his Walkman, walked off one way, Jake shouldering his shin guards, went another. George said, "Maybe I will be sick for school today." Finally they were all gone except me and Dariusz and Henry. We found a taxi and they took me to Żoliborz. It was three a.m. Three hours later Dariusz boarded the Ekspres train and went back to Rybnik with Pizza Hut's mother.

I saw Dariusz again at our next practice, on Tuesday afternoon. He had just come from work. He looked rough. About Pizza Hut he only said, "All is the same."

"How are his spirits?" I said.

Dariusz shook his head. "No, no. No drinking."

"I mean, how does he feel? OK? Not OK?"

Dariusz shrugged. Then, "But very good doctors. I tell you this."

Pete and Froggy and I had been playing catch when Dariusz showed up, and now, none of us able to say more about Pizza Hut, Dariusz went in the *kawiarnia* for a badly needed cup of coffee. Pete and Froggy and I returned to our warm-up. The other players hadn't arrived yet. (We were practicing that day on the soccer field, which was right beside the *kawiarnia*.)

After a while Pete said, "Dariusz is married to a doctor."

I hadn't known that. I knew he had a wife and small son, and that they all lived with his father—not far from Skra—but that was about it. I wondered now why he hadn't brought her to the party at the Embassy dacha. Why he never brought his son—who was nine, he told me—to practice or to our games. He said he played catch with the boy; in fact, one day he showed up with a scab over his eyebrow—the result, he said, of a powerful throw by the youngster—and I said I'd like to meet this fireballer. Dariusz said, "Of course!" But I never met him, or Dariusz' wife.

"Have you seen her?" I said to Pete.

"Last year," he said.

"At baseball games?"

"Once, I think."

"Maybe she doesn't like baseball," I said.

"Maybe," Pete said.

Of course, I thought, when would the woman have time to come sit all Sunday afternoon and watch us play? She had her work, a child, shopping, the apartment, and maybe the father-in-law needed looking after too. Indeed, when did she and Dariusz have time together? The last four days were not that unusual. Dariusz, it seemed, was always about to leave on a journey or on his way back from one—either out of town for his paper, out of town on baseball business, or just across town, across the river to Praga, to see about Jacek Małecki's cut wrist, Norbert's twisted ankle, Paweł Płatek's ankle—and these visits, including *piwo* and talk with the father, would last until dawn. So the trip with Pizza Hut's mother which took a full day and fourteen hours on the train—and which followed the Sparks' journey to Rybnik with hardly a break for much at home—was almost normal in Dariusz' life. Polish life, he might have said. But he didn't.

Now he came out of the coffee shop. Henry was with him. They came over to where we were playing catch, both of them smiling. Dariusz said, "Henry has something."

I stopped throwing and everyone gathered around to see what Henry took from his pocket. It was a silver medal about the size of a quarter—the Royal Eagle. Henry showed us the crown.

Pete said, "This is very rare. Very."

Froggy hummed approval.

Henry said something in Polish, and Dariusz said to me, "Henry presents it."

He pinned it on my shirt. Froggy and Pete and Dariusz were smiling and nodding and for a moment I couldn't remember a word of Polish except *przepraszam* (excuse me). Finally I said, "Henry, *bardzo dziękuję*" ("Thank you very much").

He waved his hand as if it was nothing. Then he and Dariusz respectfully stepped to the sidelines so we could continue practice.

Over the next several months Henry would give me more medals—medals representing Poland's past glory, her brief flame with Solidarity—and each time he brought one forth I would feel close to these men and very far from them. Closer and farther away. I couldn't explain it to myself. Except to think—with a kind of self-protecting cowboy toughness—that I wasn't used to receiving medals. I also felt frustrated at not having better Polish to thank the man.

Henry was a round man down to his belt and below that he was slim. Vicki said it was a toss-up between Henry and Dariusz as to which one was the biggest teddy bear, though she wasn't thinking of weight or shape so much as eyes and smile and how both men made her want to hug them. Henry was the quickest Pole I knew to kiss a woman's hand, but there was never anything rushed about it—nothing automatic or slavish or flirtatious; it was a ceremony he performed because it was an honor to meet the woman, or to see her again. He was Dariusz' age, thirty-two. Dariusz described him—proudly—as "a specialist for special efforts." When Whale, our Junior catcher, stopped coming to practice, for example—because his mother said no more baseball—it was Henry who got him back for us.

You wouldn't guess it by looking at Henry's plump gut, but in his youth—from the age of fourteen to nineteen—he was a champion Junior bicyclist. He rode for Legia, the Military Sports Club in Warsaw, and he was happy enough until another club offered him more money. Then he could think only of getting rich. He spoke to Legia about leaving; he was reminded that at Legia—which means "Legion"—he was protected from having to serve his military obligation. He was almost twenty. He wanted everything—glory, money, girls—but not a uniform. Finally he found someone at Legia who agreed, for a fee, to fix things for him. He could go to that other club, he was told, everything would be OK. So he left. A few weeks later he received his draft notice. He had a choice of joining the Army, the Navy, or the Milicja. He joined the Navy and served three years in Gdańsk. During all that time he was courted by a sports club there, to ride in the Seniors division, but the Navy said no. After his discharge he returned to Warsaw and worked in "show business."

"What does that mean?" I asked July, who was translating for us.

"He took tickets by the door of the Black Cat night club in the Victoria Hotel," July said. "He also organized events."

"What kind of events?"

"Henry says it doesn't matter."

I didn't push it.

July continued, "Then he got a good job in the silver factory. Then Solidarity happened. Henry joined. This cost him his job."

Henry shrugged. That was all there was to tell.

"Now what does he do? I mean besides help Dariusz with special efforts?"

"He works for a wood company," July said. "He orders supplies. He is also—I don't know how to say this—like a leader. In the union."

Henry put his fingers to his lips—a gesture to mean not silence but pleasure.

"He likes to eat and drink," July said.

"Tell him I've noticed."

"But he is no bad drinker like you see in the street. *Smakosz.* This means 'to taste.' Henry prefers *smakosz,*" July said.

Henry kissed his fingertips.

That conversation took place in mid-June, on the team bus, when we were all coming back to Warsaw from Cyprzanów— storybook Cyprzanów of the sheep meadow. Much later, in September, when Vicki had returned to the States and I was living in the Victoria Hotel, I had another conversation with Henry and July. This time we were sitting on a bench outside the train station in Łódź. It was a dreamy fall day, a day with no hurry to it, and I was happy being right where I was for the moment—on a bench in the sun in Łódź, watching quite a few pretty girls go past. It was a Friday afternoon. People were taking the electric train to Warsaw (where we had just come from) for the weekend. In a little while I would want to go with them. In a little while I would not want to go to Silesia anymore—even though we would not be going through Old Town in dark, sad Katowice and even though I would probably never again see the girl in the shoes that were too big for her, see her walking there adolescently tall and uncertain and so full of hope under Katowice's grimy sky I could weep. I had seen all I ever wanted to see in Silesia.

But for the moment, there we were in Łódź, waiting for the Kutno team bus to come by and pick us up. We were a selection of Sparks who would join a selection of Kutno steelworkers—to form the Polish National Team "B"—and together we would journey down to Rybnik, with me as the coach and Juan Echevarría as my assistant, for a big international tournament. Another tournament. Another interruption in the regular schedule. On paper, these tournaments were a wonderful idea. Competition from outside, sophistication—they were almost like a World Series. But what they finally amounted to was not very much. A colorful patch to bring home and sew on your jacket. A patch showing the flags of Italy, the Netherlands, Sweden, Austria, Czechoslovakia, Poland . . . and the U.S.A.! The problem was, after the Poles got so excited—and so territorial and duchified—that they couldn't agree on one national team to represent the country but had to form four (known as National Team "A," National Team "B," etc.—three of which came from Silesia); after they got all worked up about where the tournament would be held and who the coaches would be and which players would play; after all this brandishing of sabres and issuing of plans (and manufacturing of patches), maybe a team from the Netherlands would show up to play them. Not the Netherlands national team—just a team from Amsterdam or some other Dutch city. No Italy, no Sweden, no U.S.A. ("The U.S.A.?" I said to Dariusz. "What American team was supposed to be there?" He shrugged. "I don't know. Maybe U.S.A. flag was for you.")

The story of the international baseball tournaments in Poland that year gets a little more complicated, containing, as it cannot avoid containing, good amounts of dukish foolishness and intrigue and trickery—as well as good amounts of hope. Foolishness, intrigue, trickery, and hope have always had a lot in common, of course, but it was the hope part—separated for the moment from the other parts—that was mainly on my mind that dreamy September Friday afternoon in Łódź. Thinking about the young girl in the ill-fitting high heels walking through Katowice's grimy Old Town had started it, her awkward first steps into womanhood, the sweet, brave, frightened, fifteen- or sixteen-year-old face she was presenting to a world that was too tired, too old, and certainly too busy to be much concerned with it—this girl had come back to me from the Sparks' last road trip to Silesia—just a week previous, when we played the Rój-Zory beehive—and her image in my head, in sunny Łódź, was getting mixed up with a lot of stuff. It was getting mixed up with the pretty and far more confident girls walking past my bench with friends or alone to ride the electric train to Warsaw—girls in shoes that fit, their faces done up as beautifully as my students' faces, under fashionable hats cocked to cover one eye and make you want to see more. Her image was getting mixed up with Pete and Mark and the two Łódź girls they had invited to sit a while, the four of them flirting, exchanging addresses; it was getting mixed up with Jacek Demkiewicz—yet another Jacek—who on the train to Łódź had showed me photos of my daughter she had sent to him from the States—these, he said, and seventeen letters, plus a tape, had arrived since her visit in June, and he was very happy; although now, sitting on a bench alone, not far from the bench where Pete and Mark were flirting, he did not look happy, smoking a cigarette and gazing at the ground. The image of the girl courting hope on a Saturday night in grim Katowice got mixed up with all this, and then it got mixed up with Henry kissing his fingertips.

"Is Henry thinking about food?" I said to July.

"Yes and no," July said. "He is thinking about expensive women."

"Polish women?" I said.

"Of course," July said.

"How expensive?"

"That depends. There are several classes. The highest class are fifty to one hundred fifty dollars a night. They are in the best hotels."

"Why is Henry thinking about expensive women?"

"I don't know," July said. "Maybe he is having some fun with me. Maybe he is saying an expensive woman is cheaper than a marriage."

July was getting married the following week. The problem he was having back in May (i.e., which one was his true love, Agnieszka or Renata?) had been more or less resolved by nature: Agnieszka was pregnant.

Pete and Mark had put on their gloves and were now playing catch for their admirers, showing how throwing a baseball was done. The people going past to and from the train station gave them plenty of room. Two young boys stopped to watch, moving their heads in unison as they followed the ball back and forth. All this was going on in front of the bench where Henry and July and I were sitting. On the bench to our left sat the two admirers in white skirts and white high heels, and on the bench to our right sat unhappy Jacek D., smoking. My guess was he was thinking about my daughter because on the train earlier he confessed to me he thought about her all the time. Off in the distance, behind the young boys watching this bright white ball fly through the air, Mariusz was buying an ice cream cone.

"The most expensive woman in Poland is five hundred dollars," July said.

"How many are in this class?"

"Only one."

"She must be famous."

"She is."

"What's her name?"

"Rita," July said.

"Where is she?" I said.

"Szczecin. She drives a Porsche."

"Why can she get five hundred dollars?"

"She knows everything," said July, who seemed more interested in Henry's little joke than Henry did.

A couple more young boys stopped to watch Pete and Mark play catch. They lined up beside the first two boys and all four heads moved back and forth together following the ball. Jacek D. stood up from his bench and his thoughts and peered around as if he had just arrived on the scene: he peered around through the smoke from the cigarette that hung from his mouth, and then his gaze settled on the game of catch. It seemed to fascinate him as it did the boys. He walked over and stood behind them; he was tall and thin and despite his height and clothes and hairstyle, he seemed very much one of them. He seemed, for the moment anyway, relieved of his responsibilities and worries.

Jacek D. wore cutoff Levis and a black T-shirt with yellow and pink lightning bolts on it that spelled out HEAVY METAL. His hair fell to his shoulders; one lock covered an eye. He was a disk jockey and journalist: he played rock records on a Warsaw radio station for fifteen minutes once a week and he reviewed new albums—preferably heavy metal—for one of the city's newspapers. Back in January at Gwardia he was among the thirty-three hopefuls, but after a couple of weeks he disappeared. When he showed up again—in April or May—it was not to play baseball but to assist Dariusz. Dariusz liked the fact that he could speak passable English. Jacek D. was twenty-two and lived with his father and grandmother in Praga. Three months after Chernobyl, his mother died from cancer. There was no doubt in his mind that the Russians had killed her, just as they had killed his grandfather by throwing him in prison for being a proud and faithful Polish soldier. That was another thing: Jacek D. had his military obligation to face, a prospect he hated to think about; it was stupid serving—wasting!—two years in the Army because it was not the Polish Army anymore, everything was different from his grandfather's time! But whether that in fact was on his mind at this moment, mixed up with thoughts of my daughter, I don't know. All I can say is he stood behind the young boys watching Pete and Mark throw the ball for two admiring girls from Łódź—his head moving back and forth in unison with the youngsters' heads—and July was saying, "The women in the hotels must pay the elevator man, the desk man, the head waiter, the man in charge of carrying suitcases, and the Milicja. And sometimes these women are stool pigeons."

Henry abruptly stood up. He was no longer interested in discussing expensive women. He wanted to know why the Kutno bus wasn't there. It was almost three-thirty: we were supposed to have been picked up at two o'clock! Henry was beginning to be unhappy with Dariusz, for it was Dariusz who had talked with Walter Szymański on the telephone and arranged this rendezvous, this plan for Skra and Kutno to travel together to Rybnik. Henry said that Dariusz should have known better than to trust Walter Szymański.

Pete, still playing catch, defended Dariusz. He said Dariusz didn't want us to have to take the six a.m. Ekspres from Warsaw to Rybnik; that taking the ten a.m. electric train over to Łódź let us sleep in, and besides it was only one quick hour on the train—instead of seven on the Ekspres—and then a nice, comfortable bus the rest of the way with our friendly National Team "B" teammates.

Mark, laughing, said Pete was being sarcastic.

"It's true," Pete said, feigning innocence, "Kutno has a very nice bus."

"You trust them?" Mark said.

"Of course!" Pete said. "Why not?"

Dariusz himself was not with us because he had to work that day. He was leaving Warsaw on the night train and would arrive in Rybnik—according to his plan—long after the rest of us had had our supper there and were fast asleep, gaining our strength for the start of the tournament in the morning. (Norbert, Froggy, Adam—and Big Robert, who joined the Sparks in June—were also on the "B" team. The first three, like Dariusz, had commitments that day and presumably would take the night train too; Big Robert, the horniest man I'd met in Poland, was somewhere in the Łódź train station, where he had followed a woman.)

Henry, Pete, and Mark continued to discuss the theme of trusting Kutno, tossing in anecdotes about other trips that Dariusz had organized—all of which had in common hours spent waiting and waiting in train stations—and at that point I was thinking about my daughter writing seventeen letters since June to a young man who wore a T-shirt with pink and yellow lightning bolts on it, who was watching a baseball fly back and forth while chewing on a lock of his hair, his head in perfect sync with four other heads. I was thinking of how she had come to Poland with her three-year-old son to see me and Vicki, but also to see a young man named Don, a man she had been corresponding with all year, a man she had known back in the States, and when she arrived in Warsaw, excited and hopeful, how little time he had for her. I was thinking of her and the young girl in Katowice and of how they were both tall and uncertain and looking for someone to love them, and I didn't care if the Kutno bus never showed up. I was thinking life in Poland was not easy but it was not easy anywhere else that I knew of. I was thinking about my young daughter raising a child by herself, her faith in goodness, her idealism, part-time jobs she'd had working with the poor, people without much English, and how one of these people, a man, had put his burning cigarette to her son's hand, and how I went looking for that man to kill him—realizing as I walked the streets where I might find him that what I wanted to do stood counter to everything I had tried to teach her, and not caring, seeing only the look in her eyes when she had to tell me what the round, raw, hateful wound in Gabriel's hand really was. I wanted to kill a man for confusing my daughter's belief in his goodness.

All of that came back to me now in Łódź as I sat on a bench in the sun . . . and then my Aunt Mary came to me, sitting on her bench, in her sun, holding a tomato from my grandmother's garden and finally after what seemed a long struggle to move her lips, saying it was so pretty . . . and I concentrated on the baseball moving back and forth between Pete and Mark . . . and then I thought of the difficulty most people have in simply getting from here to there, of how often we're stopped in the middle, and of how close we were, all of us, to hurt and rage and worse . . . and of how grateful I was for never finding that man, but more than that, for my daughter's strength. And then I thought of my students, of a discussion we'd had that winter about a novel called *Fat City*. They hadn't liked it. They hadn't liked it because the story took place in California and the author, they said, made California look hopeless. Hopeless and heartless. And they wanted to believe otherwise about California. They said the author was taking away from their dreams. I said but this book is full of dreams. They said yes but they are foolish dreams. I regarded my intelligent, beautiful, sensitive, and thoughtful students who were not exactly coddled but close to it, and they regarded me. Being an American is not as easy as it looks, I said. At that point the telephone rang.

IN A WARSAW CLASSROOM CONTAINING CHAIRS

a table, and a blue telephone—
plus ten students, a window allowing
gray light and, fresh from the States,
a writer with a crick in his back—
they were searching out the American
character, its here and there, its wide
and lonely and rich and two-fisted
get up and go, when the telephone
began to ring. The writer answered,
yes? hello? But no one spoke.
The searching resumed. The tough
American character blazed trails,
made hay, made the fur fly, the sky
the limit, and desired—always—
a perfect companion for life,
someone strong, creamy . . .
and again the telephone rang.
This time the writer, impatient, raised
the handle and put it back, letting
the American character sail on,
keeping its distance, dancing its dance,
and singing those songs that can change

everything forever, or for only a night—
embrace me, I'm saving my love for you.
When the telephone rang a third time
the writer opened the room's little
garret window and put the thing out
there, on the roof, where a pigeon sat.
It was a gloomy winter afternoon, nothing new
—and regarding the blue telephone
as you and I might regard a small
animal coiled into itself at dusk,
the pigeon blinked. The American character,
now in California, in a field bright
with grapes, also blinked, having spent
a long night tossing back shots, fighting,
and finding a place to lay its head.
Its head hurt this morning,
and it was broke, but never mind
any of that. It had the sun—right?—
a knife, and fruit to pick. And tomorrow—
listen—with some luck, a new leaf,
anything could happen.

Now the students in that Warsaw
classroom—containing what it contained
plus the raw, gloomy afternoon light—
didn't especially like the sunny limb
heavy with uncertainty and hangover
that the American character had crawled out on.
And it was all the writer's fault, really.
He got mad, maybe, at the telephone interrupting.
Or his back was acting up, making him cranky.
He didn't need to leave the American character
wishing like a foolish child, a dreamer, at the end.

The writer agreed. He said the American
character might have gone to the bank
and asked for the banker's daughter,

the one whose left eye shone—always—
like a fresh-made quarter, and lived
if not exactly happily ever after
at least on a good-sized bluff
and plenty away from those Spanish
on the corner, that noisy bunch
cluttering up their yard with weepy Madonnas.
The American character might have said
look here, look at this mess,
and had its ears brought in
closer to its head, its nose
polished, corns popped off,
and its love handles wrapped
in plastic at the weekend
fat farm, munching lettuce,
sweating out the whole ball of wax
to music from a can,
and become a star, something
far, far above the crowd.
The American character, finally,
might have said to hell
with all this noise
and taken up tying flies,
tying up all the loose ends
and talking to itself
instead of tying one on,
riding a three-wheeled bicycle
for its sluggish heart, its gall-
stones rattling from one rest stop
on the reservation to another.
No more mountains to cross,
no more fields to plow.
No one bothering anyone.
No children allowed.

On my bench in Łódź I remembered saying to my students, finally, Has *Fat City* stopped you from having your dreams about

California? They said no. Has it stopped you from wanting to go to California? They said no.

But the image of a young girl in a yellow dress handed down from the Forties, a girl in red high heels walking bravely and afraid into her future, a future filled most likely with long lines and soot in her plain brown hair and soot on the white ribbon gathered around it—that image stopped me from going to Silesia. At five o'clock I got on the electric train to Warsaw. Jacek D., Henry, July, and Big Robert also got on. Pete, Mark, and Mariusz boarded the night train to Rybnik, where they planned to meet Dariusz, and maybe Norbert, Froggy, and Adam too, and play in the international tournament, if there was one.

As for the Kutno bus, we were told later that it had come to Łódź and looked for us, arriving at 5:15. To which news Dariusz only said, "Fuck Walter Szymański!"

I started this chapter with the Sparks returning to Warsaw in the early hours of Monday, May 23, after beating Górnik for their third win in a row; I had planned to tell what happened in our next three games and then got ahead of myself . . .

So there we were at our first practice following the Górnik trip. I had the Royal Eagle pinned to my shirt and was warming up with Froggy and Pete. After about twenty minutes I said, "Where is everybody?"

"Maybe they are still sleeping," Pete said.

Some Juniors arrived—Whale, Paweł Tymiński, Robert (who in June would become Little Robert, to distinguish him from Big Robert), Andrzej the pitcher, and one or two others. Of the Seniors, George, Alejandro, Marek, and Mark turned up. It was the fewest number of players we'd ever had at practice. At least half were missing.

I said to Dariusz, "We've got a big game next Sunday. Where is everybody?"

"Very big game," he said. "Kutno. I don't know where is everybody. Maybe work, maybe school." He was sure the turn-out would be better on Wednesday.

But the next day it was worse. On Thursday, it was also dismal.

Dariusz looked glum, saying, "No happiness." George, trying for a better mood, said, "Gary, Kutno is afraid of us."

"Is that right?"

"Yes, they read in the Warsaw paper how good we are."

That set me off. I made a speech. It was a speech coaches have made since way back, since the beginning of the circle. I stood in the middle of one at Skra and clichés poured from my mouth like air from a punctured inner tube you blow up and hold in a tub of water to find the leak. I bubbled forth. I was angry, sarcastic, disappointed, tough, forgiving, fatherly, and figuratively down on one knee. The most remarkable thing about the speech—to me— was that I believed every word I uttered.

On Friday nearly everyone showed up at practice and I sent them off to run laps around the track. Dariusz was all smiles. He said to me, "Gary, you listen. Big happiness. Mr. Liszka, president of Polish baseball federation, says to me Paweł, Mariusz, Norbert, and Jake the catcher—all selected for national team. To play in international tournament July two and three."

I said, "Dariusz, we have a game against Kutno on Sunday— the day after tomorrow—and these All-Stars haven't been to practice all week."

"I know," he said. He thought a minute. "Moving stars. No good."

His mistake—for movie stars—conjured up an image of plummeting, which did not make me feel good either.

"But Paweł's leg was resting," he said, defending the team captain.

"His arm didn't need rest."

"He runs now OK. You look."

I looked at Paweł and the other Sparks circling the pink track. "Right," I said. "But on Sunday I'll be looking at Norbert turning his head on grounders, at Jake not using both hands, at Mariusz swinging at high pitches. Just because we won three games, Dariusz, doesn't mean we'll win four."

He nodded, but I could tell he really wasn't listening—really didn't believe me. After all, the Warsaw papers said that Skra was like a phoenix, having risen from its ashes. Dariusz himself had been interviewed on television, and there he declared—to millions—that the Sparks were the surprise of Poland, playing like professionals this season, like men not boys. I looked at him now as he gazed fondly and with pride upon the young men circling the track. They were warriors, said his eyes. They were eagles. And four of them had been chosen for the national team! Who was I, I suddenly thought, to mess with his big happiness? Baseball was a game, right? It was supposed to bring pleasure. Well, here was a baseball man enjoying himself. And why not? We played some pretty good ball in that first game, knocked hell out of our next two opponents, and just last Sunday rose, yes, like a phoenix. And right now we were tied with Jastrzębie for second place and breathing down the great Silesia Rybnik's neck for first. I began to think: maybe George is right. Maybe Kutno is afraid of us. Maybe Juan Echevarría and his boys will be so tight on Sunday they'll quiver and snap like rubber bands. And maybe our guys, rested, relaxed, and ready to go, to continue, will perform in ways that only sportswriters and poets who believe in beautiful, fiery birds can imagine.

At the light practice on Saturday which everyone attended, Mr. Richard said we would not be playing in the stadium on Sunday—because of a track and field event scheduled there—but on the rugby field. We didn't care. We were too jacked up. We went there now, to test it, and under a warm sun we ran our laps like stallions, Paweł Płatek, our captain, leading the way. During infield practice Norbert plucked grounders out of the cleat-pitted rugby turf as if they were meteorites other men might fear but not he; Tony, shirtless, caught rays and everything else that came his way; Mariusz was also sure-handed; and Froggy at first base was a spider. Behind the plate, Jake was still using only one hand to catch the ball, but doing OK, so I kept quiet. If it's not broke, don't fix it. During outfield practice, Paweł in left, Alejandro in center, and George in right missed nothing; and Marek and Blackie did well out there too. Mark, July, Pete, and Adam, throwing on the sidelines, all said they felt good. Mark said, "Of course I feel good.

Kutno will see only strikes. And this"—he shaped a sneer that Elvis couldn't have beat. We were ready. Bring on Kutno! Bring on Rybnik! Anybody!

At nine o'clock on Sunday morning the temperature was already in the seventies—it was going to be a gorgeous day for baseball. And getting from Skra's main entrance to the rugby field was easy: the field lay in a far corner, maybe fifty yards from the teeming plaza, and a path beside the plaza, through a cluster of trees, let you avoid the bazaar altogether. On the way to the field I stopped beside a hemlock and unzipped my pants. Peeing, watching skis and bikes and other bright toys bob on backs among the crowd, I suddenly felt very lucky—not just about the game but about everything. About Vicki, living in Warsaw, my daughter and grandson's visit in three days, the new poems I was working on, the Sparks, Anna Mydlarska in Gdańsk (who had become my translator and introduced Vicki and me to Wałęsa), Anna's husband Jacek—a wonderful guy and fine painter—both of them our friends now, the readings around Poland I'd given, the students I'd met, my mornings free to work in a sunny room overlooking a garden, throwing and hitting baseballs every afternoon, curling up with Vicki every night . . . I zipped up, but stayed where I was for a while. I wasn't quite ready to leave this spot where my life had come to me in such a nice summary, where, also, there seemed to be something very different about the bazaar this week. It seemed, as I caught whiffs of roasting kielbasa and coffee and drifts of talk, like an event from my youth—the parish summer festival—and now I could smell cotton candy, hear what was surely a calliope, and for a moment a great, heroic collage from high school lit up my brain: I was on the mound, at the peak of my kick; I was at the top of the key, suspended in air, the ball I had just feathered off my fingertips falling through the net with a sound like thighs in nylons uncrossing; I was fading back after a perfect fake to my halfback, fading back ten yards, twenty, thirty— what did it matter?—I could throw this thing in my hands a mile, hell if I couldn't. I glanced around. I was looking for a Ferris wheel, a merry-go-round, a big tent like the one where the Holy

Redeemer men, chewing cigars, conducted bingo games, where the parish ladies offered their jellies and pies for sale, and where I would meet my girl and take her hand and slip her away to my car in the parking lot, her skin smelling like cherries . . . and then I saw, down in my hand, the baseball I had taken from my pocket and was gripping across the seams as if my catcher had signaled for my heater, my smoke, calling me sweet names. Suddenly I burst out. I roared. Here was the Holy Redeemer moving star, alive and well indeed, in the jigsaw of Warsaw! And still laughing, I started toward the rugby field. But under my yellow practice shirt—which I continued to favor over the peach-colored game shirt, for any odd god up there who rewarded acts of faith and hope like mine—I was sweating.

IN MY MEANEST DAYDREAM

I am throwing hard again
clipping corners, shaving
letters, dusting off
the heavy sticker crowding clean-up
clean down to his smelly socks—
& when my right spike hits
the ground he's had his
look already & gets
hollow in the belly—
in my meanest daydream I let fly
a sweet stream of spit, my catcher
pops his mitt
& grins
& calls me baby.

Chuck Powers arrived early too. We walked over the rugby field looking for rough spots, patching holes in the infield with sand—especially around shortstop for Norbert's sake. I was always glad to see Chuck at our games because we needed someone in the other coach's box—at third base—and because he got visibly, and vocally, more excited faster than I did and that helped me to keep reasonably cool. In our opener against Jastrzębie, he hadn't liked a particular call by the chief umpire and said so, at some length, and the umpire flashed a yellow warning card at him. This was the same umpire who, minutes before, had told Jake that Jake couldn't tell the batter his shoes were on the wrong feet. Which didn't please us since we had taught the Sparks that razz was part of the game. Now came the yellow card.

"What the hell does *that* mean?" Chuck said.

It meant that after the yellow card came a red card, and if Chuck got one of those he'd be expelled from the field.

"The little snot," Chuck said. "The self-important little stick of rat shit."

The umpire was not very big and Chuck compared him to a variety of small animals and their spoor on every call that went against us. Finally the umpire got wind of it all and pulled out his red card. Chuck fired off a last blast, and then with Jackson Diehl of the *Washington Post* (who had been pacing in front of our bench, reminding Chuck several times that they had a rumored demonstration in the old Jewish quarter to check out) he left.

Now Chuck and I were lining the field for the Kutno game. Dariusz was off somewhere trying to find a portable microphone, because the rugby field did not have a public address system. What with Kutno's reputation, our winning streak, his TV interview, and the fine weather, Dariusz expected a large crowd today and he wanted to explain to all assembled what they were seeing.

He returned empty-handed. "Big opportunity," he said, "but no happiness." Soon, however, his face began to take on a shine like a man's in the presence of a vision: he gazed at the Sparks getting loose in their peach and powder blue, at the bleachers fast becoming peopled, at Henry walking toward us with a smiling Mr. Richard and a couple of suit-coated gents who would turn out to be Skra Klub board members, and here came Juan Echevarría—beaming, his hand extended—followed by his Kutno steelworkers. They all wore blue and white uniforms that looked, and fit, like the real article.

"Juan Echevarría," Dariusz said, glowing.

"We figured," Chuck said, shaking the man's hand. "How are you, Juan?"

"*Buenos días,*" I said.

"*Dzién dobry!* Hello!"

"Are you ready for us?" Chuck said.

"Maybe! I don't know!"

Tony came over and Juan opened his arms. Alejandro came over, bobbing and weaving and pretending he had a punch to deliver.

"Now I am worried!" Juan said.

The Skra Klub board members, introduced, got their consonants out and seemed prepared to make speeches, and Dariusz, on full beam at this meeting of sportsmen from three countries, seemed prepared to enjoy himself for as long as the summit needed to take; but it was ten o'clock, time for the Juniors' game to start.

"Let's get going," I said.

We couldn't get going, Dariusz said, the umpires hadn't arrived yet. We waited fifteen or twenty minutes, then decided to umpire ourselves. Chuck put on a mask and chest protector and got behind the catcher; a guy from Kutno took the bases. After every inning they would trade places.

Kutno, up to bat first, was facing Andrzej Stankiewicz on the mound. Dubbed Fleetfoot, Andrzej was flat-footed, slow, good-natured, and big—almost as big as Whale his catcher—and he had a decent fastball. He also had a headful of wild, corkscrew-curly blond hair, and an intense admiration for Mark, in particular for the Senior pitcher's ability to possess from three to five girlfriends simultaneously. He tried to groom his walk, his talk, and his hair like Mark's, but he had no success. His arches were what they were, his tongue shrunk in the presence of wit—and vanished altogether in front of a girl—and his hair, wetted or waxed, sprang like a furious conductor's chasing Beethoven.

He struck out the first two batters. Then Kutno loaded the bases. When the next Kutno batter stepped to the plate, Chuck took off his mask and looked at me sitting on our bench. The batter was the pint-sized umpire from the Jastrzębie game who had yellow- and red-carded Chuck.

"Good eye, Chuck, good eye, baby," I said.

Andrzej fired three fastballs and the batter was called out. He seemed very unhappy, judging from the color of his face. I say Andrzej threw fastballs because they *appeared* to be fastballs; they also appeared to be somewhat high. But when I trotted past Chuck on my way to the first base coach's box, he said, shaking his head in wonder:

"Did you *see* those pitches?"

"Pretty good, were they?"

"Good! Hell, those were major league curveballs! Dropped in nice as pie."

The other Kutno Juniors, however, started to hit Andrzej hard. I replaced him with Robert—a fiery competitor—but he too was hit hard. And very much in the manner of Blackie, he suffered every blow as if it were an injustice, an insult, a diminishment; and like Norbert, he was wont to take a personal time-out, in the heat of a play, to grieve. Watching Robert shake his fist at the sky and kick dirt and throw down his glove, I had one good presentiment, one bad: that he was using up—for the Juniors and Seniors both—our allotment of uncool for the day; that he was promoting a nasty, uncontrollable tic.

Immediately following the game—which the visitors won, 13–5—Kutno's Seniors took their infield practice, looking nothing like rubber bands about to snap; indeed, looking very schooled and smooth under the calm direction of Juan receiving throws at first base. Then we took the field. The regular umpires had arrived, the bleachers were full (Vicki sat in a front row, wearing a red straw hat), and Dariusz, smoking a Mocne—which means "strong"—was poised over his Scoremaster book. The chief umpire cried, "*Pałka!*" Under a sun straight up and hot, Mark, on the mound, rocked and kicked and flung the first pitch over Jake's head. "No problem!" Dariusz sang. Mark got the ball back, stomped once around the mound collecting himself, then pitched a perfect inning. No hits, no walks, no runs. We came up and scored on a walk to George, a sacrifice, and a single by Tony. Textbook. In the second inning Kutno again went scoreless, while we got a single and stolen base by Alejandro, and an RBI single by

Froggy. It's such a simple, beautiful game, I thought: throw the ball, catch the ball. Which was what we were doing in the third inning. A ground out to Tony, a fly ball to Paweł. Watching the ball float out to left and hang for a moment against the tall poplars standing behind Paweł, I thought of—heard in my head, *felt*—the gravelly radio voice of Harry Heilmann from forty years back, telling me, almost crooning to me, as I sat beside my father in the car riding home to Flint from up north, from the Au Sable River, our cooler full of rainbow trout, my hands still smelling of them and of the wintergreen in the woods I had wiped off with, the smoke from his Lucky floating out the window, his elbow out the window and the slanting sun lighting up his whiskers making them suddenly golden—the same sun that was at that same moment lighting up left field in Briggs Stadium in Detroit—that it was an easy, *lazy* fly ball Hoot Evers was waiting for, and I knew exactly what Harry Heilmann meant. And still knew, watching Paweł, in Poland, wait for this one.

Then Norbert turned his head on a grounder, letting Kutno have its first base runner. Froggy dropped a throw from Tony, allowing another man on. Both runners scored on a triple. In our half of the third, we got nothing. The game was tied, 2–2.

"It's OK!" Dariusz said.

Kutno loaded the bases in the fourth and Juan cleared them with a double; it should have been a triple but age, cigarettes, and a good throw from Alejandro to Tony kept Juan at second, where he pulled up puffing and shaking his fist good-naturedly at his fellow Cubans. Mark went into his stretch. Norbert and Mariusz suddenly broke toward the batter, as if they expected him to bunt, leaving Juan free to take all the lead off second he wanted. He took a big lead; Mark threw a wide pitch to Jake, Jake threw the ball back over Mark's head toward second, where Alejandro, racing in from center field, took it on one hop and fired to Tony at third. But Juan, forty-year-old smoker or no, had already rounded third and was heading home. Tony fired to Jake and Jake had him dead except, using one hand, he couldn't hold the ball. But for the result, it was exactly the kind of razzle-dazzle the Sparks loved.

Inspired by their near-success on the play, they came up to bat and scored three times, the big blow a two-run single by Tony. The Cubans were hot and the game was close: 6–5, Kutno.

In the fifth the steelworkers got one more, but we got four and out of the corner of my eye I saw Dariusz holding one burning Mocne and trying to light another, while explaining to the gents from the Skra Klub board what everything meant. As for the Sparks, leading 9–7, they carried on as if the deed to the duchy was practically in their pockets. Blackie stood on his hands in front of the bleachers. Mariusz let his girlfriend hold his glove for a while. Marek sat quietly nervous at the far end of the bench, gripping a bat, but Mark, Norbert, Alejandro, and Blackie couldn't put down anywhere when we came in to hit. They were too lit.

Jake said to me, "You know those bubblegum cards? Maybe we should have some made of us."

"Maybe you should start using two hands, Jake."

"I know! I have a bad habit!" he laughed.

Kutno got a goose egg in the sixth. We got three walks and another run on a perfect squeeze bunt laid down by Mariusz. The play sent Blackie into somersaults. A man came up to me from the bleachers and held out his hand. "I am George Biń's father," he said. George had just scored on the squeeze. I said, "Your son's a fine ballplayer." He said, "We have a grave problem. His studies are a shocking disappointment."

Time had been called. Juan was changing pitchers. George's father was asking me if I, as a professor, had some advice I could give him. The new Kutno pitcher, a herky-jerky type, was firing bullets. He struck out Mark. He struck out Blackie. Alejandro popped up to Juan. During all this time George's father stood respectfully off to the side, waiting for me to answer. Kutno came in to bat and as I walked over to our bench, George's father beside me, I said, "When you've got the bases loaded, no outs, and the lead—and it's this late—you should squeeze and keep on squeezing."

The natural beauty of that day in Warsaw, May 29, 1988, continued. The sun, like Harry Heilmann's lazy fly ball, moved where it would after its uncomplicated fashion, and by and by it went down. The sun had caused no unhappiness, it had even helped us along toward those small pleasures of the past that belong to us always—though sometimes we forget we have them—and tomorrow it would return. That evening when Vicki and I left the Bazyliszek restaurant in Old Town, refreshed by our roast duck and Bulgarian cabernet, the stars above the Square had a similar effect: they were clear, steady, encouraging. You could tell them anything. You could tell them you had stood that morning holding your major tool under a hemlock tree. You could tell them you had spent more than half of the seventeenth century on horseback driving an invader out of your country and now, praise God, you were going home to patch up the castle. I hoped that Blackie, thinking things over, was telling the stars, or anyone, something like that. I knew that Juan Echevarría—looking at the stars or not—was feeling pretty good. He had brought in a herky-jerky knight we couldn't touch. He had got two more hits, his fellow steelworkers had got a bunch, and our 10–7 lead disappeared as quickly as the holy shine on Dariusz' cheeks. Kutno had roughed up Mark for five runs in the seventh and roughed up July, Adam, and Pete for eight more in the eighth, to knock us down, 20–10. During the debacle Norbert's head turned and turned on grounders as if it sat on a swivel, Jake, tiring, kept letting pitches get past him, and Blackie had to be put on the bench for his oratory.

As we strolled under the Old Town stars, I said to Vic, "Who told us the history of Warsaw is like the temperature chart of a malaria patient?"

"You're still thinking about the game, aren't you?"

"The shower room was real gloomy."

"Did you make a speech?"

"I told them to get their butts to practice this week. We go against Cnota on Sunday."

Attendance at practice on Tuesday, Wednesday, and Thursday was better than the previous week, though still not what it should have been—not with Silesia Rybnik, the perennial league champion, and its ace pitcher, Jan Cnota, coming up. But much worse, the Sparks seemed listless, their spirits ragged. When I suggested—not serious—that maybe they needed some vitamins, George said, "A Pole invented vitamins"—implying, by his glum tone, that vitamins were therefore worthless.

"Who invented them, Madam Curie?" I said.

"No," he said, "Casimir Funk."

I had to laugh. "That's pretty funny, George."

"What is?"

"Your joke."

"I don't understand."

"Funk means not so good, droopy, shaky. Like you guys. What's wrong? Have you all given up?"

"I don't know. Maybe there are problems at home—with work or school."

"Know what I think, George?"

"No."

"I think the Sparks are acting like babies. Like they need some tit."

He blushed. "Maybe."

Blackie was missing all week, so was Jake. I asked Dariusz if they were home brooding, spent ten minutes telling him what brooding meant, then had to change the subject: his eyes were watering. I moved Alejandro from center field to catcher. His barking picked up Mark, Mark's barking got Mariusz, George, and the others going, and by Friday the cavalry—or most of it— was back in the saddle.

Two days before, Gretchen and Gabriel arrived in Warsaw. Vicki and I met them at the airport with bunches of jonquils and forget-me-nots and daisies. Vic brought the flowers. I brought my baseball gear—in fact was wearing my uniform—because on the way back to Żoliborz I planned to hop out at Skra for practice.

"This is my dad!" Gretchen laughed, emerging from customs. She looked wonderful. Gabriel did too. "I'm three and a half," he said. We all hugged, making a ring, Gabriel and the flowers in the middle.

"So *dzień dobry! Jak się pani ma?*"

"That means hello?"

"Hello! How are you?"

"I'm just great," Gretchen said. She took off my Tigers hat and put it on her head. Then she laughed and put it on Gabriel's head.

The last time I had seen them, almost a year before, was in Flint. Vicki and I were on our way to London; they were on their way to Iowa from Connecticut. Before Connecticut (where they'd spent the summer) they lived in New York for about a year, Gretchen working in a Manhattan day-care. Before New York, they lived in Miami, in the Spanish quarter, where Gabriel was born; and before Miami, Gretchen lived in St. Paul, where she attended Hamline for half a year. Before St. Paul she lived—for seventeen years—in Iowa. At our rendezvous in Michigan, my brother had a party for us. My brother and his wife and their two children; my sister and her husband and their five children, plus a son-in-law and a grandchild; my mother and her boyfriend; my Aunt Rita and Uncle Tommy and their three children, plus a daughter-in-law and a grandchild—they were all waiting for us in my brother's big back yard in Flint where tables of food and tubs of iced beer and pop and wine had been set out and where, late that evening, I saw my mother offering my father a lick off the spoon she was mixing a German chocolate cake with (his favorite), saw her brothers raising shots of whiskey above the kitchen table and toasting "*Na zdrowie!*" and saw my Aunt Rita, just out of high school, dancing round and round in her wedding dress with my new Uncle Tommy home from the Navy. Then I saw my grandfather, big and dark in a dark suit that seemed much too small for him, gazing out over an empty pasture, and then in my brother's back yard Vicki said, "This is just like it is in Ohio. Everyone is still there when I go home, nothing changes. It's wonderful." The next day we flew to London, and Gretchen and Gabriel drove to Iowa.

Now in the Warsaw airport, in the ring we were still making, Gabriel pointed at the strips of old nylon stocking and the braided grass that tied the flowers into bouquets.

"What are those?" he said.

Vicki told him. She told him the Polish grandmas she bought the flowers from tied them that way so we wouldn't lose any.

He said he wanted some grass tied around him. I said we'd do that—next week in the mountains. And at the seashore too, when we went there.

"Will you remember?" he said.

I said I would.

"But we haven't booked you up completely," Vicki told Gretchen.

"What about these Sparks I keep hearing about? Will I get to see them play?"

"How does traveling down to Silesia seven hours on the team bus sound? Twenty-five healthy young brooding Poles and us?"

"When!"

"We leave Saturday," I said. "Spend Saturday night in Rybnik, play Sunday, then Sunday night head for the Tatra Mountains."

"Twenty-five healthy young brooding Poles and us?"

"No—the brooders have to come home," I said.

"Damn."

"The word in Polish," Vicki said, "is *szkoda*, which means 'too bad.'"

"Well, I'm here," Gretchen said, "and I'm ready."

In the taxi she said, "Have you heard from my friend Don?"

"He called," Vicki said. "He said he was very sorry he couldn't meet your plane. But he's coming to dinner. He sounds nice."

On Saturday at Skra Henry stood beside the Sparks' bus door and kissed Vicki's hand, then Gretchen's, as they stepped aboard. George took charge of Gabriel. Before we were out of the city, Gabriel was calling George his brother. Dariusz and I sat up front, across the aisle from each other. Vicki sat behind me, reading, and behind Dariusz sat Jacek Demkiewicz making his first road trip—and therefore eligible for a baptism, which Pete, two rows behind Vicki, called up to Dariusz about with horse-winking innocence, but which Jacek, no matter what Pete was talking about, wanted no part of, occupied as he was with finding the right posture and facial expression to present to the young American woman who sat behind him talking in Spanish with Tony and on whom, it was obvious to everyone, he was trying very hard to make a good impression, while at the same time trying equally hard not to appear so. Dariusz pretended not to hear Pete's question. Clearly a baptism among men was not possible with women on the bus. Jacek found the expression he wanted: it bore an uncanny resemblance to that famous one in Warsaw's Łazienki Park of Chopin's, wherein the composer is gazing off over his shoulder as if after those melodies no one but he, among mortals, can hear. Like the statue, Jacek was in touch with angels, please, let him listen to the trilling of his heart, enough with this baptism drivel. Now Henry, sitting across from Pete—and a colleague in this little colloquy—called up to the front: "Yes, Dariusz, what about it?"

Dariusz' neck blushed red. He said to me, ignoring Henry, turning to team business, "No Blackie, no Jake."

I said we were OK at catcher. But not having Blackie's bat was a definite handicap.

"What is handicap?"

I told him. He liked the word and repeated it, nodding gravely.

Henry said—loud enough for Dariusz' benefit—"Does tradition mean so little to him anymore?"

"It appears so," said Pete.

"I can remember," Henry said, "when Dariusz was a very different man."

What made all this even more embarrassing to Dariusz was that I interrupted Jacek's pose to ask him (though I could figure out the gist) what Henry and Pete were talking about.

"Some foolishness with tradition," Jacek said. "I am not hearing it."

There were titters in the back of the bus and Dariusz was squirming. Having fun with their founder—who had a large responsibility now to keep decorum on the bus—was a lot more fun for the Sparks than spanking Jacek. Finally Dariusz, deep red, stood up and went to have a word with his tormentors. On the way he bowed to Vicki, then to Gretchen. "Little boys," he said. "These are little boys back here. Big handicap, you understand?"

About halfway to Silesia the driver pulled over at a wooded rest stop. We all got out, but the players hung around the bus as Vicki and Gretchen started toward the public toilet. "Maybe," Pete said to me, "you should call them back." He pinched his nose. I didn't have to call them back. Ten yards from the toilet, they angled off, giggling, into the trees. When they emerged, the Sparks politely took their turn among the trees.

Back on the highway the Sparks entertained themselves—and Gabriel—by passing him over their heads from seat to seat, up one side of the bus and down the other—round and round—while he held out his arms like wings and squealed his favorite new word—*masło*—which means "butter." By and by I heard George telling Vicki about the problems he was having with his girlfriend and his father. Pete was telling Gretchen about his interest in Beckett and Eugene O'Neill. Mariusz settled into *David Copperfield*, Froggy into a physics problem, Norbert and Mark into comic books. To round out the literary fare, I distributed packs of Topps baseball cards fresh from the States. Dariusz told me there would be no improvisation on this trip—no handicap—because he had made complete reservations for all rooms and all meals; and just before we pulled into gray, coke-smelling Rybnik, Jacek, out of a personal blue, said, "I will tell you the truth, Gary. I do not read books. They hurt my head."

In a private—i.e., not state-run—restaurant we had a good supper (borsch and baked chicken and a chocolate cake that Dariusz had special-ordered, by phone, days before); we checked into not the sparrow-like clerk's Workers' Hotel but the Hotel Rybnik, which was right next door and cost the same but was much nicer, though according to official ratings ranked one class lower because it didn't serve breakfast; and next morning after kielbasa and tomatoes and sweetened black tea at the former—dished out once more by the busty ladies in their misty smocks—we got on the bus under a grimy sky that dripped a grimy, sad little rain and started for the game.

Dariusz had puzzling news. "Message from Mr. Cnota, manager of Silesia Rybnik. We play on old field, not new field."

"What's the difference?" I said.

"New field is fifteen minutes from here, away from city. Very good field, like Skra. Grass. But Mr. Cnota say to me grass is too high this day."

"Did you ask Mr. Cnota why he didn't cut the grass?"

"Only message. No discussion."

"And where is the old field?"

"Five minutes."

"And no grass."

"No grass."

"I'll bet the old field is rough as hell."

"Rough?"

"Not smooth."

Dariusz nodded.

"So the great pitcher is also the clever manager of this team."

"I don't understand."

"Is Mr. Cnota Jan Cnota, the pitcher?"

"No, no. Father of Jan Cnota. Very big man in Polish baseball."

Who wants to remain a very big man, I thought. I took two new balls out of my bag and flipped one back to July, the other to Mark. "Rub some strikes into those," I said. Then I asked Vic, sitting beside me, if she'd had any dreams last night. She said she had two, a short one and a long one. The short one was about setting her chair in a parking place and putting nickels in the meter for it.

"Hundreds of nickels, it seemed like."

"That was the short dream?"

"I'll tell you the long one later."

We arrived at Silesia Rybnik's old field. It was bare and black as a wet blackboard—but only smooth like a blackboard if you were fifty yards away from it. Standing on it you saw the crushed pieces of coal, the slag, the cinders, the gouges. I was furious. "God damn it, Dariusz, look." I threw a white ball on the ground to Froggy standing about ninety feet away: it squiggled and crazy-hopped like a knuckleball. I told him to throw me a grounder back. When I held up the ball to Dariusz it was nearly black.

"You know what this is?" I said.

"Ball is all dirty."

"Mr. Cnota is a first-class cocksucker."

"Ball will be difficult to see," Dariusz said sadly.

"A bitch to see. And to handle."

"Big handicap."

"I'd like to shove this ball in his teeth."

I ranted and swore some more telling Dariusz to get the bastard and poor Dariusz looked helpless and confused. He'd come to Rybnik to play baseball, a game of skill, of much quickness and beauty, a sport he harbored real hopes of seeing Poland play in the next Olympics, and he was jacked up for all that, not for dirty tricks, and certainly not for a display of anger by his American coach and friend. He didn't know what to do and I could see that—could also see, suddenly, that my lack of cool was no doubt making Mr. Cnota very happy if he was there yet and watching. I walked around in a tight circle. I recalled some stories—Ty Cobb filing his spikes knife-sharp to intimidate infielders, pitchers putting Vaseline and spit on the ball to make it wiggle; there were all kinds of stories; but this one got the prize. Finally I took a deep breath.

"Piss on it," I said.

"Piss on it," my buddy Dariusz said.

"The bastard's afraid of us."

"Much afraid."

We watched the Sparks getting loose in the grainy, soot-colored mist; watched the orange rubber practice balls—which I was not fond of—bounce too high, plop out of mitts. It was almost like watching an inept, spiritless fruit fight. To top it off, here came a dignified Jacek stalking across the outfield wearing a suitcoat over his shoulders and a white towel over his arm—the Chopin expression replaced with that of a most fastidious head waiter's; he carried a tray of cups and saucers, bottles, a cream pitcher, and a tall silver pot, and was followed single file by Gretchen, Gabriel, and Vicki carrying bouquets of wildflowers and weeds. Jacek and his little band of pilgrims paraded among the Sparks, among the bright orange Japanese practice balls flying around, and brought their wares to our bench, where they sat down and commenced a tea party.

"Ah," I said, "our new specialist for special efforts."

"Very special," Dariusz said.

The light rain quit and the Juniors' game got started. The white baseball turned black in the first inning and stayed that way until the end. At one point Robert, playing third base, missed a grounder hit right at him and then held a private brood while two runs scored. I couldn't fault him for the error (I could hardly see the ball myself), but I chewed him out for hanging his head. I caught Vicki and Gretchen throwing me murderous looks from the bench and went to inquire. "You are humiliating that boy," Vicki said. "I am trying to get—and keep—his attention," I said, and brooded some myself on the wisdom of allowing mothers to sit so close to the action.

In the fourth inning Whale, Robert, Andrzej, and Paweł Tymiński all got crazy hits and scored on poor fielding—and then in a flurry they scored again, great big lumbering Whale, vindicated fist-raising Robert, flat-footed Andrzej with his corkscrew curls gone haywire, and altar boy Paweł who, after he crossed the plate, came running over to me. "Coach, I think we knocked them down. I think we won." He seemed almost mortified—as if he might be guilty of the sin of pride—and slightly confused as well. All the Junior Sparks seemed slightly confused except Whale, who was smiling like a kid who'd got caught eating the last poppy-seed cake in Poland and didn't care. Pete and Mark stepped in and directed them to line up along third base, and then led them—since they had had no experience—in a victory yell.

I took our success in the Juniors' game as a good sign (as did Dariusz) and watching Rybnik's Seniors take infield practice I felt even better. They could not handle the ball very well on those gouges and cinders either. Of course they had Jan Cnota and his fabulous, accurate fastball (his warm-up throws were not pleasur-able to watch), and that, plus a field that would dirty the ball in a hurry, was Mr. Cnota's strategy: we'd strike out on offense and muff grounders on defense. They'd knock us down short and sweet in five innings and go drink beer.

I called the Sparks to a huddle. We were all shivering a little as you do just before a game. "OK," I said, "we came here to play baseball. Not to fight each other. Not to hang our heads if we make an error. Let me do the yelling. Tell them, George."

He told them. Then he said, "I think they are nervous, Gary."

"Are you nervous, George?" I said.

"Me? No—I have my private bat," he grinned.

"Are you nervous, July?"

"Why should I be?"

"Mark?"

"Of course not."

"Mariusz?"

"No."

"George," I said, "why do you tell me bullshit? No one is nervous. Look—even Norbert, even Marek—*bardzo spokojnie.*"

That broke the ice. Everyone laughed. Then George said, "No, I mean Rybnik is nervous."

"I'm glad to hear it. I want to make them more nervous." I knelt in the middle of the huddle going over our signs. I was kneeling on cinders, on scabby little patches of blackened weeds, focusing on Paweł Płatek's smiling face and moving my hands. Paweł, who spoke no English, who looked like Harpo Marx the man who never spoke, said "take." I moved my hands and he said "swing" and "steal" and "squeeze." I felt like a magician, a genius. I wanted to teach him other words—words like "summer" and "yesterday" and "over-the-shoulder." I wanted to take him—and Froggy and Norbert and the others—back to Michigan, to Mott Park and Ballenger Park and the diamond in the field behind Holy Redeemer where a pheasant once flew past the mound as I went into my stretch. I hadn't thought of that pheasant in years, in decades, and there it was in a burst of purple- and green-feathered glory, in our shivering huddle in Rybnik, where the Sparks waited for me to give the next command, which was to join hands. Past Paweł I could see that Cnota, on the mound, was waiting too. He had finished his warm-up tosses and was ready to go. So was the umpire. I wasn't. I wanted the sun to come out and the grass to grow. I was willing to wait all summer if we had to. I wanted to play *baseball*. But Dariusz on the fringe of the huddle was nervously calling, "Gary, Gary, we must go now." We all touched hands and broke away in a yell, and George, kissing his bat, stepped up to the plate.

Cnota (pronounced Snow-ta) was Mark's size, twenty-eight years old, and he threw the ball like a pro. Though he walked George—who stood on first base and said to me bravely, "I am not afraid of him"—he struck out Norbert, Tony, and Mariusz, and then walked off the mound like a man who simply did what he had come there to do. If there was any joy in his performance, he didn't show it. My mother would have described him as tall, dark, and handsome. He looked a lot like an actor from the Forties named John Hodiak. In addition to a powerful fastball, he owned a good curve. Mixing these two pitches, he kept the Sparks off-balance for five innings. Only in the third, when Paweł walked and stole second and Mark drove him in with a single, did the Sparks score. Cnota recorded thirteen strikeouts, two short of the maximum for a five inning game. Mark got our only hit. On defense we lunged at half a dozen squiggly grounders that eluded us like mice; those errors plus two walks, two hits, and a throwing error gave Rybnik the eleven runs it needed to knock us down and go drink beer.

The game took just an hour to play—that's counting the rather lengthy time-out I called to go out and speak with Norbert for yelling at Marek, who had thrown the ball in from left field over Norbert's head; the ball had got into left field in the first place because Norbert ducked away when it crazy-hopped in front of him, but he seemed to have forgotten that part until I reminded him. I also had to speak to Mariusz and Mark for yelling at each other, and to Alejandro for yelling at everybody. We were all frustrated.

Mr. Cnota's strategy had worked beautifully. If you took away the grounders we couldn't handle, that caromed off cinders, that skewed and bad-hopped over the pock-marked field, the score after five innings would have been only 3–1 and we could have played four more innings. But piss on whiny if-talk. And piss on that God damn knock down rule. How in hell could the Poles, who prided themselves on going against the odds—spending sixty years on horseback getting the Swedes off their backs, rising up with a ragtail home army against the Nazis squatting on their faces—how in hell could they stop a baseball game like Little Leaguers after only a ten-run spread? Didn't they know it wasn't over until it was *all* over?

Dariusz went to shake Mr. Cnota's hand. I did not. I shook his son's hand for his fine control and that was enough. I was not prepared to congratulate a man for crapping on my team in broad daylight. Also, Mr. Cnota had turned out to look—from a distance—remarkably like Joseph Conrad in the *American Heritage Dictionary*—or, had he worn a mustache, like my grandfather. I was not happy to see that. It had interfered some with my concentration during the game, and now in the aftermath it interfered with my frustration.

I wanted to get out of Rybnik as soon as possible. On the bus I told Dariusz to drop Vic, Gretchen, Gabriel, and me in the center of town, or wherever the best place was to hire a taxi, and we'd take off right away for the mountains.

"Now?" he said.

"Yes."

"What about Pizza Hut?"

"We visit Pizza Hut. Then a taxi."

"But, Gary, we must have supper. Everything is reserved."

"Ah shit, Dariusz, I'm not hungry."

"Vicki not hungry? Your daughter? The little boy?"

"We'll stop on the way to Zakopane," I said.

He looked even more disappointed than when the umpire had stood on home plate and declared Rybnik's knock down victory.

"I don't understand," he said.

"I'm being a very poor loser right now. But I know one thing," I said. "That bastard *was* afraid of us."

"Maybe," Dariusz said, "you don't like the food where we have reservation. OK, no problem, we must find food you like. In Katowice maybe—a first-class tourist restaurant."

"Damn it, Dariusz, I'm trying to bleed and you won't let me."

"Bleed?"

"Let's go eat where you have the reservation. I like that food fine."

The manager of the restaurant ushered the team toward a back room. Some of us detoured to use the toilet. Ahead of me, Paweł Tymiński was washing his hands. I asked him how it felt to win a game. He thought about the question, then he said, "To tell you the truth, Coach, it's difficult to say." He wore a studious, almost sad expression. Hell, I thought, my gloom has infected them all.

When I finished up and walked in the back room, where everyone sat at a long banquet table, there was a burst of applause. I saw big smiles on Whale and Robert, on George and Pete and Fleetfoot. I sat down between Vic and Gretchen. Across the table Paweł Tymiński was smiling too.

Vic said, laughing, "Don't you just love these guys?"

"I sure do," Gretchen said.

"I think we need something to drink," Vic said.

We absolutely did. I went out and went over to the counter where you paid your bill—and where, on shelves, the restaurant displayed samples of its drink offerings: mineral water, grape juice, cherry-flavored vodka, Bulgarian red wine.

"*Nie piwo?*" I said to the clerk.

"*Nie ma.*"

"*Szkoda. Bardzo szkoda.*" I tried to look real sad. Then I showed her a five dollar bill.

She disappeared behind a curtain. In a minute she returned, smiling.

"*Tak,*" she said. "*Piwo.*"

"*Dobrze. Bardzo dobrze!*" I pointed to the back room and drew a circle, the universal sign for a round. Then I held up two fingers and drew a second circle. She understood.

Back at the table the players were into their soup course.

"How's the borsch?" I asked Mark.

"Too much vinegar. No good."

"Norbert's finished his already," I said. "He must like it."

"It's good for Norbert," Mark said. "He eats all things."

I ate all things too, and the waiter was serving the beer, and the room took on a very nice glow. No brooding allowed!

"Now I don't want you to think," I whispered to Vic, "that I ordered this beer just because the guys gave me a hand."

"I won't," she said. "They applauded everybody who came in late."

I roared. Then I raised my glass to the Sparks. "Rybnik has to play us again," I said. "In Warsaw!"

The players cheered. Everyone cheered, and I heard Gabriel say, "*Masło!*"

After supper we went to see Pizza Hut. The hospital said only three visitors, but Henry sweet-talked a nurse into "a couple more," and then nine of us slipped up the stairs.

Pizza Hut was sleeping. He wore a big black patch over his eye like a pirate. Two other patients in the room—pale, thin, middle-aged men—sat hunched over on their beds and watched us look at Pizza Hut. Suddenly his eye opened, and slowly a sheepish smile spread across his face. The Sparks backed up: they wanted me to greet him first. I held out my hand and he slapped it, and then a young red-haired nurse stepped quickly into the room. She put her hands protectively on Pizza Hut's shoulders, saying to him—and to us—"*Spokojnie.*" All the guys laughed. Mark said Pizza Hut was too ugly to have such a pretty girl beside him, and Pete said that was no problem because Pizza Hut didn't know what to do anyway. The laughter rose and the nurse, blushing, trying to look stern, told us not to make him excited and the guys oohed and ahhed and Pizza Hut in his pirate patch was smiling as if he knew exactly what to do. I said I hoped he was using two hands, and when the laughter from that died down, he said he didn't have to use any, everything was done for him. Which got a roar. The nurse, getting into this, said, "*Prawda,*" it was true—which got the biggest roar of all. Then she gave us one more minute. We all told Pizza Hut to hurry up and come home. He said he would. Henry kissed the nurse's hand, thanking her for putting up with us, and then we filed out past Pizza Hut's two roommates who seemed almost bodiless in their big hospital smocks—and who continued to sit hunched over on the edges of their beds as if nailed there like scarecrows.

Vicki, Gretchen, Gabriel, and I rode north with the team as far as Katowice because Dariusz said Rybnik was no good for taxis—Katowice, the region's capital, was better; in Katowice, he said, we had "three combinations." (He liked that word a lot and used it to mean "possibilities" or "choices.") From Katowice, he said, we could take a bus, the train, or a taxi to Zakopane. He recommended the bus or the train. The distance to Zakopane from there was over a hundred kilometers and a taxi, he said, would be very expensive.

"Taxi will ask dollars," he said.

"I know. It's OK."

"Maybe not OK. Maybe too much," he said.

I assured him I could handle it.

He sank back, his chin all bunched up. He never wanted me to spend money when I traveled with the Sparks. If I did he would say I was guest! I would say no God damn it I was the coach. He would say of course Gary of course but. And I would say no more Polish. We are not *speaking* Polish he would say and I would say *nie rozumiem* which means "I don't understand." I knew he wanted us to take the train or the bus to Zakopane because then he could buy the tickets. A taxi—and it would cost dollars—was impossible for him.

"Look," I said, "quit brooding. You look like a *babcia* with a boil on your ass."

"I don't like this word brooding."

"Tell me how much a taxi will charge to Zakopane."

"Maybe twenty dollars."

"In the States that's what I pay to travel from my house to the airport. I do it all the time."

"Maybe fifty dollars!"

"Please, Dariusz, it's really OK. OK?"

"You listen, Gary. No happiness."

"OK. If we can catch a train for Zakopane—soon—we'll take it. If we have to wait, I'm hiring a taxi."

He didn't like it, but he nodded.

"Now," he said, "I must speak about *piwo* at the restaurant."

"No, you must not speak about it."

"But, Gary—"

"*Nie rozumiem.*"

At the Katowice train station, Dariusz sent Jacek to check the train schedule, Henry the bus schedule. It was four o'clock in the afternoon, but if you had only the color of the sky to go by you'd be lost. Under that low ratty gray it could have been six a.m. or eight p.m., or a time when clocks were no longer used because why keep track of a world that was always the same? It was a sky you saw from your sickbed when you were a kid—a sky under which nothing was going on and never would, ever. Though it was the same sky we'd had in Rybnik, there we had baseball to distract us from it; here, we had to acknowledge it constantly. Froggy was holding my bag, Pete had Vicki's, Paweł Płatek had Gretchen's, and George had charge of Gabriel. We all stood by the station entrance, on a ramp, waiting for Henry and Jacek to report. Below us in the street was a line of maybe fifteen taxis. Smoking one of his foul Mocnes, Dariusz glared down at the taxis as if preparing to do battle with them.

The reports came back: a train in two hours, a bus about the same.

"We'll take a taxi," I said.

"OK," Dariusz said, "but you please wait here."

He and Jacek went down and got in the first taxi. Then they got out and Dariusz entered the second one, Jacek the third. We all watched from the ramp. Pete laughed, "There is a word for this." Jacek returned briefly to the first taxi, Dariusz entered the fourth one. Down the line they went, moving faster than I had ever seen them move. From time to time they'd meet, confer, and Jacek would dash back to the first taxi. "It looks like that one," I said to

Pete. "Maybe," he laughed. "But maybe they are only trying to make the others nervous."

Finally Dariusz waved me down. The second taxi, he said, would take us to Zakopane for twenty-five dollars. The others, he said with disgust, wanted forty and fifty. "All thiefs," he said. "All."

Now everyone was gathered at the taxi, to shake our hands and wish us good luck as if we were going on a great journey to a land much farther up the road than one hundred kilometers or so. Mariusz said, "Mountains very clean," and George said, "I always love it there," and Froggy's cheeks seemed about to burst. "I wish I could *say* something," Gretchen said, and Pete said we must visit two lakes: Morskie Oko and Czarny Staw—"The Eye of Mr. Morskie" and "Black Lake." He said Mr. Morskie's daughter fell in love with a monk and Mr. Morskie, not approving, turned the monk into a mountain. The daughter, very sad, threw herself into the lake at the foot of this mountain—that is, into "The Eye of Mr. Morskie." Mark said no, not a monk, only a man disguised as a monk—what would a monk do with a girl? Pete said maybe Mark would be surprised. George said that lake could also be called "The Eye of the Sea," because *morskie* meant "sea." Pete said anyway Mr. Morskie, seeing his daughter drowned, began to cry and his tears became "Black Lake." But it was only a story, he said, and pulled George's hat down to cover his face. I saw Jacek, shy on the periphery, edge closer to Gretchen, hesitate ("Romeo, come forth; come forth, thou fearful man—"), and then I heard Vicki say, "I'm going to start bawling like Mr. Morskie if we don't get moving, Coach." I told Dariusz I'd see everybody at practice on Wednesday and then we left.

To go from Katowice to Zakopane is to go from the death rattle to the pink blush of health. Zakopane (which sounds Italian—Zok-o-PAHN-ee) is in the Tatras, the largest group of mountains in the Carpathian range. To the Poles, Zakopane is almost in heaven (it is also almost in Czechoslovakia) and they go there, as people have always gone to the mountains, to escape. During the war patriots hid from the Nazis there; now lovers, families share sleeping bags under the stars in Zakopane and make all the noise they want because the cramped boxy flats they normally live in are somewhere else, don't ask them where, at the moment they couldn't tell you and couldn't care less. There are two fine hotels in Zakopane, the large Kasprowy, the small Giewont, and if you have a little extra to spend and can manage a reservation, you will stay in one of these, of course. Of course! a Pole will tell you, expansive, unworried. He will tell you there are plenty of tourist homes with good beds covered with feather quilts and those are *dobrze* too! The important thing is to be here, he will say, never mind the details—tomorrow you could die, and what an excellent place for it, no? Listen, Karol Wojtyła, before he became pope, skied in these mountains! Is that so? *Tak*, and even party members come to Zakopane, to stay in their fancy dachas, though how much fun *they* are having is hard to say.

We stayed in the Kasprowy on the slope of Mt. Gubałówka, our rooms facing the town in the valley and—rising behind it—the broad shoulders of Mt. Giewont that still had some snow on them. Below the snow were clouds of mist and forests of spruce and one day we started up, following a cold rushing stream. It was not a difficult hike, the path was clear, the air cool beside the stream, and after about three hours we came to a high sunny meadow. We stopped for lunch. Vicki and Gretchen wove a rope for Gabriel out of grass and tied it around his waist. We were all quiet, listening to the wind in the trees and keeping an eye out, at Gabriel's suggestion, for rabbits. I took a baseball out of my jacket pocket and was rubbing it, thinking I might move Norbert to right field, Mariusz to shortstop, and try Pete at second base. I saw Vicki smiling at me, slowly shaking her head. Her eyes were very blue up there closer to the sky and I was thinking how many women would stop what they were doing and follow a man to Poland? Or look so sexy in a child's blue socks with red and yellow polka dots on them? (Some kid had left them at her house—kids were always leaving things there, she said—and she simply packed them.) Or what woman who taught in college and served on her community's mental health board and owned a complete set of *Gourmet* magazines would say—as she had whispered to me at the ambassador's house during a dull party—"Let's go upstairs where they've piled all the coats on that wonderful Posturepedic, and lock the door. I've always wanted to screw on a bunch of wraps, haven't you?"—and mean it?

She lay back in the grass now and closed her eyes. Gretchen was looking at Gabriel, who was looking uphill, holding onto his new rope. They sat perfectly still, the one pleasurably amused to see the other so absorbed—like figures in a painting you happen on. You wonder if they are related (she is blonde, he is dark) but more important—for the moment—you wonder what the boy is looking at, what holds his attention so, because his expression is beguiling, almost adult. The painter has done a good job not to make him cute. The painter has also managed, you now notice, to change slightly the woman's expression—he has given it a touch, a flicker, of puzzlement, uncertainty. I looked uphill and saw only meadow and spruce trees around it and above those only the blue sky—no bears, nothing threatening—but in my head suddenly I saw again the huge black and white blowups hanging on a wall in Auschwitz, and then the one that had held me: a young girl who for the instant it took to capture her forever did not quite understand something. And then her fixed, beautiful, uncertain gaze was too much. I looked down. Below her picture—below all of them—was the kind of glass-topped case you bend over in museums, to observe old manuscripts, precious stones. This one held stuffed animals, the cheap and irreplaceable dolls you find years later, in attics, in musty boxes, and remember their names.

We were on a bus, leaving Zakopane for Kraków—two hours away—and Vicki was saying, "In the late Forties and early Fifties we'd make this sixteen-hour drive from Newark, Ohio, to my grandparents' farm in Gadston, Alabama. My mother's folks. We'd leave as soon as my dad got off work at three-thirty. We'd go down and cross the Ohio River into Kentucky—at Maysville, where Rosemary Clooney was born—and then we'd scoot through Tennessee. All those barefoot kids in front of shacks and boys in gas stations looking us over. I thought those kids didn't wear shoes because it was summer, but one winter we made the drive for Christmas and those kids were still standing outside their shacks without shoes on. Every time we passed through Dayton, my dad would say, 'Here's the monkey town!' and my sister and brother would look out the windows for monkeys. I knew better, though, because my mother would sigh, 'Oh, Don.' I always waited for the next town, Soddy Daisy, because I liked the sound of it. After Tennessee we clipped off a corner of Georgia where there was a big sign for the Georgia State Game Park. I can't tell you what's there because we never stopped. We never stopped to see Rock City either. You'd start to see signs as soon as you crossed the river at Maysville—every barn, every bird house we passed had a sign on it: SEE ROCK CITY. But we never stopped. We had to make good time, my dad would always say.

"When I got older and got interested in looking at a map of where we went those summers, I discovered we could see the TVA. It was practically on our route. I'd point this out to my dad and he'd nod and say, real serious, 'One of these summers we'll have to do that.' But we never did. We never stopped anywhere except to get gas and pee and eat one meal outside the car, at a lake in Kentucky. My mother loved that. So did us kids. She'd pack fried chicken, baloney and cheese sandwiches, bananas, cookies. When we got to Gadston my dad and my grandpa would start right in on how long the drive took and how many curves the road people had straightened out since the last trip. 'You know that curve outside Crab Apple, Tennessee?' my dad would say. As a rule we'd pull into Gadston just in time for breakfast. But sometimes we'd arrive before anyone was awake. They'd get right up though and put the coffee pot on and fry eggs and marvel at what good time we'd made."

"My dad never wanted to stop either," I said.

"Are you that way too?"

I had to think about it. I guessed maybe I was at one time.

She said she missed Rachel and Jocelyn. Rachel was the daughter at Wellesley whom I hadn't met yet, the good student, the one she didn't worry too much about. Jocelyn, not quite eighteen, was the high school dropout, the high-spirited one. I had met her at Christmas when Vic and I arranged for her to join us in Rome.

The three of us spent ten days there and Vic and I saw Jocelyn about half that time: she had met a young Brit on her flight from London and he wanted to show her the sights. How can I resist? she told her mom.

Vic was sitting by the window. She looked out for a while—at the farms we were passing, the land becoming flat—and then she said, "Anyway, that was the long dream I had the other night. That drive down to Gadston with my family."

On most days in Kraków you can see very quickly why the Poles do not like the Russians. Above this beautiful city that was Poland's royal capital between the eleventh and seventeenth centuries, there rises, almost daily, a sky of filth, which then of course, piece by powdery piece, falls down. It falls on magnificent Gothic, baroque, and Renaissance buildings, on the second oldest university in Europe, on babies. It falls, a Pole will tell you, because Krakówians were too proud of their city, too proud of their past, and the filth is teaching them humility. During the war, he will say, Kraków, unlike Warsaw, was not bombed by the Nazis; its beauty was spared. But now we have this. Every hour. Every hour, also, day and night, a trumpet can be seen emerging from the taller of the two towers of St. Mary's Church in the Main Market Square. A long plaintive note begins, it rises to another, perhaps one or two more, holding you, and then, in mid-note, the trumpet stops. From that same tower in 1241, you are told, a trumpeter raised the alarm as Tartars stormed the city, and was stopped by an arrow in his throat. You are told that that brave trumpeter is being remembered—has been remembered, hourly, since the fourteenth century. Looking up at St. Mary's blackened tower and then at the most polluted sky in Poland—which comes from Nowa Huta ("The New Steelworks"), built by Stalin just east of the city—you understand that something else is being remembered too.

Vicki and I had been to Kraków twice before (in September and in April, to meet with students at the university and for me to give a public reading of my poems at the American Consulate) and both times the sky was bad. But on that early June day when we arrived with Gretchen and Gabriel, the wind was blowing the other way—toward Russia.

We strolled in the sun where Copernicus, Joseph Conrad, and the Nazis had strolled in the sun, measuring the world, stealing from it. In Wawel Castle we saw where Polish kings had warmed their feet and cooled their heels, where their queens, in bed, looked up at naked couples playing on the ceiling. High above the main altar in St. Mary's we saw the Virgin receiving her crown (the Nazis had hauled that altar off to the Reich but it was returned), and we saw Christ almost everywhere—in the manger, crucified, being entombed. We also saw Satan descending into the abyss with black skin and red eyes, with horns and curly black hair and hands like a chicken's claws and with red boils— the boils of lust—covering his face. Gretchen said, "I'm not too big on churches," and took Gabriel outside. Vic and I stayed a while longer. I was looking at the fair, rosy-cheeked Virgin, smelling all the old familiar odors—incense, candle wax, aged wood polished with human oils—and then I was seeing again the girls of Holy Redeemer kneeling at the communion rail and easing their tongues out for Father Gauthier and for me, his acolyte, who behind a basement furnace, buried deep in a wagon of hay, and in the hot, sweaty front seat of a 1946 Chevrolet had tasted this one, and that one, and oh my dear Lord that one too—and all at the trembling, glorious, juicy risk of losing forever my immortal soul. That vaporous white thing I kept getting dirty. Which hounded me. And which I could not feel. What I felt was something else, and at no time more deeply than when serving at Mass. Breaking my leg sliding into third base gave me a sharp pain and a sense of helplessness for a few moments, but that was nothing compared to kneeling at the altar and smelling flowers and candles and wine, seeing the spike through Christ's feet, hearing the choir reach higher, and feeling Delphine Bononi's skin under my surplice.

In St. Mary's Church that day Satan, for me, was the most interesting figure but the crucified Christ by Wit Stwosz from the late Middle Ages was a very close second. Carving in wood, Stwosz gave Christ the lean, muscular body of an athlete (a swimmer perhaps, or a long-distance walker); the face, however, is shockingly lined and old. It's a face I had seen in Warsaw more than once—the face of a man gazing out from a park bench with an empty vodka bottle in his hands. The detail that held me the longest, though, was the stomach; it was very feminine. I wanted to run my hand over it. Perhaps the sculptor had used a woman to model for that part, or was thinking of one.

The least interesting figure in St. Mary's was the Virgin, but how can you make her interesting? When I tried to imagine her growing old, wearing black, sprouting a few white hairs on her chin like a *babcia* and giving hell to some guy who looked like her son for getting drunk in the morning in public, I figured it was time to go.

I found Vicki in a corner, at an exhibit telling of Nazi cruelties and Polish losses during the war. She'd been crying. We went outside. The day was still beautiful, still hundreds of years old.

"It was a story about two children," she said. "Two little girls."

On the far side of the Square where some temporary bleachers and a platform-stage had been set up (probably for May Day party speeches), we saw Gretchen and Gabriel. She was sitting in the bleachers and he was running back and forth on the platform with a couple of kids his age. A little apart from Gretchen sat two women about her age. Beside the bleachers, an old woman was selling flowers, a dozen small cans of them blooming around her feet like votive offerings. Her face was pink and her expression said she was in no hurry, let the sun shine and the children play. We were not in any hurry either. We watched this little scene as if it were the thing we had come to Kraków for, as if it were glossing in ordinary, direct language more ornate or patently evasive stories elsewhere. At one point Vicki looked at it through her camera, but didn't take a picture. (She told me later she wanted to remember the scene on her own.) Finally, Gabriel came running to his mother and buried his laughing face in her lap; the other two children—a boy and girl, both blond as wheat—waved good-bye from the platform.

"Feel better?"

Vic didn't answer right away. Then, "It's hard to say, Coach. There's a lot going on. But I know I'm hungry."

We ate grilled salmon in a 400-year-old restaurant and then caught the Ekspres train to Warsaw—from the same station where Conrad in 1874, almost seventeen and aiming high, boarded the Vienna Ekspres, " . . . as a man might get into a dream," he said. But there is no plaque to remember this leave-taking. The astronomer who flung a little world into the heavens and a skiing archbishop who became pope are remembered everywhere in Kraków. So are quarrelsome kings, even the hated Nazis. But not the dreaming boy who went to school there and later described Poland as "that country which demands to be loved as no other country has ever been loved, with the mournful affection one bears to the unforgotten dead and with the unextinguishable fire of a hopeless passion which only a living, breathing, warm ideal can kindle in our breasts for our pride, for our weariness, for our exultation, for our undoing."

The first half of the baseball season ended for us the following Sunday, down on Cyprzanów's sheep meadow. Before that happened, however, the Sparks got to meet Stan Musial. So did Vicki, Gabriel, and I.

It was Saturday—travel day—and it was raining hard that morning in Warsaw. Vic and Gabriel and I arrived at Skra late; we couldn't get a taxi in Żoliborz and had to take the tram, then hoof it from the tram stop in the rain—Gabriel saying, "We're having an experience, right?"

Dariusz met us at the *kawiarnia* door. He wore a suit and tie and an expression that at first made you think of an FBI agent attending his chief; but in his eyes you could see that he was merely stunned, and that his heart rate must have been medically wondrous. All the guys were dressed in their best, and sitting down polite and shining as if word had been sent by their *babcia*s to behave. The tables were arranged in a big T, banquet style. Musial was sitting at the top of the T, tanned and relaxed, in a gray suit.

Still in his special shock, Dariusz took us over. "Mr. Stanley Musial," he said.

Musial stood up. He was almost seventy but his grip, his movements, his big confident smile said he could still tie on the spikes and take his cuts.

"How are ya?" he said.

"Hauling some water," I said.

"Who's this guy?" he said.

"Gabriel, my grandson."

"He looks like a nice guy. How are ya?"

"Fine," Gabriel said, shaking his hand.

"This is Vicki," I said.

"I used to listen to you on the radio," she said. "When you played the Cincinnati Reds."

He laughed. "Have some coffee. Get dry."

Dariusz, standing off to the side with Mr. Richard and Ron Czarnetsky—but keeping a quick eye on things—had coffee brought over. I waved to Ron. He was a Third Secretary at the American Embassy, fresh out of diplomatic school. Before that he wrestled at Brown. Today he was Musial's chauffeur.

I asked Musial if he'd met the Sparks yet.

"We were waiting for you, Coach."

"George," I said, "come up here. Pete, Norbert, Marek—"

They formed a line.

Wearing a big smile, George said to me, "Can I ask him to sign this?" He had a piece of paper.

"Wait a minute," Musial said, "I've got something better. In my bag. Where's Ron?"

Ron Czarnetsky produced a bag. Inside it Musial found a pack of postcard-sized cards bearing his picture in his St. Louis Cardinals uniform and a legend. The legend, as magical to a certain kind of believer as the Psalms are to another, said that from 1941 to 1963 Musial played in 3,026 games, came to bat 10,972 times and got 3,630 hits, for a life-time batting average of .331. (In the world we normally inhabit there is nothing to which we can satisfactorily compare this remarkable average, this feat; if you have ever tried to hit a baseball traveling ninety miles an hour straight at your face—or often what appears to be straight at your face—and having less than a second to make up your mind about it, you know.) The legend also said he won seven National League batting crowns, was named to twenty-four All-Star teams, named Major League Player of the Year (twice), named Player of the Decade, and elected to the Baseball Hall of Fame. When he retired he held seventeen major league, twenty-nine National League, and nine All-Star Game records.

George, showing his autographed card to Vicki, said, "Look, on one day he hit five home runs."

Froggy wanted to know what a Cardinal was, and Pete told him, "*Bardzo kapłan*" ("A big priest").

Marek took his card back to his place at the table, holding it carefully by the edge so as not to smudge the ink. Eventually he tucked it away in a clean sock. Other Sparks put their cards safely among the pages of textbooks, novels, and comic books.

Saying "Mariusz . . . Paweł . . . Andrzej. . . ," Musial, the son of a coal miner from Silesia and Pennsylvania, wrote these names across his photograph, wishing them all the best of luck.

When he was finished, he said, "You know who gave me the idea for those cards? John Wayne. I was having dinner in a restaurant and he happened to be there and came over to say hello. That surprised me—I mean, I knew who *he* was. Anyway, people started coming up and asking for his John Henry. A few asked for mine too. I'm using matchbooks and napkins to write on, but he just takes a card out of his pocket with his autograph already on it. Printed there. Saved him a lot of time. My autograph is printed on my card too—see?—but I don't mind writing it again."

A television crew showed up and shot some film.

"Tell us, Mr. Musial, your opinion of baseball in Poland."

"We're happy to see the interest, we're always happy about that. Baseball's a great game and the Poles are a great people and we're happy to see what's going on over here . . ."

The rain stopped and we all went outside. Holding one of our American-made aluminum bats, getting a feel for it, Musial took a couple of casual half-swings.

"Aluminum," he said, "I don't know. I like to hear wood on a ball."

"Who gave you the most trouble?" I said.

He cut his eyes at me, then got into a slightly more serious batting stance, not quite his famous crouch but close.

"Guys who threw junk," he finally said. He moved his shoulders around, looking off to where a pitcher would be standing. "Curt Simmons gave me some trouble. Johnny Vander Meer."

"How about the guys who threw hard? Koufax? Robin Roberts?"

"Hell," he said—and now he was in the famous crouch, looking over his right shoulder—"the faster it came, the better I liked it."

I felt little pinpricks in my neck, waiting for him to swing. But he didn't. He straightened up and looked at me. Then he laughed.

"Here you go, Coach"—tossing me the bat—"I hope there's some hits in that thing."

Ron Czarnetsky came over and said Musial had a tight schedule.

"I guess that's right," Musial said. "And after Poland we're meeting the pope. How about that?" He wished us all good luck, then Ron took him away in a blue Ford.

Dariusz watched them go, his face relaxing.

"Your friend," he smiled at me.

"Did you think we were friends?"

"You are friends," he said.

"That's the first time I met him."

"But you played baseball with Stanley Musial."

I had to laugh. I put my arm around his shoulders. "Let's go, Dariusz. Let's get those damn seven hours on the bus over with."

He said to Vicki, "This is a joke. I understand."

"America's a big country, Dariusz," she said.

"I know, I know. I also know Americans joke," he said.

I looked at him, at a man who was inventing me while I was trying my best to play it straight—which was hard enough—and I said, "Dariusz—" and then I stopped. I didn't know where to begin except at the beginning, or at least with names like Cy Young and Walter Johnson, and then Cobb and Ruth, and then DiMaggio and Williams and Aaron and Mays and of course Musial, and already I felt exhausted because reciting those names wouldn't help him see very much at all. He needed to be about nine years old, he needed a cap which he hated to take off at night, a ball which came more and more to fit in his hand like no other thing and which he could hold and turn round and round for hours at a time listening to a voice from miles away tell about a ball just like it, the same white leather, the same raised red stitches you couldn't find the beginning or end of, a ball that was blazing or curving or turning into a lazy fly, into a hot smash, a lucky bounce, a liner with eyes, into a long drive that was going, going, gone. But not forever. Because tomorrow they'd all be back—Big Train and The Babe and The Kid, Bad Henry and The Georgia Peach and Jolting Joe and Stan the Man. They'd all be back, in one way or another, and everything, or almost everything, would be like always.

"Dariusz, Musial and I never played baseball together, but you're absolutely right, we're old friends."

"I know," he said.

We watched the Sparks playing catch on the plaza, waiting for us to give the signal to get on the bus. I started counting heads.

"George," I called, "who's not here?"

He came over. "Blackie and Jake," he said.

"Have those guys quit the team?" I asked Dariusz. It was two weeks since I'd seen them.

"I don't know," he said sadly. "Maybe problems."

"Where's Alejandro? Where's Tony?" I said.

"I telephone," Dariusz said.

"You will or you did?"

"No answer," he said.

"It's two o'clock, damn it."

He lit a Mocne.

Vic said, "Maybe I should say good-bye now and get Gabriel some lunch." She was baby-sitting him that weekend while Gretchen went to visit her friend Don in Skierniewice, where he taught English in an agricultural school.

Then George said, "I will say good-bye too."

"What?" I said.

He looked at the ground. He said his parents had ordered him to stay home and study.

"Great," I said. "I have no third baseman and no catchers."

"I'm sorry, Gary. I yelled all week to convince them, but they are too strong."

"Did you know about this, Dariusz?"

He looked at the same gray cement that George was looking at, and nodded.

"How can we play without a catcher?" I said.

"Maybe Alejandro will be here," Dariusz said.

Then it struck me: the Cubans weren't there because of Musial's visit—which Dariusz had announced at practice on Friday. Playing under an American coach was one thing, but being photographed with an American hero was not necessary.

"*Kupa*," George said, "maybe I will run away."

"You will not run away," Vic said. "You will come have lunch with me and Gabriel at the Victoria."

"Why didn't you tell me about this before, George?"

"We didn't want to worry you. We thought maybe we could convince my parents."

"I wish I had a nickel for all the maybes around here," I said.

"I do too," George said.

Just then Alejandro came bopping across the plaza wearing a big smile.

So we went down to Silesia without Blackie, Jake, George, and Tony, spent the night in Rybnik, and early Sunday morning drove the ninety kilometers to Cyprzanów. The day started out gray and smelly and flat and turned sunny, green, and rolling. And then time seemed to more or less stop—or pause as it does when you are looking at old photographs by yourself in an attic. In the pretty village—which is not important enough apparently to be on the map—people were just leaving Mass, the men in shirtsleeves, the younger women in white dresses and babushkas. We followed the red brick road and came to a creek; we crossed over a bridge that the driver was nervous wouldn't hold us, and there was the sheep meadow, and on it a diamond.

It was something, when you were a kid, you'd dream up: a perfect green field, bordered by woods and a stream. Walking there, watching the villagers begin to cross the bridge and collect on the grassy bank behind third base, I felt both very small and large enough to be in several places almost at the same time. I felt a pleasant tingling sensation under my scalp. I saw myself in my grandfather's apple orchard, not hiding exactly but not eager to come out and meet my parents who had come to fetch me. I saw my father standing with one foot on the bumper of his gleaming black Chevy, about to light a Lucky. I saw my mother unpin her big white hat in front of the barn and shake her sunny hair. I saw Uncle Joe holding two hens by the feet, their broken necks dangling down, and I saw my grandmother sitting on a stool in the yard, her ruby hands emerging from a steaming bucket to throw the chickens' bright guts to the brown dog. I saw myself straddling the granary roof, straddling the broad hay- and sweat-smelling back of Nelly, while my cousin Donny held the bridle. I saw myself looking at these pictures in our attic, the rain beating on the roof, my baseball glove under my head for a pillow, and finally I came to my grandfather, buttoned up tight in his dark suit, the one he wore to church; he stood gazing out over his pasture, a man whose clothes seemed far too small for him. What was he looking at? There was nothing out there, nothing at all. And you couldn't see much of him either—much of his face—because whoever took the picture shot it almost straight at his back. All you could see was a man in a dark suit standing at attention before an empty field, a woods in the distance, and a couple of fleecy clouds in the sky. And I? I was no longer spending my summers on his farm and brooding in the orchard when it came time to leave; I was staying in Flint now, playing baseball, waiting for the rain to stop, thinking as I lay there on the attic floor and seeing myself under my grandpa's bridge, out from under the sudden windy storm that wrinkled the creek like skin and made a million pock marks on the wide place where Prince and Nelly came down to drink, where my grandpa, going in with them, washed the hay-dust off his scarred back—I was thinking, then, how far away those summers were, but now, in Cyprzanów, forty years later, how close and sweet and gone they were.

On the bus that night riding back to Warsaw we drank a fair amount of *piwo*; the first half of the season was over, what the hell. We saw convoys of Milicja heading toward us, toward the coal miners who had gone on strike; the players stared at them, mumbling *kupa*, giving the finger, but otherwise not saying much. Dariusz conked out soon after supper and slept all the way home. I got Henry, with July's help, to tell me about himself. Only when we stopped to pee under the stars did I think about the game. I thought of how we all had stopped, in the eighth inning, to wait for a train to go past on the tracks above the grassy bank, of how the engineer had tooted his whistle and of how we all had waved to the passengers. The Sparks were behind at that point, 9–3, but Janusz Rzytki, Cyprzanów's star pitcher, was now gone from the mound and we felt confident. We *liked* coming from behind, right? We promptly scored three runs in the eighth and then in the ninth had the bases loaded, nobody out, with Pete, Paweł, and Mariusz coming up. They all hit the ball in the air. The first two were infield flies—easy outs—but Mariusz, our slugger, delivered a blow that seemed headed for Czechoslovakia, a grand slam if I ever saw one. We'd win, 10–9. Their center fielder went way back to where the bright woods began, he stood there looking up—he stood there long enough, I thought, for all the mothers and wives in Cyprzanów to put supper on for their sons and husbands who would soon come home from the sheep meadow, from a Sunday afternoon given over to a small pleasure some of us would never forget—and then he caught the ball.

4

Froggy had half his body under the hood of his car, ministering to the engine. You would not see another car like this one anywhere. He had built it himself out of various junk parts and painted it the color that inspired his nickname. It even resembled a frog—a squarish frog—and now it was making a noise like a frog croaking its last. Dariusz, Marek, Mariusz and his girlfriend, and I sat on a bench beside it, watching, waiting for it to expire. A little wind came through the poplars behind us and speckles of sunlight and shadow played on my hands. We were supposed to have been on the field at four o'clock; it was now four-thirty and only three Sparks had shown up. Twenty minutes earlier, Froggy and his jerking, choking, sputtering car had arrived on the Skra plaza, and Froggy immediately dove under the hood. He held a screwdriver and a small hammer. In the kind of silence reserved for interment, the rest of us watched him. At quarter to five I saw Pete and Henry enter the main gate. Pete was hobbling on a stiff leg. This was the last Monday in June.

The day before, we had taken the electric train to Łódź and played an exhibition game against Kutno. It was the first time at least nine Sparks had gotten together since losing to Cyprzanów two weeks earlier, and we looked awful. We made eight errors in the first inning and lost, 13–1. If the game hadn't been stopped after three innings so that we could catch the last train to Warsaw, the score probably would have been worse. On the way home I told the Sparks I was disgusted. I asked them how in hell they expected to play decent baseball if they didn't practice. They all hung their heads. Eight of us were sitting in a compartment and three or four others were crowded around the door. Finally

Dariusz, jumping up as if stuck by a pin, said he had a plan. He waved his arms and spoke about a training camp the first two weeks of August—to get ready for the second half of the season!

"You listen, Gary," he said. "Two combinations. First combination: we go south to mountains. Second combination: we go north to sea. But no vacation, you understand, only baseball. What you think?"

"I think we need to practice tomorrow," I said. "And the day after that, and the day after that."

"You hear?" Dariusz said, looking around at the players.

Now, at Skra, Froggy was trying to make his car stop sputtering, Dariusz, Marek, and Mariusz and his girlfriend were watching him, and Pete was hobbling across the plaza. He had a cast on his leg.

"Dariusz, look," I said.

"I see," he said.

"Hi, Coach," Pete said.

"What happened?" I said.

"Nothing," Pete said.

"What do you mean 'nothing'?" The cast went from his toes to his knee.

Froggy, still under his hood, suddenly goosed the engine into a roar; the squat little car shook and shook, as if it meant to make a great charge. It would live. Froggy emerged, beaming—until he saw Pete and the cast. Then Henry said something I didn't understand and everyone smiled.

"OK," I said to Pete, "what the hell is going on?"

He shrugged. "Next week I must present myself for my Army examination. This is for them. After maybe two or three weeks my friend will take it off."

The ruse, like a spectacular play in a game we were losing, changed everything. We could practice now. The Sparks, or one of us anyway, had pulled off, or was about to pull off, a slick one.

So we all went into the stadium. Froggy, Marek, Mariusz, and I played catch. Then I hit them some grounders; they lobbed the ball back to me. I noticed that Jacek Demkiewicz had arrived and was smoking on the sidelines with Dariusz. "Hey, Jacek," I called, "get the catcher's mitt and take these throws for me." He came and stood on home plate, with the cigarette in his mouth, and took a couple of throws, dropping both. "If you flip that butt," I said, "you won't have smoke in your eyes." He tossed it away, took some throws—including a few stingers in the pocket—and then he said, "I think my hand is not strong today." I kept hitting grounders. Finally he said, "I'm sorry, Gary, I must quit."

"Quit?"

"Yes." He eased out of the mitt, as if out of a torture device, and looked at his hand. It was a little red, but otherwise OK.

"I'm sorry, I have too many sad thoughts in my head." He walked over to Dariusz. I watched him put another cigarette in his mouth, light it, then stand, hands on hips, in a kind of pose that said even though he'd quit, even though he had sad thoughts, he was still among the living.

"Some practice, Dariusz," I said.

Pete hobbled out then, volunteering to take the throws. Then Jacek came out and stood behind Pete in the same cigarette-in-mouth, hands-on-hips pose; then Dariusz came out and stood so close I couldn't swing the bat.

"No problem, Gary, no problem!"

"Right," I said. "I've got three guys in the field, a catcher in a cast, and Humphrey Bogart."

But Dariusz went on—it was seminar time—telling me he had found two new players who would show up any day now. Big talents, he said, you see. I said what about Norbert, George, Paweł, Mark, Adam, July, Alejandro, Tony, Blackie, Jake, Greg, and all the others? Dariusz waved his hands, he had big news to give me! Why hadn't he told me before, I asked, out on the plaza? He waved that question away too. And then, so that I might get the real beauty of his news, he bent over like an infielder and hopped sideways, back and forth, to demonstrate that these new big talents possessed much quickness. "Monkey-monkey," he said. "Big monkey. You see." Then he told me he had spoken to the chief of Skra about his training camp plan for August, and that the chief liked it and would find us a good field either in the mountains or at the seashore.

"How many players will be there?" I said. "*If* there's a training camp."

"How many? All," he said confidently.

"Uh-huh," I said.

"And two new players. Very big talents, Gary. You see."

What I could see was a man trying to keep his American coach. I figured Pete's little ruse had something to do with his enthusiasm too—one invention inspiring another—and no doubt the *piwo* Dariusz had had before coming to Skra had inspired him as well.

But the next day a new guy appeared. His name was Robert Szustkowski, he was twenty-five, six feet tall, well built. He told me—through Dariusz—that he had grown up in Venezuela, where his father had worked as an engineer, and that he had learned baseball there.

He said—according to Dariusz' translation—that baseball, for him, was like food.

What position did he play? I asked.

Infield or outfield, he said.

Did he have a glove?

Of course. He removed from a plastic shopping bag a mitt with five equally fat fingers and hardly any pocket. It was like the mitts you see in photos of Pie Traynor and Rabbit Maranville, mitts circa 1920, except this one had SEARS ROEBUCK stamped on the thumb and was designed for a small boy.

I asked when was the last time Robert had played in a game, and as near as we could determine it was junior high. But he had been practicing a lot lately, he said.

How did he practice?

By throwing a ball in the air and catching it, he said. Then he took from the plastic bag a red rubber ball about the size of a golf ball.

"What you think?" Dariusz said to me.

I couldn't begin to say what I thought. We got him a better glove, then went out on the field. The same guys were there as the day before—Froggy, Marek, and Mariusz (plus Pete in his cast and Jacek Demkiewicz with his sad thoughts: he was miss-

ing Gretchen)—and we played catch with the first of Dariusz'
new finds. Who turned out to be not bad. Rusty, a little wild on his
throws, but he knew what he was doing.

"You see?" Dariusz said.

"I see," I said. "I also see we have only four players today."

"Pete is five," he said.

"Damn it, Dariusz, you know what I mean."

"But I tell you, you remember, vacation is very important to
Polish people."

"Isn't there a big tournament in Kutno this weekend? Don't we
have four players on the national team? Mariusz, Norbert, Paweł,
and Jake? Only one is here as far as I can see."

"Always problems in Poland. I *think* about this, believe me." He
lit a cigarette. I threw a grounder to Robert, who took it nicely on
the short hop. Dariusz shot a fist to the sky.

"You see!" he said. "Big monkey! I tell you this."

"How did you know he was a big monkey?"

"I know," he said. "I feel it."

I told Marek to put on the catcher's gear (which he was not
eager to do) and then I threw a few warm-ups from the mound.

"I am not happy," Marek said.

"Sure you are."

I told Pete to put on a mask and chest protector and stand behind Marek and talk to him. "Keep telling him to watch the ball
and not turn his head." Then I told Robert to get a bat.

I served up the fattest pitches I could. Robert missed a couple,
fouled off a couple, then put one about four hundred feet into center field. It was a shot good enough for an old-fashioned movie—
in the just-in-time scene. The whammer, the wonder, the whop-
ping innocent the local guys needed to pick them up and carry
them to glory had arrived. He had walked out of the jungles of
Venezuela with his little boy's glove and red rubber ball and found
his way back to his native land and been revealed, with one
mighty swing, as the curly-haired hero. "You don't believe," a
voice over my shoulder was saying, "but now you see." Oh, I believed all right, believed more than Dariusz could begin to imagine. And the next day when another new player showed up, a kid

barely five feet tall but muscled like a college wrestler and afraid of nothing—not bad-hopping grounders or fastballs under his chin—I was ready to write the script for the greatest baseball movie ever. The kind that only taciturn bartenders and carpenters and math teachers and poets who never got to play with Stan Musial can write. I even started toying with the notion of attempting a comeback.

All jacked up we had very spirited practices the rest of the week. I put Robert—Big Robert—at third base and Mariusz at shortstop. Froggy of course was at first. The newest player, Jacek Kołak (who became Little Jacek and who was not Dariusz' other find—just a seventeen-year-old boy who had found *us*), I put at second base. I told Marek he was our new catcher. He said, "Coach—no." I had him throw the ball to all the bases. "You're as good as Alejandro," I said. He wasn't, not yet, but I believed he would be; his arm was strong. Mark and Adam showed up. They apologized for being absent but Mark said he'd eaten some bad food and had been in bed for three days; Adam, he said, had had a misfortune too but was now OK.

"What happened?"

"It's OK, it's OK," Adam said, dismissing the subject.

What happened, I learned weeks later, was that Adam had stepped on a broken Coke bottle; the glass went through his sneaker and a sliver of it lodged high in his heel and would stay there for a while. But he practiced hard that day and the next day too, as did the others. Mariusz would solve our shortstop problem. Though he was no Tony, Robert could speak Spanish *and* zip the ball over to first. I was crazy about fearless Little Jacek at second, who thought nothing of knocking down a sharp grounder with his chest (and who would make a perfect leadoff batter). Froggy's growing confidence at first and with a bat was a thing to behold, and Marek, whom we peppered with praise, was behaving like a real catcher. As for the outfield, Mark and Adam could play there just fine when they weren't pitching. Pete could too. So if nobody else showed up, we were only one player shy of a full team. On the mound throwing batting practice, I reached back more than thirty years and it didn't feel all that long ago. Taking cuts at the plate against Mark, I slapped ropes up the alleys in left and right that told me straight out, hell, it wasn't that long ago at all. I finished each day shagging flies in the outfield or spelling Froggy at first, feeling like a man with a sabre strapped to his belt.

"Guess what, Vic?"
"You're hungry now."
"I hurt all over."
"Everywhere, sugar?"
"Even there. But the universal pain feels real good."
"You big ole nasty powerful ballplayer, you."

On Sunday morning I sat with Dariusz in the bleachers at Kutno, waiting for the Polish National Team "B" to play a Swiss team. This was for third place in the tournament. On Saturday the Polish "A" team had defeated the "B" team, and a Czech team defeated the Swiss. On Sunday afternoon the "A" team would play the Czechs for the championship. Our guys were on the "B" team, which otherwise consisted of Juan Echevarría's Stal Kutno players. The "A" team was composed of players from Silesia. Dariusz, agitated, explained all this to me and then tried to relax and enjoy what he had come for—baseball. But like Gaul—or like Poland during Partition—he was feeling pretty chopped up. First, he hadn't been consulted about anything for this tournament; he'd simply been told that four Sparks had been chosen to play. Second, I had not been asked to help coach—a big error, he said, which he blamed on Walter Szymański, calling Szymański a moving star and a provincial. And finally, Juan Echevarría, whom he respected—but not so much anymore, he added sadly—was using only his own players. "I speak yesterday with Echevarría about this. I tell him for me to sit here and not see Warsaw represented is a very big handicap."

"He didn't use any Sparks yesterday?" I said.
"Only Mariusz."
"Well," I said, "if Norbert, Paweł, and Jake don't come to practice, they won't be playing for Warsaw either."
Dariusz stared at his shoes, sucked on a Mocne, and nodded.

But when the "B"–Swiss game started he brightened considerably. Norbert was at third base, Mariusz at second, Paweł in center. (Our fourth all-star, Jake, was still a mystery. When I asked Dariusz where Jake might be, he just held up his palms.) The Swiss hit first and the third batter bounced a big-hopper to Norbert. He fielded the ball OK, but then fired it over Juan's head at first base. Paweł made a nice catch over his shoulder to end the inning. In the second inning, however, with two outs and a runner on first, he tried to shoestring a low liner that got past him for a triple. Juan let Norbert and Paweł each bat once—both struck out—then he replaced them. Mariusz stayed in the game.

Walter Szymański sent a messenger over, inviting Dariusz and me to join the players and coaches at the big mid-day meal after the game. Then on the P.A. he pointed out our presence and asked the crowd to give us a hand.

Dariusz snorted, "He tries now to make everything OK."

I said, "What do you think of Walter's explanations?" Szymański, like Dariusz in the press box at Skra, though considerably less voluble, was helping the crowd understand what was going on.

"Moving star," Dariusz said.

Norbert and Paweł joined us in the bleachers. They said they were no good today. I said they needed to practice. No, no, Norbert said, they were only nervous. I didn't try to explain the connection, though I did tell Paweł he should never attempt a difficult catch like that with two outs and a runner on base. He knew, he said in Polish, but it was for me that he had tried it. A gift, he said. For my coaching.

The Poles won the game in the ninth inning on a two-out two-on double by Mariusz. "You see! You see!" Dariusz shouted. We could go eat now, with honor.

At the restaurant he directed me and the Sparks to a table next to the Czechs, and introduced me to the Czech coach—a stocky man with yellow hair and a yellow mustache. The coach said it was a great pleasure. He had heard about me—a colleague of Stanley Musial!

Dariusz said, "They come from Ostrava, Gary, just near the

Polish border, and they play very, very good baseball. Like you. Like Mr. Musial."

The Czech coach was pleased to hear that his team played like the Americans.

"Yes," Dariusz said, "they are very near. Very." And then in a move slick as any car salesman's he managed to link up me and Musial and the Sparks in a wonderfully warm relationship and then rode that relationship, or so it seemed, into the Tatra Mountains come August—when, he said, we would be very close indeed to Ostrava—and before our soup had arrived I was shaking hands with the Czech coach to play two games, at his place and at ours, wherever that might be. Dariusz, beaming, wrote down the man's telephone number and said no problem, he would take care of everything. Then the food came and we turned to it, all of us, like warriors. Never mind the details, or the snubs, the bad throws and the failed circus catches: Skra got a big hit today—a game-winner—and the Sparks added another bright combination to that hopeful sky up ahead. As always we were looking to fly. And it didn't hurt—I could tell from Dariusz' satisfied grin—that somewhere in that restaurant a certain provincial moving star was no doubt wondering what the Duke of Warsaw was tucking up his sleeve.

On Monday—the Fourth of July—Vic and I went to a picnic at the Embassy dacha. It rained, none of the Americans we had gotten to know were there (Chuck Powers was in Gdańsk covering the strike, his wife Cheryl was home working on a book, our fellow Fulbrighters were seeing the sights in Eastern Europe before calling it a year), and Vic got a case of the homesick blues.

"I can't help it, Gare. I want to be out in my back yard wearing a big apron that says something corny on it and turning over pieces of chicken on the barbecue. I want to be barefoot. I want to sit in the grass later and ooh and ahh with all the little kids at the fireworks squirting and popping in the sky. Then real late when the teenagers sneak away and are breathing hard in the bushes, I want to go upstairs and fall in bed happy and let you take off my apron."

We had a hot dog, a beer, and when Ron Czarnetsky—dressed up as George Washington—brought out a candle-blazing red, white, and blue birthday cake, we had some of that too. We watched the Marines play volleyball in the rain. First chance we got, we hitched a ride back to town.

On Tuesday, at practice, Norbert and Paweł showed up. I told Paweł no more tries at shoestring catches; the best gift he could give me was not letting the ball get past him. I had Norbert and Big Robert trade off between third base and right field; otherwise everything was the same as the week before. We got in five days of good work, then after practice on Saturday everyone gathered in a circle. Dariusz said, "Players go on vacation now. Must go, Gary. But you listen: July 30 we all leave for training camp."

"For sure?" I said.

"For sure."

"In the mountains?"

"Maybe. First combination: mountains. Second combination: sea. For sure."

I looked at the players. I said I didn't want to waste my time waiting for nothing. They said they would be there.

"And a new player," Dariusz said. "A monkey like Robert. Name—Zbyszek."

"And me too, Coach," said Pete.

Earlier that week Pete had given us a report on his Army exam. He said they had looked at his cast and at him and he had presented a proper sad face. Finally they said to go away and come back in one month. By then, Pete told us, he would think of something else.

So Vic and I had three weeks to do a few things we'd put off, like visit Budapest and Vienna and Prague. But we didn't go anywhere. Though we were curious to see them, we even missed Mr. and Mrs. Gorbachev when they came to town. We seemed, suddenly, to have lost all our juice. "But why would you want to see Gorbachev?" our neighbor Alicja said. "So boring. Only those workers went who are paid to go, to stand in the street like idiots. Save your energy."

Vic boxed up some stuff and mailed it back to the States. I worked halfheartedly on a couple of poems. We saw a few movies. One movie was *Carmen*. Leaving the Palace of Culture, where it was shown, we noted that it was a Spanish story, created by a Frenchman, and put on film by Italians.

"With Polish subtitles."

"In a building paid for by the Soviets."

"And thanks to Senator Fulbright, who represented a State with an Indian name, we got to see it."

I guess the point of our litany was that we felt sort of everywhere and nowhere. We wondered if we could hold out until August; if Dariusz' training camp—to which Vic was also invited—was only his fantasy. We wondered if maybe the party was over, we'd had it, and it was time, maybe, to find our coats.

We'd done a lot that year. In the fall we were off to something almost every night—the opera, a concert, a play, dinner with Polish or American friends, a party. We went to Kraków and Zakopane. To Auschwitz. When the leaves changed color we went up north to Sopot on the Baltic, and at a long lovely stretch along the shore where the flaming hardwoods came down a group of hills to the sand, we ran and ran. The week before flying to Rome for Christmas we saw *Tosca*, *The Magic Flute*, and *Boris Godunov* and I rented a tuxedo for a dinner dance (the first tux I'd worn since college). I saw fifteen operas that year, Vic even more. I saw our guide at Auschwitz scoop human bone from the dirt and play the pieces over his palm. In the Great Theatre I got a crush on Elżbieta Hoff, a stunning soprano, and called her for an interview. We sat on her sofa sipping tea, looking at her scrapbook, at her flashing eyes as Floria, Leonora, Carmen, Rosalinda. In January Vic began teaching a course at the university, acting in a film for Polish television (playing the role of a bitchy New York fashion designer), giving talks around town on American popular music, U.S. education. Elżbieta Hoff was telling me she stayed in the shower for two hours on the day of a performance, alternating hot and cold water. Thirty minutes before going on stage she ate steak Tartare. "Raw meat gives me courage," she said. I worked on a long poem about Auschwitz, on other poems. Vic was jogging and shopping and catching trains with me for readings in Gdańsk, Poznan, Lublin, Opole. We canceled plans to visit Hungary and Czechoslovakia—things kept coming up: a British production of Kapuściński's play *The Emperor*, the International Jazz Festival, Dariusz knocking on my classroom door. At the Catholic University in Lublin when I invited questions from the audience, a blushing girl asked, "Are you happy?" Another girl asked, "Do you believe in God?" A boy burst out, "Do you have a car in America?" I took the easy one first: yes, a 1946 Chevrolet! It looks just like a big eggplant. When I got back to the States, I said, I planned to take Vicki for a spin into the Iowa countryside. To buy apples! Then I told the blushing girl I thought I was happy. If my father, the son of a German immigrant, had not pursued and married my mother, the daughter of a Polish immigrant, I would not be there. I was happy that her brothers informed my father that Grandpa enjoyed a little whiskey, and that my father never came calling empty-handed. I was also happy that my crush on Elżbieta Hoff had stayed only a crush, and I was happy I had gone to the post office back in December, because the bureaucratic reception I received had helped me make a poem.

STRING

The women in the Polish P.O.—their clusters
of bunched-up consonants exploding
and ricocheting off the walls like so many Chinese
firecrackers—sent me reeling in the dark
with my three mailers of books back and forth
between the two stations they commanded,
until this hard fact slowly shone through:
neither woman wanted me: my mailers
were too big for one, and for the other
I had no string around them—string
being essential, required by law, without it
everything would fall apart during the journey
and then where would I be? said the string woman,

who moved her pretty Slavic fingers with such nimble
and lacy grace to help me understand this impossible
situation, that I now felt something like the fuzzy
combustions of love burning under my scalp.
I needed to respond somehow, to show her
this time everything was different, not to fret,
that what I'd laid on her scales was tough as nails.
So getting a good grip on my biggest American-
made mailer and then dipping into the classic, slowly
uncoiling crouch that discus throwers have burst from
since the beginning, I flung the unstrung thing up, up
and away, toward the Gothic rafters of that Polish P.O.
Oh, it flew and flew and no one at that moment
could have been more possessed by his power
than I was, and when it almost reached
where no man would ever dream to touch,
I began to reflect on a law I never had much use for
—i.e., objects in motion tend to remain in motion.
I didn't believe it in my youth when all smacked
baseballs and all spun-off hubcaps soon stopped dead
in the weeds somewhere, and I didn't much trust it now
watching my discus-mailer of hardbound books, run out of
gas and glory, begin its heavy, necessary journey
down from the ceiling, toward a tiny, ancient, white-
haired grandma, who sat, composed as porcelain,
at a table, writing; surely she had come in
from the cold with only one thing in mind:
to send sweet wishes and high hopes for many
healthy tomorrows to her loved ones far away—in Puck
perhaps, or Łódź—for indeed it was Christmas week
and who among us wants to hear about misery.
I saw myself hauled off by the Milicja,
and I saw the headline: American Brains Innocent *Babcia*.
They'd throw the book at me, of course, I deserved it,
a hot-headed Yankee off his nut. And no nice poppyseed
cakes, no *piwo*, no luscious pierogi stuffed
with cheese, meat, or creamy potatoes where I was going—

And then my mailer came down with a great whack
to the floor, landing inches from the little *babcia*'s feet.
Slowly she raised her eyes and regarded it,
then around till she found me,
then back to her writing as if the flat brown thing
and the man gripping his hair didn't exist,
that nothing in fact had happened—or if it had,
so what, she had seen bigger noises fall from the sky.
My fires were out, cold; it was time to pick up and go.
Turning to the other two women, I saw that
they had somehow gotten together
and were blushing, blushing like impossible peaches!
And pulling dozens of loose strings out of nowhere.

As for the question about believing in God, I said maybe the
best answer I could give—right now, anyway—was in another
poem I had written recently, called

CABBAGE IN POLISH

Cabbage in Polish is kapusta—ka*poos*ta.
Street is ulica—oo*leet*sa.
                              Our street,
Ulica Staffa, is named for a poet,
Leopold Staff (the extra *a* means possession).
To honor our luck, and his, we have invented
two dishes: cabbage leaves neatly wrapped
around meat, called Kapusta Staffa Stuffa,
and a cabbage-and-meat concoction, all chopped up,
called Kapusta Staffa Loosa.
The latter results when the former fails.
This little ditty intends to say nothing more,
contains no hidden meanings, no subtle
references to freedom, madness, or long delays in jails.
The rhymes are only goofy, like stuffed cabbages
that end in a mess. Give them a good name,
eat them, brush the crumbs away, and slip off to bed.
Steal a kiss. Dream your dreams. Don't forget.

In March we met Anna Mydlarska. She had come to my reading at the University of Gdańsk; she wanted to translate my short
stories into Polish—in fact had already started, she said, was that
all right? We were at a party after the reading, drinking wine. It
usually took about eight years for a writer in Poland to see his
book published, she said—that is, eight years *after* it was accepted—but she could move things faster than that. "This is
true," said Jacek, her husband. "Anna does not hear no." We must
come back to Gdańsk soon, they said. Visit longer. Maybe, she
whispered, I would give a reading in the underground? Maybe
Vicki and I would like to meet Wałęsa? We said of course. She
said it would be arranged. Anna has very dark eyes; her hands
move almost constantly when she talks. "I began, years ago, in
theatre. It was good training—especially for those times I must
deal with people who think they are in charge. When you come
back," she said, "we can also visit Jacek's new pictures, they are
wonderful."

The last week in April, after the Sparks defeated the Rój-Zory
beehive in the snow for their historic first win and after Vic and I,
on her birthday, finished a reading tour of Galicia, we went back
to the Baltic to give an underground reading and to meet Lech
Wałęsa.

"You see that house?" Anna pointed. She and Jacek had met
our train in Sopot, and now we were walking down Ulica Pstrowskiego—the street they lived on, in the same house that Anna
grew up in. But at the moment she wanted us to notice another
house. "Isn't it marvelous? Like a castle. And the fence, those
lions and horses—how do you say?—wrought?—in the bars. As a
child I invented stories about them. But the best story of all, which
was true, was about the beautiful woman who lived behind that
fence. Sylvia. She had long red hair and very white skin—perfect
skin—and she invited to her table, and then to her bed, the captains of the ships docked in Sopot. Now this part is unclear. Did
she invite such men to her house before her father became blind,
or afterwards? We debated the issue for years. In any case, her
father was the Chief of Police in Sopot, a very powerful man
physically. Then he was shot in the face by a burglar. After this

happened, he sat in his yard in fine weather, or in the house when it was cold, and did nothing. We could see him there by the window, a large dark shadow of a man. And behind him, Sylvia, in her long red hair . . ."

We arrived at Anna and Jacek's house. Their house, in fact, is the top floor of a handsome four-story red brick building from the last century. We started up. Anna said, "Twice she went abroad for lengthy visits—to Canada, it seems, to California—and both times her pimp came to care for the father. A very faithful man, this pimp. Preparing the Captain's dinner, helping him to bed. Now of course the father, after a long and mainly dark life, is buried. And that dazzling woman is gone for a third time, possibly forever."

We reached the top floor.

"I will make tea," Jacek said, showing us in.

"Where do you think she is?" I asked.

"It is a little mystery, like so much in Poland. And there is an emptiness in the street. But not a total emptiness—her faithful pimp is still there. Now, the children. Jurek! Sophie! Come, please, greet our friends from America!"

Jurek, who was nine, played his guitar for us. Sophie, thirteen, helped her father serve tea. At the public stables that morning, she had ridden a difficult black gelding named Josef and been thrown (but not hurt) and now was thrilled to reveal this news. "What next?" Anna said, fluttering her hands. Jacek said, "Very fine." He would go for a ride himself, he said, while Anna took us to meet Wałęsa. "Anna loves him very much, you see, and I only normally. Besides, the room will be small, and he is big."

Wałęsa is big, but not tall. He is burly, about five-ten, a beer-barrel of a man. St. Brygida's Church in Old Town in Gdańsk—twenty minutes by taxi from Sopot—was where we met him. We sat at a small round oak table in the room where, once a week, he received visitors. The room had the rectory odors of candle wax and old books, of dark suits and serious talk. Wałęsa sat in the kind of high-backed upholstered chair you'd expect the pastor to use, the bishop, not an electrician. It had polished wooden arms. Positing his own arms there, Wałęsa sat up straight, ready, sometimes tapping his fingers waiting for the next question. On the fingers of his left hand he wore two large rings—one turquoise, one topaz—and in the lapel of his tweed sportcoat he wore a gold cross, the red and white colors of Poland, and a silver Solidarity pin. On the table in front of him was a cup of black tea.

I sat at his left, a French journalist at his right. The journalist had a translator, and Vic and I had Anna. Anna's face was glowing—like Delphine Bononi's at the Holy Redeemer communion rail, like Dariusz' at Gwardia when the gym was full of Sparks, the balls flying. Half a dozen men stood behind Wałęsa—associates, bodyguards; one looked constructed well enough to play in the line for Notre Dame. I wished we could have met Wałęsa almost anywhere but there—in a park, over a *piwo* in a neighborhood bar, on the sidewalk just passing by. Sitting at the round oak table in St. Bridget's, hearing the journalist ask about the future of Solidarity, where it was going politically, and what role its leader expected to play, I thought of how much these meetings and the stories that resulted from them must prick the government; I knew they certainly cheered the Poles—cheered a lot of people; but all I wanted to do, I realized, was shake the man's hand and say good luck, stay healthy. I didn't care to see him holding forth from an upholstered rectory chair that the bishop—proffering his ring to be kissed—might also use.

I drifted. The harmonies and not unpleasant clashes of Polish, French, and English let me slip off a ways, much as I do at concerts, and while I was out there I saw a beautiful blue cup fall to the floor. It broke into three or four pieces. I picked them up, to fit them quickly together. But Sister Good Counsel, the principal, caught me. She said, "Oh my, I believe we have an allegory here. This cup represents your immortal soul. Look what you've done to it." I said, "No, ma'am," for I was older now, bold. ("Brazen," Sister Good Counsel would have said.) "This cup represents language and I am trying to drink from it. It's not easy. It's especially not easy when I try to pass the cup to someone else. How can I, with my thumbs and fingers all over it, trying to hold it together?

I'm struggling, Sister, and making only one thing clear: this cup that is broken is broken."

Wałęsa was looking at me. I said I'd heard he was a fisherman. Did he prefer flies or worms? He seemed puzzled for a moment. Then he laughed, and Anna laughed, and I was given the picture of a fish followed by a man followed by his bodyguards followed by the Milicja. A parade! said Wałęsa. In any case, he said, he used whatever he had, flies or worms, but that he threw most of his fish back, especially if they were smiling: they were having as tough a time as we were. One of his associates, noting the time, reminded Wałęsa of a dinner he'd been invited to—the dinner to which so-and-so and so-and-so (apparently a couple of big shots) had also been invited. Did he plan to attend? No, Wałęsa said, he didn't think so—there were already two mushrooms in the borsch. When we left, he gave us each an autographed picture of himself.

The underground reading the next day was held in another church in Old Town, St. Nicholas'. I always take the word "underground" literally—or to mean "secret"—and was therefore surprised when we arrived at the church entrance to see fixed to the outer bricks a large blackboard all chalked up with details of our caper. Knowing that the event was sponsored by a magazine forbidden by the government to publish, I said to Anna—indicating the advertisement—"Doesn't that make anyone nervous?" She laughed. "This is only a religious meeting, Gary. Don't you feel religious?"

There was a reading a month—each one viewed as an issue of the magazine. I was reading in Number 14. We followed a series of narrow hallways and climbing stairs that seemed to go round and round, and ended up in what looked like an attic. It was packed, and warm. Seats had been saved for us in the front row.

The reading began at five p.m. and lasted three hours. It didn't seem nearly that long. A journalist sat at a small table and spoke just above a whisper. A man in the back said louder; she was not an orator, she said, and continued as she had been, reading an account of a boy's murder by the Milicja. When she was finished, a professor stood up and shouted a sheaf of statistics related to the 4,500 Polish officers found buried in a mass grave in the Soviet Union in 1943—executions for which he blamed the lying Russians, not the Nazis. Then a young poet pulled from his pocket a folded manuscript, unfolded it quickly, and recited half a dozen short poems with his eyes closed. When he opened them he seemed to want to apologize for taking our time. His fingernails were chewed almost off. The poems he had recited—and which he now folded back up and sat down with—were filled with images of skulls that wouldn't stop talking, caged birds, corpses colored like oranges.

Anna was next. She read her translations of my story "Tornadoes" and my poems "Cleaning the Oven" and "String." Then it was my turn to read the poems in English. Anna reached in her bag for the originals, found "Cleaning the Oven" but not the other one.

"How stupid. I must have left it on my desk," she said.

"That's all right," I said. "I'll just read 'Cleaning the Oven.'"

"No, no—we must have both. And especially 'String' for the humor."

"But, Anna, I don't know my poems by heart."

"Impossible," she said, and before I could stop her she announced to the audience that I would read one poem and recite the other. Then to me, "If you have trouble, I will coach you."

In the early hours of the following morning, none of us was feeling any pain. We had gone from St. Nicholas' to drinks in Old Town to drinks in Jacek's studio to more drinks and supper at Anna's table. Then from Ulica Pstrowskiego and the single light that Sylvia's pimp left burning, we went down to the Sopot beach and along the beach under the stars to the *molo*, the wide, white L-shaped pier. During the day children came there to throw bread down to the swans and ducks bobbing below. And lovers and tourists and the old came there, to stroll on the brightly painted boards. The *molo* was deserted now except for us and a fishing trawler tied up for the night. We went all the way out to the end, maybe two hundred yards out, and leaned on a railing; in the distance we could see the tiny lights of the freighters passing from Russia toward Scandinavia. The wind made our eyes water. Jacek said we need not worry about the elements—about anything—we were protected by the honey mead. We all agreed that honey mead was an excellent drink, even when it was the only drink available, and that we were not drunk but very satisfied—*bardzo zadowolony*. We would be very happy, we said—*bardzo szczęśliwy*—except that happy was too hard to say.

"In Poland," Jacek said, "satisfied is OK."

"He means plenty," Anna said.

"Is very fine," Jacek said.

"To say you are happy requires *work*," Anna said. Then she laughed at herself. "Oh dear, I think I just said something critical. Or philosophical. Or both!"

"Anyway, happy's a mouthful," Vic said.

"Yes," said Anna, "even for us."

Back on the beach in front of the Grand Hotel where Vic and I were staying, we sat in the sand and Anna said she and Jacek used to come down there and walk on the *molo* every night when they were courting. Yes, said Jacek, and every night he would dream they had a room in the hotel—especially in the winter. We all laughed. Vic said our courtship was on a beach too, on Little Bay de Noc in Escanaba, Michigan. For three days.

"Gary found a baseball."

"Vic didn't want to get her hair wet."

"The same with Polish women!"

"Jacek to me was an ordinary boy—until he told me he was a painter."

"Anna one time kept me waiting five hours. She forgot our appointment."

"Completely! Then I went for a walk, and there he was—flat on his back!"

"I studied the clouds," Jacek said.

I thought of when we had visited his studio the first time— before the reading—and of what he had said about the new pictures he was showing us: that they had taken him almost twenty years to discover. They were swirling, lyrical skyscapes, brilliant with light, and if they were not happy or at least very satisfied, they were certainly courting. I thought of the student in Lublin the week before who asked if I was happy, and I thought of how easy it was to be happy sitting on a beach under the stars with honey mead in your brain after surprising yourself reciting a poem you never thought you could to an audience that laughed in the right places, and having good companions who could work twenty years for something they might never discover, and discover it, and hearing a woman you enjoyed as she enjoyed you, saying, "Here's to the clouds, Jacek." Here's to the clouds indeed, I thought. I saw Anna's beaming face in his studio, in St. Bridget's, then Wałęsa in his upholstered chair sitting up straight, wary, shouldering the burdens of love and fame, and then I saw my students' faces in Warsaw, their creamy perfection. I saw my Aunt Rita rosy on her wedding day, dancing, my grandfather there too, off by himself as always, but smiling, I thought, and then my mother saying, "This is your Aunt Mary, Gary, Donny's mother," and I remembered her taking my hands and holding on tight and smiling as if she were more glad to see me than anyone in the world, but not saying one word, and the tears rolling and rolling down her red cheeks.

In the morning Anna and Jacek met us at the hotel for breakfast. We promised them we'd return to Sopot in June, with Gretchen and Gabriel. Then Vic and I caught the early LOT flight to Warsaw so that I could make it to practice at Skra on time.

Two months later, following the Sparks' 9–6 loss on Cyprzanów's sheep meadow, we were back. The first half of the baseball season was over, classes at the university were over, Vic's work in the Polish film was completed, I'd finished my readings. Gretchen and her friend Don were also finished, apparently. Sopot, however, like resort towns everywhere, was just getting started. Young girls were washing windows in the ice cream shops, souvenir kiosks had new posters up showing bathers in blue water, freshly painted furniture for the beach was brought out. A disco advertising FUNKY JAZZ was ready to roll.

We stayed at the Grand and strolled on the *molo* and Gabriel,

With Gretchen and Gabriel on the shore in Sopot. That's the molo
behind us.

with his shovel and pail, hauled sand from one part of the beach
to another and back. We went to a showing of Jacek's pictures in
Gdańsk, bought one, stayed up late at Anna's table, walked to the
hotel under the stars with Gabriel asleep on Jacek's shoulders.
The tourists had not yet arrived in earnest, but they would come,
Anna said, as would a big strike by the workers. Of the few things
that were certain now in Poland, that was one, she said. But that
mid-June when Jacek and I rode horses in the morning and Anna
worked on her translations and Vic ran and Gabriel and Gretchen
fed bread to the swans squabbling for it beside the *molo*, we were
all of us thinking of other things mainly. Departure—in most of
its meanings—was high on the list.

Back in Warsaw, Vic took Gretchen to the beauty salon in the
Victoria Hotel—"We need some tending to"—and I brought Jacek
Demkiewicz home for dinner after practice. The dinner was a
complete success, Vic pointed out to me later, because neither
Jacek nor Gretchen could stop talking long enough to eat. I said
I'd noticed. Next day he met us in Łazienki Park with flowers, and
strolling there, and elsewhere over the following afternoons, I
thought they must be the tallest, shiniest couple in Poland. At the

zoo, Gabriel said to Vic and me—as we waited for Gretchen and Jacek to catch up—"Some guy painted them, right?" We did a double take; he hadn't meant the glowing lovers at all, of course, but the zebras he'd spotted. Vic said, "Some guy sure did." Jacek took Gretchen to meet his father and grandmother in Praga. Then at practice he said to me, somewhat frantically, "It is her last week in Warsaw!"

"I know it's her last week," I said.

"This is terrible."

"If you keep sighing so hard, Jacek, you'll hurt yourself."

Then she and Gabriel flew back to Iowa, the Sparks went on their vacations, and Vic and I had three weeks to kill.

One afternoon George telephoned.

"I think I am lonely," he said.

"I think we are too," I said.

"Maybe we can play catch?"

"Why aren't you on your vacation?"

"I don't know."

I invited him over. Vic said she'd bake some cookies and left to buy chocolate chips at the Embassy commissary. Minutes after she'd gone, I answered a knock on the door. There stood Christina, stylish as always but looking more desperate than ever.

"Oh, Gary," she sighed, "how good to see you. I hope I have not come at a bad moment."

Back in October, Vic and I were riding the autobus home from the commissary. It was Halloween in the States and we had a can of Libby's pumpkin among our groceries and a craving for a pie. Standing in the crowded aisle we were having fun talking about the construction of our pie, when I noticed a woman next to us smiling.

"Do you speak English?" I said.

"Of course," she said.

"We are discussing something very American," I said.

"I understand quite well." She smiled again.

"Do you know about Halloween?" Vic asked her.

"You wear charming costumes."

"I love dressing up," Vic said.

"We have what is called All Souls Day then. We visit our graves," the woman said.

"Yes, we know," Vic said. "We're planning to visit the cemetery near Żoliborz."

"Perhaps Powązki?"

"The biggest one."

"Powązki," the woman said. Then, "I wish you success with your American pie," and she got off the bus.

Vic said, "Damn, we should have invited her over for a piece. She seemed interesting. And very stylish. Maybe she's famous. Maybe, Gare, she's an s-p-y."

The next evening, which was very cold, we took the tram to Powązki Cemetery. We joined the huge, silent, orderly crowd entering a gate in the high wall. Inside, our way was lit by candles burning on the graves. Some graves had so many candles you could warm yourself; and some, on the main path, called the Alley of Merit, you had to step back from because of the heat. The Alley of Merit is a wall of monuments as long as a football field, and here, side by side, lie poets and composers and architects and engineers and actors and soldiers. We filed past them keeping warm. We filed past a large stone cross that remembered the 4,500 Polish officers found buried in a hole in the Soviet Union in 1943—the heat there was so great a man had to use a long stick to push his candle among the others—and we filed past a monument remembering those who fell in the 1944 Uprising, where the heat was also painful. We stayed in Powązki Cemetery a couple of hours. At one point Vic and I got separated by the crowd and I saw the stylish woman from the bus. But when I caught up with Vic and took her back to where the woman was, the woman was gone.

A few nights later at a concert in Old Town we saw her again, during the intermission. We introduced ourselves. She said she was only in Warsaw briefly, to settle some business matters, then she was returning to Italy, to Princess Somebody's villa.

"But we must have lunch tomorrow," she said.

I couldn't. I had a date with an editor of the magazine *Litera-tura Na Świecie*, then I had class; but Vic and Christina arranged to meet at the Europejski. Late that afternoon, Vic was waiting for me when I got out of class.

"How was lunch?" I said.

"Buy me a drink and I'll tell you."

We walked over to the Bazyliszek.

"So we started at the Europejski," Vic said. "She wanted some-thing that wasn't on the menu. The waiter apologized. She told him he was incompetent. 'Come,' she said to me. We went out-side. 'That waiter knows who I am,' she said, 'and he knows I will not tolerate such behavior.' She asked me if I'd ever eaten at the French Embassy. I said no. 'We will go there,' she said. In the taxi she complained that Warsaw was intolerable and she couldn't wait to finish her business and return to Italy, to her princess friend and the princess' wonderful villa. The view, she sighed, was breathtaking.

"At the French Embassy the guard said there was no public dining. She said of course, of course, but *we* were not just any-body. This got her nowhere. She was fuming. I said, 'Look, I'll buy us a hamburger at the American Embassy.' I was starving. So we get to Piękna Street and go in past all the Poles lined up for visas, and I ask the Marine for a guest pass. He says the Embassy dining room is only for employees and Fulbrighters, but I can take her next door to the Eagle Club. 'Food's better over there anyway,' he says. 'They make a great cheeseburger.' 'Oh, right,' I say. The Eagle Club was what I'd had in mind in the first place, but I'd got turned around a bit. Suddenly this woman, Christina, *lays* into the Marine. Her remarks to the Europejski waiter and the French Embassy guard were only warm-ups. She tells this poor guy he's a fool, a moron, an idiot, and a dozen other things I don't want to remember. I was so embarrassed. And she wouldn't quit until she'd had her say. God knows why they didn't throw her out. Probably because of me. Finally I got her away and into the Eagle Club.

"Now this is the amazing thing, Gare. She looked absolutely fine over there, as if nothing had happened and we were having a splendid time. But what she told me was: the Marine had refused her a pass because he recognized her. He knew who she was and he knew her power. This is her power, Gare: she can read minds, predict the future. She had a hand, for example, in choosing the pope. She's telling me this, you understand, and enjoying her cheeseburger. Then she put on fresh lipstick. It's scary how attractive and well tucked-in she looks. A lot like Ava Gardner. Anyway, she wanted my help. She wanted me to recommend a good private detective, and she wanted to borrow fifty dollars. Just five minutes before I saw you, I managed to shake her."

But the woman wasn't shaken off. We had casually told her where we lived, and she had come and spoken to our landlady, Pani Trawinska. She told Pani Trawinska we had sent her around in the belief that Pani Trawinska could help her find a flat for a few weeks. Pani Trawinska put her in the apartment of a relative who had gone abroad—an apartment in the next block—thinking she was doing us a favor.

In the months to come we would suddenly see Christina in a movie theatre, a shop, walking behind us on Marszałkowska Avenue. When we flew to Rome for Christmas, she was at the Warsaw airport, pretending not to see us. Once she was waiting for me under the Royal Eagle after class. It was snowing, already dark, and she was wearing an equestrian get-up, slapping her palm with a riding crop. "Oh, Gary," she said, "this is most embarrassing, but could you let me have a few hundred dollars?" Before I could answer, Magda came up to me. "Ah," Christina said, "I see you have other friends—and so young and pretty." She turned on her heels and left. At least once a week she would telephone Vicki and suggest they fly to London, Paris, Madrid. She would complain that the apartment Pani Trawinska had put her in was filthy and cold, that Warsaw, unlike former times, was full of animals.

Now she was standing in the doorway. She was twirling a parasol on her shoulder, and dressed in the kind of suit that women wore around the turn of the century. A row of buttons ran down the front. She had a bustle. There was a Polish film playing in town then, called *Łuk Erosa* ("The Bow of Cupid"); it was set during World War I, and the main character wore a suit much like the one Christina had on. During a celebrated scene in the film, a professor takes the woman's clothes off and lays her on a table filled with flowers and fruit. I told Christina that Vicki was not home and that I was just leaving myself, to go play baseball. She continued to twirl the parasol, and smile. Her bright red lipstick was not quite on the mark—maybe she'd been in a hurry—and she appeared to have two sets of lips. Her eyes had dark pouches under them.

She touched my arm. "Gary, your life is in danger."

"Probably," I said.

"I can help you. I know where you can go to be safe. I will take you. The air is very clean there, very clear. You will be able to think and write your books and become famous."

"Can Vicki come too?"

"Of course. Though her life, I must tell you, is not in danger."

"Maybe I shouldn't take her then."

"I don't advise it," Christina said. Her lips and her lipstick made two smiles.

"Wait here." I collected my practice gear. Then I ushered her down the stairs and outside.

"My friend George should be along soon," I said. "We're going over to the Sports Academy."

"But *we* must go," Christina said.

"I'm passing on your offer. It sounds fantastic, but a game of catch will do me a lot more good. Thanks all the same."

She gripped my arm. "Don't be stupid."

"I can't help it," I said. I also couldn't help feeling sad. I wished I hadn't been so glib with her.

I saw Jan coming up the street. Jan and his wife Ewa lived in Pani Trawinska's basement. They taught at the School for the Blind. Ewa taught music and Jan taught English.

"Hello, Jan," I said. "I'd like you to meet Christina."

He bowed. She glanced at his deformed hand—at the fingers that lay off to the side like feathers—and then she turned and walked away. Jan and I watched her. I saw him look at her bustle and blink.

"Are you enjoying your vacation, Jan?"

He sighed deeply. "We have bad news. Pani Trawinska is putting in our apartment a big computer and we must move. Maybe we will have to live with Ewa's parents."

We spoke a few more minutes—he said he and Ewa were taking their students to the shore for two weeks—and then George showed up.

Walking to the Sports Academy, I asked George how he was doing.

"Not so good," he said. "My girlfriend is having a mood."

"What's wrong?"

"It's difficult to say. Things go along very well, then she has a mood. I don't know when they are coming. Such humors are painful."

"What do you suppose it is?"

"I wish I knew. I try not to think about them. I work on my boats then."

"Your boats?"

"I build model ships. I have three: a fire ship, a tug, and a cruiser. Maybe I will build a hospital ship now, during this new mood."

At the Sports Academy we ran a few laps around the soccer field, played catch, took turns hitting each other flies. After about an hour, we lay down in the middle of the field and covered our eyes with our caps. George said that women were a big mystery.

"You don't want them any other way," I said.

"Maybe."

What were mysteries to me, I said, were Jake the catcher and Blackie. And Greg. Had they just disappeared? George said Jake went to Sweden and Blackie went to Japan. Why was I learning this now? George didn't know. He only knew that Jake went to earn money and Blackie went because maybe it was necessary. He said Blackie became very angry in Poland sometimes. But he would be back, George said. As for Greg, he heard that Greg took a wife. He wouldn't like to have a wife, he said, you couldn't do anything then.

It was warm lying there under the sun, and I was feeling sleepy. I heard George say, "I'm sorry I haven't been to practice, Gary, but my parents made me study. Then my girlfriend invited this Russian to come visit. She says he is only a boy from Leningrad. I don't know what to think."

A dog appeared and sniffed at the mitts under our heads. Then it ran off.

"Are you still disgusted with the team? Dariusz is worried you won't come to our training camp."

"Will there be a training camp?"

"Maybe."

I was very relaxed now and told George I was closing my eyes for a few minutes.

If I think much about the word "camp"—as in deer camp—I think of northern Michigan up around Houghton and Higgins lakes forty years ago, and the town of West Branch nearby where I was born. My father was born there too, and went to a country school until the third grade, when his formal education stopped. "Rheumatic fever . . . chores on the farm . . . and my dad starting up the lumberyard—I helped him on that too." It was just the way things went, he told me, not inclined to elaborate and certainly never bitter. His most common gesture, common enough, was a short shake of his head, which sometimes meant something didn't work and he'd have to try another way, but more often expressed his amazement that something did work and he was lucky. "Gimmicky" was one of the few adjectives he used; "gingerbread" was another. He wanted the bubble in his level in the middle, his doors and windows to open and close without squeaking, his tomatoes juicy. He'd plant anything, but he wanted to eat it—or wanted somebody to. He had sky-blue eyes—those eyes, my mother often said, were why she married him.

Thanks to the lumberyard, which was doing quite well by the time I came along, my grandparents were among the most prosperous citizens of West Branch. My grandfather—my mother called him "the old Dutchman"—would sit behind his desk in the big knotty pine office smoking a cigar, the desk littered with papers held down by arrowheads, his feet among them, a stuffed bobcat snarling on the boxy black safe at his side, the bookkeeper Lavina—"Vi"—laughing at something he'd just said, and my Uncle Carl behind the long counter, waiting on a customer, laughing too. Maybe laughing at me trying to manage my hammer, the pieces of wood I'd collected near the buzz saw out back, and the spiky fistful of nails I'd just helped myself to from one of the bins under the counter. I was not old enough for school yet, but I was old enough to drive a nail and old enough to run up to the corner gas station—bait shop—grocery store with Grandpa's dime for a cigar and a Dixie Cup ice cream; and I was old enough to climb in the truck with him to make a delivery to one of the lakes and on the way back enjoy the pickled ring baloney and crackers and pop we'd buy at a beer garden and take into the St. Helen woods where, if we were quiet, we'd see some deer, and where he unlaced the black shoes that came up over his ankles and took a little snooze. He had lumps on his arms like the lump on the neck of the old farmer kneeling bent and nut-wrinkled in the church where I went with my other grandparents. An *egg*, Grandma whispered.

My mother and father and I lived in the lumberyard—in an apartment above the office. Before that we lived a few streets away on the top floor of a three-story apartment building where one snowy day when I was still quite small, my mother frantically wrapped me in her muskrat coat and ran down through smoke and flames licking the walls and continued on to Frei Dieboldt's garage two blocks away, where my father was holding up the rear end of a Pontiac that had slipped off the jack so that the other mechanic who worked there could squeeze out from underneath.

It may have been another make of car my father was holding up as he looked helplessly at my crying mother, but a Pontiac was what she seemed to remember him telling her. We couldn't confirm it because when she remembered this scene my father was dead. He'd been dead for several years and she was reminiscing about West Branch, got around to the fire, how they lost everything, how she ran in the snow carrying me in the coat to find dad—all of which I'd heard before—and then suddenly here was this fresh, unlikely, *funny* detail. Forty years later.

"Oh you can laugh now," she said, "but that day you were bawling your head off. Your pants were full, which you hated, and you were hungry, mad too I was holding you so tight—and I was bawling like crazy myself, yelling, 'Ted! Ted!' But he just stood there blue in the face, couldn't talk, couldn't move or that poor devil underneath would've got more than his ribs busted, and I didn't understand any of it."

What my mother did understand—not right then but soon enough—was that she didn't want to live in the lumberyard, or in the little house we moved to later, or anywhere in West Branch. She wanted to live in Detroit where she was born, where people didn't keep tabs on every cough and sneeze, where her older sister Helen and her older brother Andy lived, and where my dad could do better than be a grease monkey for Frei Dieboldt. A couple of times before we did leave West Branch, my father had to drive to Detroit and fetch my red-haired Polish mother, and me, back.

What *I* understood soon enough was that she didn't like me scooping minnows out of the bait tank on the corner and bringing them home, because after they died she didn't like finding them under my pillow. I understood that we called my other grandparents Grandma and Grandpa Standish—which was the town that their farm was near—because my uncles and aunts and especially my cousins in West Branch couldn't say Szostak right. They said "*Shoe*-stack." "*Shoe*-stack!" I once saw my mother yell at the ceiling, pulling her hair. I understood that when we visited Gram Gildner I was not to try and eat any more of her fruit on the dining room table, because it was all like the wax pear I had left my teeth marks in. I understood that when we drove the twenty miles down to Grandma Standish's house there would always be a fresh coffee cake or a pie as soon as we arrived. I understood that Gramps enjoyed coming upstairs after the lumberyard closed and eating supper with us, and many years later I learned—and could make a pretty good guess why—he liked to watch my mother nurse me. I figured it was for the same reason he liked to make Vi the bookkeeper laugh, or for the same reason he liked to tell me about his turkey shoots with the Ojibway, and drink a schooper of beer up at the hotel at noon, and eat pickled ring baloney and then take a nap in the woods with his shoes off. Like my father, his firstborn, he had sky-blue eyes. He came "down from Canada"—which is all I knew, or know, about his origin—and married Grams, a local girl, who was thin and wiry (and "particular," my mother said) until the day she died at the age of ninety. Still driving her own car. Gramps, on the other hand, was as round as you'd expect a man to be who appreciated a regular snooze on the sunny ground that the white-tailed bucks, ramming and rutting, had kicked up sandy enough for him to work his shoulders in just about perfect.

After my father came Dorothy, Ralph, Russell, Carl, Edwinna, and Raymond. My father was named for Theodore Roosevelt, who was in his last year as president, and though he had none of the Rough Rider's bluster and charge, he did own a big Indian motorcycle and he brought deer meat to the Depression table and of the seven children he was the only one who ever really left West Branch. "I'll tell you *exactly* who your dad looked like then. Alan Ladd." My mother has always been fond of—crazy for, she would say—the movies. Thus my sister and I were named for Gloria Swanson and Gary Cooper, though my brother, she says, was named for Gregory Peck *and* a pope.

"Which one?"

"The tall one!"

But before she met my father, before she saw him astride his big Indian, a boy came to West Branch, or maybe he was there all along—a poor boy, an Italian—and he could play the piano like nobody's business. Angie. He'd play at the roadhouses over by Houghton and Higgins lakes, and he played this tune everybody was crazy for. When I was in high school, not paying much attention, this tune would come over the radio, come from a long time ago, and one of my parents would say, "There's Angie's song." And my mother might sing along. "*Sleepy time gal, you're turning night into day . . .*" It turned out, after a lot of nights had turned into a lot of days and I was paying more attention now, that Angie had written this song. Written it, according to my mother, during the time when he and my father would take their girlfriends to a roadhouse by a lake, and he'd play this song for his girl, who was as pretty and rich as the daughter of a banker could be; and of course they were crazy about each other, my mother said, just like in the movies. But the old German, the banker, was against his daughter marrying someone like Angie, my mother said, and sent her off to college. Everyone said Angie should take his song down to Bay City and sell it and go to college too. It was a great song, he could make a lot of money from it. But he wouldn't do that, my mother said, he'd wait for her. Besides, it was her song. Well, you guessed it, she came home after college married to somebody else, a college man, rich like she was. Then Angie did sell the song, practically gave it away, and my mother didn't think he ever wrote another one.

Less romantic and a good decade after the Depression—after Gram and Gramps had left the running of the farm to Uncle Raymond and moved into the big, modern brick house they'd built on a hill on a wooded spread you could see town from, or at least the cross on St. Joe's Church, and Gramps drove his new Hudson Hornet to the lumberyard where Carl and Ralph pretty much ran things OK and he smoked his cigars and got Vi to laugh—the bank in town went bankrupt, and after that, Vi told my mother, everything was different.

Everything was different for me too then, because we lived in Flint—where we'd moved right after the war—and I only saw Gramps and Gram during the summers, sometimes around Christmas. We never stayed long. The longest we stayed was the week he died and was buried. I remember walking in the woods behind the house with my dad and stopping at the salt lick Gramps had put up for the deer (he could see it from his favorite chair), and I remember my dad working a piece off for me with his car keys and how sharp and hot it tasted. I remember following him in the garage, how he stood there looking a long time at Gramps' Hudson, until finally he raised the hood and checked to see if the battery had enough water. I was sitting in Gramps' leather chair in the living room (watching the salt lick through the front window) when Gram came hurrying out of the bedroom where Gramps was—walking like she always did, as if something were about to boil over on the stove—and then she stopped. She took off her glasses and was wiping them so fast with her dress I thought her hand would fly off, and Aunt Dorothy rushed over with a hankie but Gram wouldn't take it—didn't want Dorothy's arm around her either, she just wanted to clean her glasses. Then my mother and Aunt Jeanette, Carl's wife, came out of the bedroom and Gram was crying now and they took her back in. My dad and Carl and the others followed. On the table beside his chair were some *True Detective* magazines, and a pair of binoculars, and a big pink seashell with a long woolly cigar ash in it like an almost perfect caterpillar. For years, my mother once said, Gram would not forgive her for being the one whose name Gramps had called, and the one whose hand he had held, at the end.

We were not given any warning about Grandpa Standish. He was heading toward the outhouse early one morning with a lamp (and a book by Conrad) and his heart stopped. He fell in the hollyhocks. Looking at him in the satin-lined coffin—his mustache trimmed more tidy than I had ever seen it, his cheeks scraped and painted—I could hear him shouting the curse Grandma always swept me away from: two spitting syllables that translated into "Dog's blood!" In his orchard sitting in a tree, or sprawled on the log bridge the cows crossed over, leaning way over facing the creek, watching my mouth reflected there and pretending to be mad, I never could make those angry foreign sounds come out right. Unlike Gram's when Gramps died, Grandma Standish's parlor and kitchen were filled with candles and flowers and food, with old farmers smelling of whiskey and manure, their razor-nicked faces flushed red and their fingers thick as brown rope keeping track, bead by bead, of the Sorrowful Mysteries on their rosaries. All in Polish. While pennies lay on his eyes and a smell like sweet cherries rose up when my mother's blonde cousin and her daughters from Chicago came in to pray. Outside, my uncles Andy and Joe and Johnny passed a bottle, and smoked, and across the yard, his foot on the pasture fence, Donny drank from his own bottle. I stood there with him and looked at the black bull. You could see the chain hanging down from his wet nose. I remembered how it swung when he ran beside the fence, chasing me, and once how it got caught in the barbed wire, just in time, when all I had in my hands was the sapling I'd pulled the bark from, until it was white and slick, for a fishing stick. Donny asked me if I remembered the time he led the bull in the barn and let him mount that milker's bony haunch—remembered that pink cock long as a hoe handle, long as a God damn sword, come sliding out.

Gramps' wake was down in Gram's basement, where he had planned to make a recreation room, line the walls with knotty pine and build a bar. But he never got that far with it. Lost interest in it, Carl figured, after the bank failed. My mother and Aunt Jeanette came down for a beer and a furtive cigarette. Gram didn't like to see women smoke. Aunt Dorothy brought down ham sandwiches. She said Gram insisted on making them herself because other people left too much fat on.

The day my father was buried, there *was* a recreation room all finished off in knotty pine for people to eat and drink in, but since it was a nice sunny spring day we all went out to the back yard, under the trees he'd planted. He'd put in white birch and silver maple and Norway pine and apple and pear. The birch were his favorite; I helped him dig them out of Gram's woods and wrap their roots in wet burlap and haul them down to Flint in the pickup. He didn't put up a salt lick but he did put up exactly the kind of house my mother wanted—brick—with lots of cupboards and two fireplaces and a rec room in the basement. She said it cost her twenty years of harping, that house.

They met at a dance. She didn't know why he was there—getting him to dance, even at his own wedding, was like pulling teeth! Even though I know exactly whom my father looked like when they began courting, I don't know how old she was then, because she keeps changing her age. I do know he was about ten

My mother and father.

years older, and that he rode his Indian all the way from West Branch to leave notes in the Szostak mailbox beside the highway, and that when we came to Flint after the war he exchanged his monkey wrench for a carpenter's hammer, and that he promised to build my mother her dream house and, twenty years after they were married, he did. He wanted to do it right, he said, on the right spot. I also know that whenever I test a new pen, without thinking about it I always write "house" several times in a straight column. As for pulling teeth, I once saw him tie one end of a chalk line around an aching molar and the other end around his hammer, and then make a single swift strike as if driving a spike in for good. A dentist, he said, would have taken a lot longer, made him feel bad the rest of the day, and charged him for it too.

While we still lived in the old house, winter nights after work he'd go down in the basement, shake up the furnace, then lie in front of a heat register in the dining room, saying, "Jeanie, wake me when you're ready." You knew when the week was over because the pencil mark in the gray hair beside his ear was at its darkest. In the new house winter nights after work, he took his before–dinner snooze on the floor in front of the fireplace in the basement rec room.

One winter day a dozen years after the house was finished, while I was trying to untangle a dozen sled dogs in upstate New York, my father was in his back yard trying to right a birch tree knocked over by an ice storm. My lead husky had spotted a woodchuck and gone after it into a thicket, taking the rest of us with her. My father, not quite sixty, felt that a horse had suddenly kicked him—as one had once—and woke up in the hospital. When I got there he said, "You know what I was just thinking? How you'd squeal and yell when I pulled your sled. I thought you wanted to go faster. Hell, I didn't know it was the snow I kicked in your face that got you so excited." Four years later he died, in the spring, while my mother was making a pie for dinner and he was tilling his garden. She said she looked out the window and saw a pheasant run across the yard and then she saw my father. At first she thought he was taking a nap.

5

Chełmża is a small town about 250 kilometers west of Warsaw. It is pronounced helm-sha and means "helmet," and like a helmet Chełmża has a hardness to it, a 1940s "News of the World" feel. Approaching its narrow cobblestone main street, the gray buildings jammed together, the old people in clothes the color of grief, you almost expect to see battle-sore GIs on tanks and on foot coming through, and to hear again that ponderous, grim background music which was relieved for a moment, maybe, by a GI handing a candy bar to a kid beside a pile of rubble, by a young woman in a babushka holding a baby and waving a small stars and stripes. That was what you focused on back then, the soldiers, the kid, not the town, because the town—the street— was just like the one last Saturday and the Saturday before that: no trees, a few people leaning out of windows, a steeple in the distance, a toothless old man, a woman with flowers in a can, and maybe, on the way out of town, beside the tanks, a boy leading a cow. Nothing like West Branch.

Before you arrive in Chełmża, if you are coming from Warsaw, you pass through Toruń, which is twenty kilometers to the south and a city of some size—well over 100,000—and of no small historical importance. Mikołaj Kopernik, whose *De revolutionibus orbium coelestium* put the earth in its proper place in the heavens, was born there, in 1473. A university is there, named in his honor, and much Gothic architecture, and a famous gingerbread factory, and just outside of town, in a woods, is where the body of the slain Jerzy Popiełuszko was found. Oh yes, almost any Pole can tell you about Toruń, at length.

But Chełmża? Where is it? Not even the driver is certain, for after leaving Toruń he must consult a map. No—wait. Fleetfoot, our Junior pitcher, knows. He went there once with his parents, long ago, to see the lake.

So it has a lake, says Mark. *Dobrze*. Does it have any girls in the lake?

Does it have a *kino*? says George.

What do you want, says Pete, Warsaw?

It has a very fine soccer field, says Dariusz. Maybe the best in Poland.

How do you know?

I telephone.

The Sparks, who are traveling not to the mountains, not to the sea for their training camp, say *dobrze*, Dariusz, *dobrze*, as if he is taking them back to a time before Copernicus, back to when, if you were foolish enough to venture out far enough, you could fall off into the void.

But after a stretch of rye fields and an occasional cow tethered beside the road, we only came to Chełmża. The big touring coach, slowing down, eased its way in. We passed the train station; Mark said if the bus failed to return for them in two weeks, the Sparks at least would not be stranded. We passed a *kino*—a movie theatre—and George said, "Look, Piotr, just like Warsaw!" Then the cobblestone street became narrow, twisting, and the bus groaned up in a low gear. We passed a shoe store that had three pairs of shoes in its window. We passed the treeless town square where two cement soldiers about seven feet tall—a Polish and a Russian—stood shoulder to shoulder, and where, on a bench, a couple of old gents warily looked us over. We groaned past the gray, jammed together buildings I had seen on Saturday afternoons at the movies more than forty years before—men and women were leaning out of second- and third-story windows for relief from the late summer heat—and beyond the roofs of these buildings, just before the street curved sharply and began a sudden descent, we caught a glimpse of the red brick bell tower and steeple of a church. The street took us down past two cemeteries, one on either side of us—walled-in, tree-filled, flowering places that looked like estates for princes—and just past these, to our right, lay the lake, a huge lake, and it changed everything. We were out of town now on a sun- and shadow-speckled road that followed beside a wooded park, and down through the trees you could see the lake, and across it, rising majestic as a cathedral, the church. Fleetfoot said he knew exactly where to go and stood beside the driver, pointing. He directed the driver into a lane so narrow tree limbs brushed the bus like scrubbers in an automatic car wash, and then we arrived at the soccer field and what looked like a motel. Whoever spoke with Dariusz on the telephone about this field gave him the right dope: it was the prettiest green field I'd seen in Poland—as pretty as any I'd ever seen.

OK, so we didn't have mountains or the sea, but we had the essential thing—a good place to practice—plus a beautiful lake. We all left the bus in high spirits. Dariusz and Henry went to find the manager, the rest of us started for the field. We couldn't get on, though. Surrounding it was a six-foot chain fence, topped with a foot of barbed wire, and inside, waiting behind the gate George tried to open, was a big black, suddenly barking German shepherd. Oh well, we'd check out the field later.

Meantime we checked into the Chełmża Sports Klub, which looked pretty much like a budget motel in the States. Each room had three single beds, a table with chairs, a bathroom; you wished after a few days of practice that the tub had been long enough to stretch out in, but it wasn't: you sat up with your charley horses and bruises. Each room opened onto its own private balcony, where we hung our underwear and jerseys to dry. Vic and I were in Room 1. It looked out over a hayfield that was being mowed, and beyond that a valley where farmers, tending their sugar beets and rye, stopped to watch Vic run by on her way to visit some storks she discovered. She ran every morning during those two weeks and every morning the farmers held their reins or their pitchforks for a moment and watched her. She turned brown and freckles she'd forgotten she had came out, and toward the end the farmers waved.

The Klub manager wasn't in that Saturday afternoon when we arrived from Warsaw, but two women who turned out to be his wife and mother-in-law gave us room keys and toilet paper. There were twenty-six of us all together: Vic, me, Dariusz, Henry, Jacek Demkiewicz, and enough Sparks for two teams, with three left over. My plan was simple: fundamentals for two and a half hours every morning, and every afternoon a nine-inning game. We'd learn some baseball. Right now, though, after the five-hour bus trip we were hungry.

Where do we eat, Dariusz?

In Chełmża, he said, and some players groaned: what could be in Chełmża? No, no, you listen, he said, a very good restaurant.

How did he know?

It's private, he said, and the groaners changed their tune—private in Poland always means good. He said we'd be taking all our meals there.

So most of us went back to town on foot, figuring we might as well get used to the thrice-daily hike right away, while Dariusz and Henry rode back on the bus. (After the driver ate, he would return to Warsaw.) It was about a kilometer and a half from the Klub to the restaurant, or about two miles round trip per meal. Most of the walk was beside the park—with the lake down below and the church beyond—then up past the two cemeteries and into the cobbled main street. Walking, Vic and I saw more than we had when coming through on the bus. We saw a beauty parlor, a beer garden, a greengrocer's in whose sunny window pieces of onionskin shone like chips of gold, and a butcher shop where a picture of a chicken hung among the empty kielbasa hooks. We saw a clothing store, a wine and tea store (boxes of Chinese black tea filling the window), a sports shop that had two *palant* balls in the window (so some Poles were still playing that ancient game), a window where, when it was open, you could buy an ice cream cone, and in the largest window of all we saw three crystal cream pitchers and a dozen crystal sugar bowls. Vic said she didn't know how she missed seeing *that* store the first time through. The others had been easy to miss because their display windows were little more than ordinary house windows, with very little in them; there were no signs (perhaps because everybody in Chełmża knew where everything was); and since it was late Saturday afternoon there were no lines: the shops either had sold out their fresh offerings for the day or were closed.

The beauty parlor, however, was open—through the doorway we saw two women under hairdryers—and the beer garden was open. First we smelled the beer, then coming to the entrance and stepping in we saw men—only men—standing up drinking at high wooden tables built into the walls at regular intervals; there was nothing else in the room, no chairs, no pictures, only the men, their mugs, the fixed tables, some smoke, and a general low grumble and growl as of humans mimicking dogs. Then we noticed off to the side another, much smaller room where three formidable women stood behind a counter beside a keg and two soapy washtubs. The one nearest the keg had her arms folded across her bosom—a visible *nie ma*—the other two women were elbow-deep in soapy water. Before the counter was a man with an empty mug and a lost look. Suddenly the beer garden fell quiet and everyone but the lost-looking man was regarding us. We left. The beauty parlor was just up the hill from the cemeteries, around the corner was the beer garden, and across from the beer garden half a dozen women were leaning out of their upper-story windows for the air and perhaps for signs of their husbands. Farther up the street the two old gents continued to occupy their bench under the cement soldiers, and not far past the square we heard a rhythmic whoosh-and-clacking noise come from inside a shop whose window I had to stand on my toes to see through. "What is it?" Vic said. "Some blind people are making brooms," I told her. Then we passed the crystal shop and arrived at a doorway where George and Pete were waiting for us.

"In here," they said.

The restaurant was half a story up from the street and on entering you might have thought, seeing so much polished pine and light, you had come to the mountains after all and here was a

Vic in the Pomorzanka.

ski lodge. Dariusz and Henry stood at the bar, beaming, finishing off welcoming shots of vodka the manager had poured. He poured two more, for Vic and me. "What you think?" Dariusz said. "No, no," Henry said. He wanted us to eat first, then tell our opinion.

There were four dining rooms. The one which became ours for the two weeks was off to the side, very private and plain, but the food served there was first-rate, the soups, game stews, pierogi, puddings, smoked fish, cheeses, and sausages as good as the Bazyliszek's in Warsaw. Tastier, I thought. Homemade. And the girls who brought round the platters and bowls were cheerful and very happy, judging by their flushed cheeks, to see so many young unmarried men in Chełmża. All in one place. The boys from Warsaw were savvy to the scene. Mark, clearly the most knowledgeable (just ask him), never failed, for any meal, to be bathed and combed and dressed as sharp as he could be. Big Robert, the one married Spark, and July, whose wedding was six weeks away, had their experienced antlers on and their cool wits out as well. And on down the line to Fleetfoot, trying his best to keep up, despite that bramblebush of hair falling into his face. But it was shy Froggy behaving as his *babcia* had taught him, waiting politely for his food, who made the first contact, the second night we were there. As she was passing behind his chair, a waitress with big round brown eyes and a bouncy step skipped her fingers quickly over the back of Froggy's neck. No one missed it. Froggy turned red as Hungarian pepper, the Sparks roared, and the girl acted as if nothing had happened. That night and every night thereafter she sent the first baseman home from the restaurant with extra rolls. The name of the restaurant was Pomorzanka, which means "the girl from near the sea," and the name of the girl who chose Froggy turned out to be Sylvia.

Vic said, "I'm starting to get a real good feeling about Chełmża."

That evening Dariusz and I met with the Klub manager, who was also the Klub's soccer coach. He was in his early forties, tall and lean, jumpy as certain coaches are jumpy; the kind of man who, while you talked with him, worked on specific areas of his body—twisting his torso, for example, to keep his middle region fit; the kind of man who, it would not surprise you to learn, wore his whistle to bed.

I told him we'd be using the soccer field from nine to eleven-thirty every morning and again from one-thirty to four every afternoon. *Dobrze, dobrze,* he said. He would use it—for the two or three soccer matches coming up—after we finished for the day. His team, he said, would practice on the dirt field at the edge of the park. Perhaps we'd seen it? We had. It looked, I thought, like a parking lot for trucks.

One more thing, the manager said: did Dariusz remember about the shoes? *Tak*, Dariusz said, and then he explained to me that he had agreed on the phone we would wear *soft* shoes, no soccer shoes, to help protect the grass. I asked Dariusz to ask him what his soccer players wore on their feet. Also, I said, we didn't play our games in gym shoes, why should we practice in them? Also—our footing wouldn't be as good. But I didn't press these issues because I could see that Dariusz didn't want to get into a squabble. "Gary, Gary, we can do this," he said. I said OK.

Dobrze, dobrze, the manager said, and we all shook hands. He said he'd put the dog in his kennel behind the grandstand every morning. Then he took off for his nightly run in the park.

Our first day of practice was sunny and hot and the Sparks were ready to sweat. We didn't have Jake and Blackie, or Tony and Alejandro (Tony had Embassy duties, Alejandro was in Cuba for the summer), but we weren't going to suffer, either. We'd picked up Big Robert and Little Jacek, and Dariusz' other promised monkey player was with us—Zbyszek (pronounced Za-*bish*-ick)— fresh out of the Army. A compact, muscular, quiet guy, Zbyszek like Norbert owned a powerful arm, and like Little Jacek was afraid of nothing. Afraid of nothing on the field, that is; in the Pomorzanka, around females, was another matter, because he had no front teeth. When we took our meals he sat in the farthest corner, near our private exit, kept his eyes mostly on his plate, his mouth carefully closed, and was the first to leave. His eyes, however, were so blue and beautiful, Vic said, that a girl would be out of her mind not to be crazy about them. All he needed was a good dentist. "Promise me," she said, "you'll take him to one when we get back to Warsaw." I promised. Meantime, I tried him at third base and he loved it, went after everything hit his way like the monkey Dariusz said he was, and though he was no Tony for finesse—and never would be—he had plenty of grit and enthusiasm. So we had two worthy contenders for third—Zbyszek and Big Robert—and when Marek began to shine as a catcher, filling the hole left by Alejandro, Paweł, our captain, wanted me to know he was very happy— and he gave me the entire mouthful—"*bardzo szczęśliwy*"—because now, he said, we would be *all* Polish.

After lunch that first day, I divided the players into two teams:

TIGERS	YANKEES
Paweł, cf	Little Jacek, 2b
Pete, 2b	Norbert, ss
George, c	Marek, c
Mariusz, ss	Mark, p
Froggy, 1b	Big Robert, 3b
Adam, p	July, 1b
Zbyszek, 3b	Chris Płatek, cf
Jacek Małecki, cf	Dariusz Krzyżanowski, lf
Little Robert, lf	Fleetfoot, rf

Jacek Małecki, who had chauffeured Norbert and me around Warsaw that day we deposited the forty dollars—and who in March cut his wrist falling into junk glass—was back with the team. The purple scars above his pitching hand looked raw as angleworms, but he said, "I am good, Coach, I am strong." Paweł's younger brother Chris, who was twenty-one, was with us too; cheerful, always eager to play when he showed up, Chris was like a mascot you kept forgetting you had. He was very proud of his brother and wanted, like Paweł, to be able to catch anything; but the trying sometimes exhausted him, in body and in spirit, and he'd have to stay away for a while. Dariusz Krzyżanowski was a Junior, as were the three extra players: Wiktor Koliński, Piotr Poławski, and Paweł Wawrzniak.

Dariusz Krzyżanowski was the best of them, and not bad, though when he ran he tended to leap, like a little kid hurtling a series of mud puddles. He was our young Baryshnikov. Wiktor Koliński, stroking, almost constantly, his adolescent mustache, was our budding Adolphe Menjou, and Piotr Poławski, who rarely said a word, appeared to be our philosopher. Often I would see Piotr turning a baseball over and over on his fingertips, following the red stitches round and round as if they might lead to the Question, his gaze thoughtful and not a little pained—and in the foreground, as counterpoint, suave Wiktor, twirling a bat like a silver-knobbed walking stick, keeping tabs on his lip fuzz. I told them they were metaphorically on the right track, more or less, but first they needed to learn to throw and catch and use both hands.

As for Paweł Wawrzniak, he was etched deep in all our memories for an incident that occurred on that dreamy May day when we hosted Kutno. He got hit on the leg by a pitch, staggered back to the bench as if shot, then fell, moaning what seemed his last, to the ground. He lay there in a fetal, silent heap. Everything stopped. The Skra rugby trainer happened to be watching the game; he rushed to the scene and the struck Spark, still alive, said he needed a bandage, a bandage. The trainer wrapped his leg in a wonderful bandage from high-thigh to ankle. When the game resumed—I put in a substitute for him—Paweł somehow got up and hobbled slowly over to the bleachers to visit his girlfriend, then he hobbled slowly back close to the field and sat with his leg stretched out in a direct line between the crowd and home plate— a good visible spot. When I told him the sun was very bad for his bandage and that he must cover it up, he seemed crestfallen.

Word in Chełmża had gotten around that we were out there on the soccer field playing this *nowy palant* ("new palant"), so for our first intersquad game we had about twenty spectators in the grandstand, including the two old gents from the town square and half a dozen teenage girls in their Sunday best. Closer to us, their fingers gripping the wire fence, were several small boys, some of whom had watched us in the morning and now were back with friends. Quiet, their grave faces cross-hatched by fence shadow, they seemed like etchings in a long series illustrating a dark, unhappy tale. But over the next few days they began fetching our fouls for us, at first handing the balls back at the gate, then, braver, venturing onto the field. We got them to try on our mitts, to throw, to swing a bat, and by and by they were cracking smiles and bringing us apples.

Before the game started, I gathered the Sparks together. I told the pitchers to throw strikes, the batters to swing only at good pitches, and above all, I said, no arguing, no heated seminars. We're here to play baseball, OK? They said OK. Henry was our chief umpire. Jacek Demkiewicz took the bases. Dariusz sat in the grandstand with Vic and his Scoremaster; he sat there like a man who possessed a magic jug that contained amazing things, and now he pulled the cork, and now he was explaining to all assembled what they were seeing.

The sun over Chełmża was bright, the grass was green and smooth and gave true bounce to the ball, and the Sparks were loose—and for three days it seemed as if we *had* come forth from a magic jug. Or been touched by one. Or something. Good workouts in the morning, swims before lunch, and three games that were remarkably well played—without any verbal sabres—and close. Beautifully close. Nearly all the games we played in Chełmża, it turned out, would be close. Better yet, neither team could manage to win two in a row. We changed our names every day (after the Tigers and Yanks, we became the Red Sox and Mets, Cardinals and Dodgers, etc.), but we kept to the same sides and after our final game in Chełmża the series stood at 7–7. Being so evenly matched the two teams released plenty of competitive heat, which produced a lot of good, sharp play, and also, inevitably, a clash of swords. Before that happened, however, we got into a duel with the Klub manager.

On Wednesday—our fourth day—the sky clouded over and by mid-afternoon there was rain. Not a serious rain, not one that would stop a game during the regular season, so we kept playing. Afterwards the manager complained to Dariusz that we had torn up his grass. We hadn't torn it up so much as *slid* it up, rubbed it muddy here and there, because our gym shoes had no bite. If we'd been using soccer shoes, Dariusz pointed out to him, the wear and tear would have been minimal, acceptable. The manager agreed. Nonetheless, his grass was badly damaged, he said, and if there was no sun tomorrow we could not use the field.

He and Dariusz had had this exchange right after the game, and Dariusz reported it to us at supper.

"Very provincial man," he said. "But no problem. Sun will be out." He recommended I move our diamond to the field's far end, to give the grass where we had been playing a chance to recover.

By the time we finished supper and were walking back, the rain had stopped and a nice brisk wind was blowing over the field. Later the moon appeared. Vic and I opened our balcony doors and went to sleep on the bed closest to it.

In the morning on our way to breakfast, passing the field (the German shepherd walking beside us on his side of the fence), we saw the manager and another man examining the grass. The sky was a cashmere gray but the gauzy sun, you could see, would soon burn through. Also, the wind was still doing a nice drying job.

When Dariusz joined us at the Pomorzanka, he said he'd just spoken with the manager. He said he'd agreed that we would use the dirt field near the park today—"only today, Gary"—to give the grass more time to dry completely.

"That other field's all right for practice," I said, "but for a game it's terrible. It's too small."

"I know, I know. But for politics, you understand, I make this concession."

"Why can't we practice there this morning, then move to the good field for our game? Look"—I pointed to the window—"the sun's already out. This afternoon that grass will be fine."

Dariusz spooned around in his kasha, and sighed. "He is nervous, this manager."

"What's he nervous about?"

"Our shoes. He says if grass is not dry for sure, they are no good. He says"—Dariusz snorted—"soccer shoes would be better."

"So we wear our soccer shoes."

"Not possible." Dariusz looked sad.

"Why not?"

"I tell players to leave them in Warsaw, because of contract."

"And now, maybe, he would like us to wear pillows tied to our feet."

"I tell you, he is very provincial."

I thought about sending someone to Warsaw to collect the shoes. Jacek D. could go, take the three Junior extras—Wiktor, Piotr, and Paweł Wawrzniak—to help. But then I thought, hell, we were here to play baseball, on a field we had a contract for. And the manager said we could use it if the sun was out—and it was—and if he didn't like our shoes, that was his problem. I said all this to Dariusz.

He nodded and sighed, then said, "Only for today, Gary. Only one time. We can do it, to make happiness."

The dirt field lay in a deep hole beside the road that we took back and forth to town; it was more like a big gravel pit than a parking lot, about the size of a soccer field but with no foul area whatsoever. A bowl . . . and snug. It was good enough for infield practice, and deep enough to left for fungoes, but in our game that afternoon we had only half a center field and hardly any right. The right fielder stood about twenty yards behind the in- fielders, his back against a high, steep wall of dirt that led up to the road. As a kind of consolation, the top of that dirt wall became lined with kids; they sat shoulder to shoulder with Dariusz and his Scoremaster, with the two old gents from the town square, and with Vic, back from her run to her storks, in a big straw hat. Dariusz wore a black cap with a lot of fancy gold scrambled egg on the bill—Admiral Dariusz—and the whole gang of them, pink in the sun, was pretty to see. (The teenage girls, off in their own cluster, were also pretty to see.) The sun stayed out all day and in the bottom of that hot hole, the Braves and the Angels, keeping their feathers intact, went back and forth, 7–6.

On our way to supper later, a man was spreading grass seed on the good field. On our way home he was putting up two rows of sprinkler pipe from end zone to end zone. I asked Dariusz what was going on. He spoke with the man and was told that the seed needed some moisture. "No problem, Gary. Very hot today and ground is very dry."

Next morning the pipes were squirting; they'd obviously been squirting all night, because even standing outside the fence (the dog eyeing us) we could see that the field was soaked. When

Dariusz and I knocked on the manager's door, his wife told us, "*Nie ma.*" She didn't know where he was.

All day the manager was gone, and all day under a hot sun the water pipes squirted, the dog patrolled. The Sparks had no choice but to stay in the dirt bowl.

"Manager *must* have good reason," Dariusz said.

After supper he produced a string of *kino* tickets and said maybe Vicki and I would like to relax at the movies, with the players. So while Dariusz and Henry went to camp at the manager's door to discover his good reason, several of us went to see Robert De Niro abandon his sword for a Jesuit's robe in *The Mission*. (Pete, Mariusz, Marek, and Adam enjoyed the film, but Mark said it was poor, a fantasy, he preferred films like *Crocodile Dundee*. George said *his* all-time favorite was *Ghostbusters*.)

Back at the Klub I found an agitated Dariusz in his room, in shorts and admiral's cap, drinking a *piwo*.

"Manager is deaf and crazy," he said.

"So we can't use the field tomorrow."

"He tells me he must protect the grass."

"How can he keep us off it—he rented it to us?"

"I know."

"Did he think we were going to use the field without touching it?"

"Gary, you listen. Chełmża is very poor. You see this. But field is very good. Manager thinks he must keep it like"—Dariusz snapped and snapped his fingers for the word he wanted—"like I don't know. Holy place. You understand?"

He said early tomorrow he and Henry would meet with the chief of the Chełmża Sports Klub, the man who actually signed the contract, and try to resolve all this.

In the morning the water pipes were shut off, the sun was shining, and on our way to breakfast we gave a cheer. But when we got back and were ready to practice, the German shepherd was still guarding the gate. Fleetfoot opened it anyway, slowly, cooing to the dog. The dog sat down and let Fleetfoot scratch his head. Then Norbert went in and petted the dog, followed by the rest of us. We all petted the dog. Froggy produced a bread roll from his bag and the dog took it to a shady corner and flopped down to eat it. *Dobrze*! The field had some spongy spots but in a few hours it would be dry enough. We went back to the dirt field; after lunch, however, we planned to remove the pipes ourselves and play our game on grass.

Which is what we did, with the dog watching. Dariusz and Henry weren't around—hadn't been at breakfast or at lunch—so Vic kept the scorebook and Jacek D. umpired behind the plate. I took the bases. Vic sat in a shady spot just outside the fence with the two old gents, our teenage groupies, and the boys who brought us apples. Everything was going beautifully. Then in the fifth inning we had a near-crisis. Crouching too close to the batter, Marek got hit on his left triceps on a hard cut by Zbyszek. No bone was broken, but he'd have a prize bruise, it was already starting to color. "I am no catcher!" he declared and unsnapped his chest protector and threw it down. We wrapped the bruise in a big bandage, Pete gave it a kiss, Captain Paweł made a speech about happiness, and Marek went back to work. In the next inning, Jacek Małecki, pitching for the Brewers, walked three Phillies in a row and the Phillies began riding him, especially Mark. The game was close, the series tied, 3–3. Jacek walked one more and Mark strutted along the sidelines like a rooster. Jacek stood on the mound and glared. Mark crowed and Jacek fired the ball at him, just missing his head. I told Jacek he'd worked enough today and took him out. In the seventh inning a soccer team came onto the field and started kicking a ball around in our outfield. It was the Chełmża team. The players said they'd been told by their coach (who would soon be there) to warm up for their four o'clock match. It wasn't even three-thirty, we said. But they were told, they said. Finally, Mariusz and Paweł diplomatically got them out of our way and we finished the game. We finished a little after four. As we were leaving the field, the Klub manager appeared at the gate, in shorts and cleats, whistle in mouth, and watched us, making sure we all got off. He was breathing so hard his breath rattled the little ball in his whistle and the whistle whined. Then we saw Dariusz and Henry. They looked exhausted. All three had met with the chief, and with several sub-chiefs as well, and after much discussion and a careful examination of the contract, it was decided that the Sparks could use the field if it was dry, but that we had to be off by four o'clock sharp. This decision took most of the day. At the end of the official discussion, Dariusz and Henry kept the manager occupied in unofficial discussion until they saw we had finished our game.

In the Pomorzanka that night, which was Saturday night after all, there was *piwo* and roast chicken and a new waitress. Her beauty—in the Miss Polonia class, the Sparks declared—was taken as a sign that our first week in town was indeed a grand success. Further, that little Chełmża was much bigger than anyone could have guessed, and that they all owed it an apology. *Przepraszam*, the Sparks bowed solemnly. Pete and George suggested we change our names tomorrow to something special, then made up a poster with crayons announcing a Super Sunday *Bardzo Bardzo* Baseball Game between the Crazy Ducks and the Drunk Sharks—which all of Chełmża was invited to witness. They put the poster in the Pomorzanka's biggest window. Back at the Klub, Vic and I sipped brandy on our balcony under the stars while Mark's portable radio produced the proper background music and while the Sparks—how many it was hard to say—explained the finer points of the game to some of our fans here and there in the darkness.

Maybe fifty people, including Sylvia and the new waitress, were watching us on Sunday—under a perfect sky—and the Sparks put on a show. Paweł raced back to the field's deepest reach and caught a towering fly belted by Big Robert that the crowd, gasping, thought was intended for heaven. I did too. On three successive pitches, Zbyszek stole second, stole third, stole home, each time arriving head first on his stomach and bouncing up wearing that old man's toothless smile—for no one in particular, just his joyful self. Froggy sliced a wicked liner to left that bit a divot out of the manager's holy grass—good for a triple—and later he made a wonderful catch of a high foul, looking directly into the sun. Adam and Mark, the opposing pitchers, each had a couple of sparkling innings in which they fanned everybody, their fastballs shimmering with heat; then Mariusz drove one of Mark's heaters over the goal post and over the fence more than 400 feet away, and circled the bases in a lope as graceful and self-assured as Joe DiMaggio's. "*Bardzo*," I said, "*bardzo dobrze*," slapping his palms at the plate. We'd come a long way since Górnik, he and I. Everybody had, I thought, and in the Chełmża sunshine that day watching Mariusz smile—watching Froggy, Adam, and even tough little Norbert (who had become our most consistent hitter) enjoy their moments too—I couldn't remember ever being happier. I looked over at Vic and Dariusz in the grandstand, she in her straw hat, he in his admiral's, the small boys sitting around them, the two old gents, the pretty groupies, and then she waved.

"Where are we?" I called.

"You mean which inning or something else?"

"I feel pretty good."

"Dariusz says no problem. He says we're winning."

In the midst of this I remembered a day I played catch with Gretchen in the back yard. She was fourteen, already tall, a flowering ungainly lovely stringbean, and she was stepping out and following through, getting better and better—she insisted on it—she knew how it looked to throw like a girl and would have none of that—telling *me* to throw harder, it was OK. I know what I'm doing, Dad, I know what I'm doing. I remembered the lilacs were out, the new leaves on the trees all feathery, the delicacy of that day, its sweet smell. I had just cut the grass and she came out with my glove and ball and threw me the ball, not saying anything, wanting to surprise me, show me her savvy, her motion, something, she finally said, she'd been thinking about for a long time . . .

Before the game was over Henry, umpiring behind the plate, caught a foul on his toe and had to be replaced by Jacek D., and Marek eased too close to the batter again and got whacked on his triceps bruise—and after the game several of us discovered our rooms had been entered and things were missing—but neither the mishaps nor the losses stopped the Sparks and me from taking a second dip in Chełmża's pretty lake—this one in the buff—to celebrate down to our skin an afternoon the likes of which might never come again. Though of course we believed otherwise. We were playing real baseball and getting lost in it—no maybes, no *nie ma*s, no Polish life—and lost we knew exactly where we were; or as Dariusz said, "This day we make big, very big happiness."

Then the Milicja came. Much later I figured Henry might not have reported the break-ins if our losses had been only a few T-shirts and rock tapes, but when I mentioned that my gold money clip and $40 were missing, he said, angrily, that the Milicja must be told. I suggested we let the matter go. It was just kids, I said. I shouldn't have left the money lying around. (And privately I was relieved that no one had looked in my shaving kit, which contained my wallet and several hundred dollars.) But Henry and Dariusz felt awful, felt responsible; they said forty dollars was not for kids, it was a fortune. No, no, they said, for me, for everybody, the Milicja must be told.

They appeared soon after supper that Sunday. Three of them. They sat in Dariusz' room asking questions and filling out a report. At first their presence was like a damper, an old unfunny bitter joke. The Sparks put on special faces. Faces that said we are anonymous.

Now I was feeling bad. These cops had nothing to do with getting lost in throwing and catching and meeting the ball in the sweet spot and going back deep. They were humorless, official, they had their thumbs hooked over wide black belts watching their colleague, the one with the pencil, record our names and addresses, birthdays, occupations, marriage dates, number of children, parents' names, if living, where, our losses, the values. On and on. In no hurry. Making sure our genealogies and losses were spelled right.

Besides me, Dariusz, Henry, and Jacek D. (who was translating), three Sparks were there. One of them was Pete. I don't know how much time had passed, but finally I said to him, "Maybe we should ask the other players to come in and keep us company?"

"You think?" Pete said.

"Sure," I said, "it's lonely here. Tell Vic too. Tell her to bring the baseball cards from my duffel bag."

Vic brought the packs of cards. They were the last of the stash I'd been saving for an occasion. This seemed to be it. The players came in, slowly, wearing their special faces. The cops looked at them. I unwrapped a pack of cards, broke off a piece of bubble-gum, put it in my mouth, then gave the rest to Pete. "Have a chew," I said. He did. I passed around the other packs, telling the guys to pick a few cards, have some gum.

"George," I said, "somebody told me you blow bubbles like a drooling baby."

"That's not true," he said.

"*Prawda*," I said. "*Prawda, tak?*" I said to Pete.

"*Prawda*," Pete said.

George said, "Look," and blew a perfect baseball-size bubble.

"Well, I'll be damned," I said.

The cops watched George suck in his bubble. Then they looked at the rest of us. We were sitting on the three beds, leaning against the walls, crowded in the doorway—some of us blowing bubbles, some of us only chewing and keeping our special faces on, but all of us filling the room with the sweet odor of Topps.

The next night the cop with the pencil was back, but so were the Sparks—to baseball and their sunny selves. "The Smurf," they cracked in the hall, pointing to Dariusz' room where the cop spread out a clean sheet of paper. About thirty, blond, with a blond mustache, he looked a lot like the Czech coach from Ostrava, like a guy from next door. And unlike his two colleagues from the night before, he had even smiled, finally, when George and Pete tried to outdo each other blowing bubbles. Why he came back—and kept coming back—was of little concern to the Sparks. He was a Smurf, that's why, they said, and dismissed him, the *kupa*. Dariusz' theory, after the third visit, was that the man was fasci-nated by us. Henry agreed. How many stolen gold money clips shaped like big paper clips would he investigate in Chełmża? No, no, Dariusz said, it was the *baseball* that attracted him. Vic's the-ory was that he was lonely, plain and simple, and she supplied a drawing of the money clip for his report after I said I'd seen enough of the guy. In any case, he came out to the Klub five nights in a row, plus a couple of afternoons, and unbelievably wrote down on fresh sheets of paper the same, unchanging gene-alogies and losses.

As for the Klub manager, he continued to be obsessed with us too. Every morning the water pipes were on the field, squirting away, and every morning before breakfast we took them down. We ran laps and played catch and pepper on the track circling the field until it was dry enough to practice on. He never confronted us. But one night the Sparks, feeling cocky, confronted him. They challenged his team to a soccer match; they told his players they could beat them wearing gym shoes or no shoes; they said—rubbing it in—a soccer match would be relaxing after playing baseball, a much more difficult sport, all day.

Everything was arranged. The Sparks wolfed down an early supper and returned to the field. Henry, hobbling on his sore toe, was their coach. Dariusz was not keen on this match; he feared injuries.

"We are not prepared," he wailed.

"How good is Chełmża?" I said.

Just then the ball shot past Mariusz, the Sparks' goalie, into the net.

"You see," Dariusz said. "One minute, one goal." He said the Chełmża players, though young (eighteen years old and under), were strong. They would teach us a lesson, Dariusz said.

But they didn't. We tied the score, they went ahead, we evened it again, and then in the closing seconds we put it away. Dariusz couldn't help himself. "Sports characters!" he cheered. "Even Jacek!" Jacek D., his hair flying, had been a star, as had Little Robert, Zbyszek, Froggy, Paweł and Chris Płatek, Mark, Mariusz, and Adam, who continued to carry around, though I didn't know it, that piece of Coke bottle in his heel.

"I think we are perfect," George said.

Next day I gave them the morning off. That afternoon we played a terrible game. George hadn't jinxed us; Marek had simply gone back to Warsaw—his sister was getting married—and we were minus a catcher. Wiktor Koliński also went home, complaining of a sick stomach. Though I missed Wiktor's theatrical motions, I—all of us—missed Marek's abilities a lot more. And while everyone else knew that he would be leaving camp early, I didn't, and therefore I had no substitute ready.

Why wasn't I given any warning?

"We didn't want to worry you, Coach."

I tried to make an instant catcher out of Piotr Połowski, our philosopher. He handled the ball OK warming up, but the game, with its pressure, was another matter. And his errors, like germs, infected almost everybody. It was as if we were back at the beginning, all the way back to Gwardia. I put Big Robert behind the plate; he fared better, but it was too late. The game was sloppy and would continue sloppy, and in the end the Sparks were gloomy and snappish.

That was Friday, our next-to-last full day in Chełmża. At breakfast on Saturday many of the players looked hungover and no doubt were; at practice they were listless. I made a short speech.

"OK, what's wrong?"

No one could say.

"Are you tired?"

They said no, of course not.

I told them what I thought: that as long as they were riding high—*dobrze, bardzo dobrze*; but the minute they fell off their horse—*kupa*, everywhere and everything and everybody *kupa*. I said I'd be on the field at one-thirty if they wanted to play that last game.

Lunch was real quiet.

On the way back, Vic bought a bunch of daisies from an old woman selling flowers on the street. When we came to the cemeteries, she said, "Let's go in this one for a minute."

Just inside the gate she showed me that the first group of graves—very small—all were of infants. The next group were of children. The farther we went in, she pointed out, the older people got. At the end of the cemetery was the lake. "I thought this order might interest you," she said. Across the lake I could see where the Sparks and I took our noon swim. In a moment I could also see that if we swam this way—all the way—and came ashore in the cemetery, and then walked up past the graves to the gate, we'd be enacting a little rebirth story. It didn't take much reflection to see that I was already in that story—and had been in it at least as far back as Gwardia.

"Oh, look," Vic whispered, glancing toward the gate.

"What?"

"Let's go see."

She took my arm and we strolled up the sloping path to the first graves. She pointed to a plot the size of a loaf of bread; it bore no headstone, no marker of any kind except a crude homemade wooden cross. At the foot of the grave was a jar of daisies and some fern. "It's the only one in the whole place that doesn't have a name," she said. She took the daisies out of the jar and put the fresh bunch in, arranging them among the fern. "I've been coming here every day, right after my run. I'm a little late today. A couple of days after I got the jar and first started leaving flowers, someone else started leaving the fern. I think we just missed her."

Vic gazed around at the other small plots. "Look at these two," she said. They were side by side, brothers. The first one was born on December 18, 1934, and died the next day. The second was born seven months later, and died on his first birthday. Vic said, "Their headstone says, 'These children make bigger the society of angels.' But I'm sure it sounds much better in Polish. Jacek helped me translate it. He didn't like how it came out either."

Then she looked back at the unmarked grave, giving a final touch to the daisies and fern. "Don't they go nicely together?" she said.

At one-thirty I was on the field. Everyone was there except Dariusz, Henry, Jacek Małecki, and Paweł Wawrzniak. While we waited for them, I called the guys together.

"I hope we can shake off that bad mood and play baseball," I said. "Also, Vic wants to take a team picture and I hope you dukes can smile. Mariusz? Pete? Froggy?" I said all their names. "How about it?"

They said they were ready to play, but I could tell something still wasn't right.

"Where are the others?" I said.

Several Sparks hung their heads.

"What's going on, George?"

"Something," he said.

"Well, tell me."

"I don't know how."

Jacek D. said, "It's nothing, Gary. There was an accident. It's best to forget about it."

"George," I said, "please go get Dariusz."

Meantime, the players warmed up. We were at the far end of the field; just inside the fence, sitting on the grass, were the two old gents, the young girls, and the small boys with a bucket of apples. I went over and thanked the old men for coming. I said we were leaving tomorrow. They stood up, bowed, shook my hand, and thanked me, all of us, for coming to Chełmża. They were toothless old men with watery blue eyes and it occurred to me that they were brothers, perhaps even twins. I held out a baseball. Please, I said in Polish, take it. They took turns holding it, very carefully, as if it were precious, breakable—but saying, "Very strong, very strong," and gesturing with fists. "*Amerykański, tak?*" they said. I said yes. "*Dobrze,*" they said solemnly, "*bardzo dobrze,*" and shook my hand again, vigorously, and then returned my gift, insisting that *I* must keep the very strong baseball.

Dariusz came walking across the field like a man who was not happy. I went over to him.

"What's going on?" I said.

"Nothing."

"Bullshit. There was an accident."

"Nothing for you to worry about," he said.

"I'm trying to get our game started and we're a player short. Where are Jacek Małecki and Paweł the Junior?"

"In their rooms."

"Why?"

He shook his head. I called over Jacek D. and asked him to explain the accident.

Dariusz said, "Please, Gary, we are feeling not OK."

Jacek D. said, "Jacek and Paweł were angry. They said words. But now it's finished."

"Are they coming out?"

"I don't know," said Jacek D.

"I've only got seventeen players on the field," I said. "I want eighteen." I started for the Klub.

Jacek D., beside me, said, "Please, Gary, Jacek kicked Paweł in the balls. Now Paweł is resting and Jacek is too ashamed to show his face. We are all ashamed, because you tell us not to fight and we fight."

"What a shitty way to end camp," I said.

"Believe me, I know. We all know."

"OK, let's get an unhappy picture, play an unhappy game, and go back to Warsaw feeling as miserable as possible."

But when Vic came out with her camera, Jacek Małecki and Paweł Wawrzniak also came out, with Henry, who had his arms over their shoulders; and after the game—maybe the best one we played (with Adam and Mark dueling beautifully on the mound, and Piotr Poławski, our philosopher, hauling in a high fly out in right for the final out)—the Sparks and I went swimming. It was a wonderful swim. And how to explain it? And the game? The sudden leap from low to high? Polish life, Coach.

After the swim, Dariusz and Henry threw a party.

Vic and I had gone to many parties that year. We went to student parties where the vodka and the dancing gave out around dawn, where, if you began to feel a lack of energy, it was recommended that fresh pepper be introduced to your glass. We went to parties given by older Poles who set food on the table that cost a month's wages or more—served on their finest plates—and who played Chopin for us on the piano, recited Mickiewicz' verses, got misty-eyed showing us photos of the pope ("Papa") when he came to Gdańsk, and who worried about the future of Poland if America elected a president who was not as tough as Ronald Reagan toward the Soviets. It would be better if Mr. Reagan stayed in office as long as he wished, they said. It was *good*, they said, that he spent so much money on defense. When we pointed out that only so many bombs were necessary to blow up the world and that we already had more than enough, they said yes, yes, but. We also went to parties given by our university colleagues which were not unlike parties given by professors almost everywhere—where about equal measures of *ex cathedra, excursus,* and refreshment obtained—and we went to the official American affairs, where the food and drink was always excellent and plentiful, the settings very nice, but where something often seemed to be missing, something just out of reach—the song you could only remember one line of, the body of the small voice at the other end of the short-wave, saying, *Come in, friend, come in.*

The best party, by far, was the one in Chełmża, in the Pomorzanka, in "the girl from near the sea." We were not anywhere near the sea, but we were close to a lake and moonlight and many other things which move the heart, and we figured we'd go a long way before finding another party like it.

There was food of course—a banquet table of it—and *piwo* and vodka and the Sparks passed a batting helmet for champagne. You can buy a lot of champagne with a batting helmet full of *złoty*s. And there were many speeches—long toasts, really, to baseball and Poland and ourselves—and Mark brought his radio for dancing. He also disappeared briefly and returned with more partners: it would be a shame, he said, if Vic and Sylvia and Sylvia's colleagues became exhausted. Vic, her shoes off, said to him, "Who's exhausted?" To me she said, "I missed my high school prom—no one asked me—but this makes up for it—plus." All the Sparks bowed and begged for the honor of a dance with her—all except Zbyszek. He kept to his place at the table. But he didn't leave; he stayed till the end, raising his glass to the bravery of one and all but especially to the bravery of Henry—who hobbled through a number on his sore toe—and then on the way home, he raised his mitt to the moon, crooning he was going to catch it. We were all together, all around Zbyszek, waiting for the moon to come down in his glove, taking our last evening walk through Chełmża; and I knew we were all there because Dariusz, holding up an imaginary pencil and an imaginary Scoremaster, counted us.

In many ways that's where the story should end. With nineteen Polish baseball players and their founder, plus two specialists for

At the end of our two weeks in Chełmża. In front: Mariusz
Szpirowski. Second row (l–r): Norbert Gajduk, Jacek Kołak (Little
Jacek), Jerzy Biń (George), Piotr Załęcki (Pete), Arkadiusz Lipiec
(July), Paweł Płatek (Capt.). Third row (l–r): Robert Hajdon (Little
Robert), Krzysztof Płatek (Chris), Adam Jaworski, Tomasz
Małkowski (Froggy), Piotr Połowski. Back row (l–r): me, Jacek
Małecki, Robert Szustkowski (Big Robert), Marek Gierasimowicz
(Mark), Andrzej Stankiewicz (Fleetfoot), Henryk Pytlak (Henry),
Zbyszek Sekuła, Paweł Wawrzniak, Dariusz Krzyżanowski, Dariusz
Łuszczyna, Jacek Demkiewicz.

special efforts, waiting for a dramatic catch, a catch unlike any
other, involving earth and heaven. And if I were writing a piece of
fiction, that's where it would end.

But the next day we went back to Warsaw. And the day after
that, August 15, Vicki flew home. She missed her daughters terri-
bly. Dariusz, Jacek D., Henry, George, and Pete were at the airport with flowers to help me see her off. Jacek also gave her a
letter for Gretchen.

"I'm *not* going to bawl, Coach."

"I know you're not."

Henry gave me a tissue to give her.

"I'll see you in October," I said.

"Not unless I see you first."

    Before regular season play resumed on September 4, Dariusz tried to arrange those two exhibition games with the Czech team from Ostrava, but Skra said it couldn't afford to send us there. So he set up a pair with Kutno for the weekend following our return from Chełmża—Saturday in Kutno, Sunday in Warsaw. He and I were both eager to test the results of our training camp; the Sparks seemed eager too. That week I held a couple of light workouts, just to stay loose. Some of the guys said they had work to make up, family gatherings to attend, bruises to heal, and could practice maybe one day, maybe for an hour—but all would be at Centralna on Saturday morning to take the early train to Kutno. I said no problem. I needed to ease off some myself. I'd pitched a lot of batting practice in Chełmża and carried a couple of bruises as well, including a peach on my thigh from one of July's fastballs. (When it struck, my throat closed up, my eyes watered, and I had an immediate and intense inclination to see what surely must be a very large gouge in my thigh; but after all my talk to the Sparks when *they* got hit—hell, American ballplayers don't even rub it—I could only send out a stream of spit, and say, "Throw strikes, July.") I also spent time that week locating a private dentist for Zbyszek. With help from my neighbor Alicja, I got one lined up, and a date set, but Zbyszek didn't come to practice at all. Nor was he at Centralna on Saturday morning; nor were Mark, Pete, Norbert, Mariusz, Jacek Małecki, and the other guys who lived in the Bródno section of Praga. The Bródno Bunch, Pete called them, the gangsters. Only Adam, George, Froggy, Paweł Płatek, and Little Robert showed up at the rendezvous time. Even if I played we'd still be three short for a game. So after the train left without us, Dariusz, puzzled and hurt, telephoned Juan Echevarría and with great embarrassment canceled the two games. I went home, telling Dariusz to call me when he found out what was going on. I couldn't believe, after the euphoria of Chełmża, that we were back to square one.

Sunday morning I sat among the lush purple grapes on my balcony and, listening to the church bells and remembering something one of my students had said, I wrote

"PRIMARILY WE MISS OURSELVES AS CHILDREN"
—a Warsaw student, overheard

I miss the toad poking up in the mud.
I miss mistaking the mud for the toad.
I am now in a house in Poland, I had
oatmeal for breakfast, I had oatmeal for breakfast
in America, in 1942. I was late for school.
Brownie my collie followed me to school.
I sat in a circle, I slept on a rug.
I smelled milk on my fingers, brown pieces of mud.

Go to sleep now, Gary, go to sleep, go to sleep
and when you wake up we'll be at the farm.
The long road to get there, counting telephone poles.
Szostak, Szostak was my grandfather's name,
he lay his head on the cow when he squeezed out
the milk, and the cats came around.
My fat cousin Robert who couldn't say Szostak
said Shoe Stack What's That and pissed

in the mud, pissing and pissing filling a hole.
He's Sleeping, they said, Your Grandpa Is Sleeping.
He picked me up and gave me the reins.
Around and around the hayfield we rode.
Shouting Gee and Haw he patted my head.
He picked me up and gave me the reins.
In a wider and wider circle we rode.
I watched him climb in the apple tree.

Leave Him Be, Grandma said, Leave Him Be.
In late sunlight I followed him down to the creek.
In the late sunlight minnows skittered away.
Like little brown clouds they all moved away.

In the honeyed glow of a kerosene lamp on the table
he opened his book and we all moved away.
He lay his face on the water.
In the last light he entered the water.

On Monday night as I was finishing dinner, Dariusz, Henry,
and Jacek D. appeared at my door with flowers.

"For you, Gary, your birthday!" said Jacek.

Then they sang a Polish song that wished me one hundred
years of health and happiness.

"Only one hundred?" Dariusz laughed.

None of them was feeling much pain. I got a bottle of vodka
from the freezer. After several toasts—to my mother and father, to
my pitching arm, my coaching, "to Gretchen and the little boy,"
and to Vicki—they wanted to go to Old Town for more celebration. But first, Dariusz said, a discussion about the team. He was
all fed up, he said, with handicaps. The exhibition games with
Kutno he'd had to cancel—did I know what they were? They
were *kupa*, he said. The players were little boys, not men. OK.
Here is what we do, he said. They miss practice any more—
except for serious reasons—out! No more bull shit. Finished.
Complete. What did I think? I said fine. He said good. There was
a long silence. Finally he said, "This does not bring happiness,
Gary, but what can we do?"

It turned out, according to Dariusz, that not all of the Bródno
Bunch had purposely missed our Saturday rendezvous. Some had
depended on friends to wake them and were not wakened. Some,
though, had other concerns: Marek needed to meet his cousins
arriving from Canada (also his triceps bruise, he felt, needed
more time to heal); July needed to do something related to his
wedding in September; Mark needed to obtain some important
papers; Big Robert needed to do this, Little Jacek needed to do that.

And Zbyszek? I asked.

Zbyszek was a mystery. No one, Dariusz was deeply puzzled to
say, knew anything.

As for Mark's trip to Italy, Dariusz had a combination to discuss.

What trip to Italy?

Sheepishly, Dariusz explained: A long time ago Mark signed up for a two-week Polish Youth excursion, by bus, to Rome. It had been scheduled for July but, as always in Poland, something went wrong and now the bus was leaving September 1. Which meant of course that Mark would miss our first two games. Dariusz told me (here was his combination) that he could maybe reschedule our first game—against Jastrzębie, a team he feared—and then we'd be without Mark for only Rój-Zory, a team not nearly so strong. He said Jastrzębie might be eager to play us later, because its best hitter was suspended for the first week of September for having put his hands on an umpire in the last game of the season's first half.

"Wait a minute," I said. "How can you and Jastrzębie monkey around with the schedule like that?"

"Maybe we can!"

"So would this mean the Sparks wouldn't play anybody on September 4? That we'd start the second half on September 11 and then go one week longer in October?"

"Yes."

"No," I said. "We'll play Jastrzębie on September 4 and pitch Adam."

"But Gary, Adam maybe is no good."

I had to laugh. "Didn't you see him throw in Chełmża?"

Then Dariusz told me about the glass in Adam's heel, and that an operation to remove it was scheduled for August 25, ten days before the Jastrzębie game.

"He needs ten days—minimum time—to be ready!"

"He'll have them."

"But this is Poland! Who knows when doctor will operate?"

"If Adam's not ready, we'll pitch July and Pete. Or me," I said, pouring out more vodka. "But for sure we're not going to sit on our asses while Mark eats pasta in Rome. Remember: no more *kupa*." I raised my glass to Dariusz, Henry, and Jacek D. "By the way, how did you know it was my birthday?"

"Vicki told us," Jacek said.

That night I dreamt I was on the mound, waiting for a magnificent cock pheasant to get out of the way so I could pitch to Musial.

I had a lot of dreams over the next several weeks—dreams that became more lush, more sensual, closer—and sometimes they were not dreams. There was my dark-haired student Kasia and her marvelous shoulders, performing for me (she confessed later), while her mother, also beautiful, a doctor, gently screwed an acupuncture needle in my hand, saying, "You will feel everywhere a rather pleasant sensation." I did. I was all skin, abuzz, floating, full of wine and horny, watching Kasia slip her sweater off one creamy shoulder, then off the other, cover them up, then bare them both, over and over as if dancing. Her father sat beside her, smoking, proud of his wife's abilities, his daughter's loveliness, and the presence of a professor, an athlete, in his home. This was not a dream—they had invited me to dinner—and yet I dreamed it too. Nor was blonde Irena, the prostitute, a dream. I was living in the Victoria Hotel then, and five nights a week when I stepped from the elevator, there she was in the hallway, on her sofa, waiting. "This time maybe?" Nor was the woman in the riding habit a dream.

Images I had tucked away began to collect themselves—

TO LIVE IN WARSAW

is to look at breasts on the walls.
I'm talking about breasts just waiting
day after day to be held—
from the skinniest side street to the Palace of Culture.
I'm talking about the watch repair shop,
the place you take your key to be copied,
the cubbyhole where serious collectors tweeze rare issues
out of little wax envelopes and catch their breath, the first
air mail, the first Chopin—I'm talking about shimmering
full-color calendar trills on the walls, on walls barely
big enough to hold a whole damn year of the usual
stand-in-line, come-back-tomorrow rigmarole,

let alone simple business. If you can afford it,
go for a piece of garlic chicken, a spare part of anything,
and see what I mean. The other day though,
for a change, I took the Number 2 tram to the zoo—
it was spring, finally, after a long, long winter.
The tram was packed, and I stood squeezed among three
cabbage- and apple-breathed *babcias* heaving their bosoms
and bristling out to the curly white hairs on their furious chins
because a man, also among us and smelling of gin,
was weeping. *Where is his brain? He should be ashamed!*
Like a turtle he pulled his head in a little—
I think he was ashamed—but he continued to weep, he
couldn't help it, lost in a thing he seemed to have lost,
searching his pockets. Wrapped up
several times over so that only their eyes
shone through—like big perfect grapes—two babies
in buggies lay just behind us, fixed between
their pretty mothers. The mothers were both made up
very nicely in rouge and lipstick and lavender hats
whose wide, fashionable brims covered one eye.
They bent down and loosened their babies' blankets
for it was now quite warm on the tram.
The man, too, was dressed rather well
in a suit and tie—his tie a shade of the babies'
blushing cheeks, the suit a suit you'd see
on a businessman back in the States, gray. Sober,
shaved, his hair combed, he'd have been OK maybe,
but he continued to weep, to pull from his pockets
old bus tickets, coins, keys, looking at them
one by one as if they might mean something
other than what they were. All the way across
the river and to the zoo, while the three *babcias* took turns
saying how bad he was, the man examined his bits of
metal and paper, and wiped the quiet
tears rolling out to the end of his nose.
Then the tram stopped and most of us got off.
The day was beautiful still. I saw an elephant stand

on one leg for a piece of popcorn, and a young lion mount
his mother and get nowhere. I saw two seal pups
rolling in mud, rolling over and over, wrapped tight
in their baby-white skins like marvelous cigars,
stogies you can't buy anywhere, squealing,
until they found lunch to suck.

I had a special paper from the university which allowed me to stay in any Polish hotel at the same rate the Poles paid, and though during the year a couple of hotels had grumbled about my paper (certain *robotnik*s were always ready to strut and fret) no one had denied me a room. The Victoria did not deny me either. But the particular clerk I drew when I arrived to check in was not happy to see that I would be staying seven weeks in Poland's best hotel—its international showpiece—at a rate of, in effect, $3 a day, including breakfast. Foreigners—from the West—typically paid $80 or more.

The woman in the riding habit appeared about a week after I'd checked in. I had just come from practice and got on the elevator in the lobby to go up and shower and change for dinner. She got on too. We had the elevator to ourselves. She seemed in a hurry about something, slapping her crop in her palm and sighing heavily. Christina in *her* horsy togs flashed in my head. This woman too was very attractive, like almost all the women you saw in the Victoria—done up to show good fortune, their glittering eyes—and if they were impatient, as this one seemed to be, it only added to their presentation. But I wasn't paying that much attention to her, I still had some things on my mind that I'd brought into the elevator, principally Pizza Hut. He'd been coming to practice the last few days—not to work out, of course, just to visit and watch—and afterwards he'd ride along in the car when Froggy or July dropped me off at the hotel. I was thinking about the pupil of his injured eye; it was easily twice the size of the other one, a large brown berry; and I was thinking about what he said: that he couldn't see so well to the side with it or far ahead. I was also thinking about his big shy grin, a grin harboring no bitterness, when he came across the field and we all gathered around.

"Pizza Hut, how are you?"

"*Kiepawo*"—which made everyone laugh.

"What does that mean?"

"Not so good, not so bad."

He had some color photographs that were taken back in April, by his father, during our season's opener against Jastrzębie. Mainly the pictures show us milling around on a bright green field looking a little lost, as if we are part of a pageant that has gone on without us. I am in almost all of them, tying my shoe laces, drinking from a bottle of mineral water, searching in my duffel bag. In only one photo can you see something of the game: I am standing on the mound with my arm around Adam's shoulders—his head hung in dejection. I thanked Pizza Hut for showing me the pictures. "No, no," Pete said, "he wants you to keep them. For memories of your adventures in Poland."

At the sixth floor—my floor—I got off the elevator. Irena was not there yet to show me that look that said very little in this world could make her happy. The woman in the riding habit also got off.

"Excuse me," she said, "but where is the restaurant?"

I told her there were two—one on the main floor, one on the second.

"You are living here?"

"I am."

"And you are a sportsman?"

I told her I coached the Warsaw baseball team. She told me she was just in Hungary for volleyball. Then speaking very fast she told me she had to meet someone, how long it would take she couldn't imagine, she had no interest in this meeting, none, she was in room 330 (she showed me her key), I could maybe come there later or she could come to my room, whichever I preferred, OK? Then she was back on the elevator, slapping the crop in her palm, smiling and saying she would come to my room, bye bye, as the door closed.

The next day, which was Saturday, September 3, a chartered bus took the Sparks down to Silesia, to face Jastrzębie. Adam, who had had his operation on schedule and worked out with the team on Thursday and Friday, said he felt strong, he could pitch, no problem. Blackie, back from Japan, refreshed by the Orient, said he also felt strong. All week he had been telling me that, and whacking hell out of the ball to prove it. "What did you do in Japan?" I asked him. "I breathed," he said, flashing a smile. All the Sparks were smiling. We didn't have Mark; we didn't have Marek (his cousins from Canada invited him to go back with them and he went); we didn't have the Cubans (whose absence Dariusz considered a handicap, though Captain Paweł did not). Nor did we have enough Juniors to play a preliminary game—which was too bad. But we had beautiful, warm, dreamy fall weather and clear skies over Silesia. All that blue up there was no doubt due to the miners' strike, and though the strike seemed to be settled now, and though the dirt might—probably would—come back, for the moment at least things were looking pretty OK. The Sparks whooped at the Milicja vans leaving Silesia, giving them the finger and singing. They felt relief, the renewal of hope, for the moment—which was all they could have—but in the midst of that moment they felt they could beat Jastrzębie this time, beat anybody. Having caught their rhythm, and having lucked past the woman in the riding habit and maybe a couple of nights in jail—or worse—I felt the same way.

She knocked on my door two minutes after I had returned from dinner. She didn't wait for an invitation but strode on in, still in her riding get-up though minus the whip.

"Where shall I sit?" she said, not really asking. "Ah, here, I think," she decided and took the sofa. Almost at once she popped back up, pulled the window drapes together—"Much better, no?"—then returned to the sofa, sighed, and removed her black velvet helmet. She had blonde hair fixed in a bun. She crossed her legs.

"Now," she said, "please," and patted the cushion beside her.

Still standing, I said, "This is very nice, your coming here, but what is it you want?"

"Yes, yes, very nice. Nice room, like mine"—opening her hand to show me her key again: to *really* show me she was truly a guest, not a hooker—"but tell me, where are you from?"

"Iowa. Where are *you* from?"

"I don't know this I-oh-wah—a pity—please, you are not comfortable, sit. You have dollars, we can change money, have fun." She recrossed her legs and, after glancing at the bed, looked at me, stroking the velvet helmet in her lap.

Why it had taken me this long to figure out the game, I don't know. But it was clear to me now that as soon as I had her marked *złoty*s in my pocket and my pants off, we'd have company.

"*Szkoda*," I said.

"*Szkoda?*"

I wanted to tell her she had very nice equipment and that yes, *szkoda*, it was too bad she was either a stool pigeon or a spy trying to get me booted from my nice room; but all I said was I needed sleep, I had a long bus ride to Silesia in the morning. I opened the door. As she passed by, sighing and looking at me sidelong—her face painfully pretty—I almost pulled her back.

At breakfast on Sunday morning in Rybnik, where the ladies in their misty smocks served us tomatoes and eggs and tea, and where the sky was blue, Dariusz was telling me he had slept with a beautiful dream. "You listen, Gary. Many, many home runs—all by Warsaw—and much good grass, very green, very smooth. I don't want to leave it, you understand?" At the next table, July, Big Robert, and Jacek D. were discussing the verb *ruchać* (to fuck). Hearing them, Dariusz said, "Little boys."

July said, "It is a Russian word, not Polish."

Big Robert said, "*Ruchać.*"

"You see," said July, "he says it 'roo-hots'—like they do in the northeast region that is now Russian."

"We lost the war," said Jacek, "but not our language. Our language is strong."

"*Ruchać*," Big Robert said.

"Still Russian," said July.

"But he does not have Russian," said Jacek. "Only Polish and Spanish."

"A mystery," said July.

"No mystery," said Dariusz. "Big Robert is like dog. Every day he must *ruchać*. It is his trick."

We got 10 hits and 12 walks against Jastrzębie, plus 4 men on base via errors, for a total of 26 runners. The coal miners got 17 hits, 8 walks, and 2 on via errors—or 27 runners. That's a lot of activity on a green field under a brilliant sky on a Sunday afternoon perfect for strolling and dreaming and feeling hopeful, feeling anything deeply. I remember looking at Dariusz in the seventh inning as he sat on our bench making furious marks in his Scoremaster, and thinking, for just an instant, of an artist I used to see on Sundays in the Place des Vosges drawing the white stone mount under Louis XIII, filling his big sketch pad with dozens of charging, leaping, flying horses, page after page in the bright Paris light, while young mothers in spike-heeled pumps paraded round and round the monument, pushing their sleeping babies. The Sparks in that inning were trailing 15–6, dangerously close to a knock down. But they came up to bat and, in the role they were born to, struck back, as driven as the man in the Place des Vosges who may indeed have been a Pole, an émigré like all the other Poles I had met in Paris, longing for the homeland, or an idea of the homeland, where Chopin's waltzes issued daily from the radio, where Mickiewicz' verses burned in almost every brain, and where farmers still used horses to break the soil and haul their produce, their coal, themselves and their loved ones. Thirteen Sparks came to the plate in that seventh inning and Dariusz recorded their flights as some people record rare birds, musical notes. He was red from the sun and his passion. He was urging us on with his ballpoint like a man with a baton, calling for more boom from the tympani, more sweetness from the strings. He wanted to win—no doubt about that—but more deeply he was in this thing, whatever it was, for the beauty. Like Kant he knew, or felt, I'm sure, that happiness did not come from reason but from the imagination. We had scored seven times and had the bases loaded and nobody was out, and simple arithmetic told us that when those three runners came in we'd be ahead, 16–15. But what we were most alive to right then was something else. Winning was not it, we expected to win. "Remember Górnik!" I kept hearing the Sparks yell, and my own brain, or part of it, was back there too, re-running our big inning—seeing George kiss his bat twice, seeing Blackie cross the plate in a handstand—and now in the seventh inning against Jastrzębie I was crooning, "No problem, no problem." Just like Dariusz. But what filled our blood was something larger, imagination, style, the charge for the castle that was rightfully ours, and I, caught in this thing as much as the Sparks were, signaled for Blackie to lay down a bunt, a squeeze, because Jastrzębie wouldn't expect it, not from a man who swung from his heels, from so far back you could almost see eleven hundred years of Polish history flash past. He bunted the ball—too hard—straight to the mound. The pitcher threw home for one out, the catcher fired to first for the double play. The next Spark popped up. It all took about two minutes and we were stunned. Worse, our juice was gone, and with it the mazurkas and burning verses, the flying horses and charging knights in our hearts. The last two innings we couldn't even get a man on base. Having followed our passion and lost, we could only go back to where we came from.

The following weekend we returned to Silesia to play Rój-Zory. We took the train—Skra for some reason was unable to rent a bus for us—and this time we won, 25–9, in a five-inning knock down. Mariusz hit a grand slam—the first ever for a Spark— and Adam, after a couple of innings to find his groove, settled down and was near-perfect. But the game was so devoid of conflict, so easy to capture, we didn't even take showers.

The weather that Sunday was near-perfect too, and the Rój-Zory field, beside a cemetery, where a little breeze came from, smelled of roses and carnations, and I thought of the girl in the yellow dress and ill-fitting shoes I had seen the day before in Katowice. The team had had to change trains in Katowice and since we had an hour to kill, we walked over to Old Town, and there she was, tall and uncertain and wearing a white ribbon in her hair. The street, the buildings all around, had the color and feel of a huge coal cellar from which the coal had been shoveled out and now people were attempting to live there. She came toward us in all that sooty gray as if none of it existed or mattered, as if the world were new and exciting and though it didn't quite fit her yet, or she it, she knew everything would soon be good and fine and, please God, don't let me fail. Her yellow dress was made of a shiny material and had padded shoulders and perhaps someone in the Forties had witnessed a wedding in it—in Connecticut or L.A.—and then put it in a box, along with soap and chocolate and vitamins, and then sent it here to this poor place where hope was small. Perhaps the red shoes, whose heels seemed long and sharp as spikes, were in the same box, a box thrust in a cellar after the soap and chocolate and vitamins were taken out, and there it waited until this girl appeared, this girl feeling a new strangeness, a flowering. She was about sixteen, and if the Sparks noticed her they said nothing. Tall and thin and awkward, she was only a girl pretending perhaps to be something she was not.

I thought about her on the train later, and that night, and on Sunday when the sweet scents of roses and carnations came across the Rój-Zory diamond from the cemetery next door. I thought about her a few days later when Irena turned my hand over to read my fortune, and I thought about her the following weekend, outside the train station in Łódź, while Pete and Mark played catch for their pretty admirers and Jacek D. was lonesome for Gretchen and July told me about the famous Rita of Szczecin who drove a Porsche and knew everything. I also thought about her one Saturday after I ran into Zbyszek on Marszałkowska Avenue; I hadn't seen him since Chełmża—none of the Sparks had—and when I said we missed him and wondered if he was ever coming back, he only shrugged and said he didn't know. I wanted to tell him that whatever he decided, I would never forget our last night in Chełmża when he tried to catch the moon, but I didn't trust my Polish enough. Nor did I trust it enough to mention the dentist. He said he had to go to work, and we shook hands. After he boarded his tram I regretted not taking him by the shoulders and barking, "Now, God damn it, about those rotten teeth—" But how can you do something like that? And how can you wrap your arms around a young girl in the street, a stranger, and tell her she is beautiful and that you love her?

Following our game with Rój-Zory, Dariusz told me that there were two changes in the schedule. First, we would not be playing the next Sunday—September 18—because that weekend there was a big tournament in Silesia, with the national teams of Italy, the Netherlands, Sweden, Austria, and Czechoslovakia coming to play the four Polish national teams. He was very excited and happy to announce that I had been selected to coach the "B" team—composed of players from Warsaw and Kutno—and that I must choose eight Sparks. I chose Mariusz, Pete, Adam, Mark, Froggy, Norbert, Paweł, and George. Paweł and George couldn't go, it turned out—Paweł's brother Chris was getting married, George's parents said he had to study—so I substituted July and Big Robert. As for the other schedule change, Dariusz said that our game against Cyprzanów—slated for September 25—was moved to October 30, the day before All Souls. I remembered how bitterly cold it had been the previous All Souls, and I wondered about the wisdom of playing that late in the year, but I said nothing. I was surprised at myself—later—that I hadn't complained about the Cyprzanów date being changed, or even asked why.

After I took the electric train back to Warsaw from Łódź— instead of going to Silesia on the night train with Pete, Mark, and Mariusz and coaching the "B" team—I gave my hand to Irena who wanted to read my fortune. She said I had a long life and could expect to have luck, but then, of course, why not, I was an American.

"Even so," she added, "it seems you can be passionate."

"Where did you learn English?" I said.

"Everywhere."

"If you don't get a client," I said, "I'll buy you a drink later."

She gave me my hand back.

"Go away," she said.

"I didn't mean to upset you."

"I lied. You can be passionate, true. But also like ice."

Back in my room I got a beer out of the refrigerator, and turned on the television. There was Vic—looking at some photographs with another woman. Vic was saying, ". . . this dress is much too long . . . this blouse is ugly . . . no, no, no, these shoes won't do . . . we must change everything."

"But here, this outfit is rather attractive," the other woman said, "and the model has a nice smile too."

"We're not in the nice smile business," Vic snapped, "we're in the fashion business!"

It was the TV movie she'd been invited to play the bitchy American in, and I had to laugh: she was bitchy—almost—as the witch in *The Wizard of Oz* is witchy. But a lot prettier, and I missed her. I missed her even more when I remembered the story of Amaretta. Vic had gone to a department store that was going out of business, to buy some manikins. "I had this idea to build a doll," she said, "and I figured manikins were like cars—you know, mass-produced—and that their parts were interchangeable. I'd buy several and use the parts I liked best. Well, when I got them home and started in I learned it wouldn't be easy. I finally got this great dame built, though, and my mother, who doesn't drink of course— her church forbids it—named her Amaretta. After Amaretto, that sweet liqueur. She'd discovered a wonderful recipe for cheese cake that uses a little of it. Or—now that I think about it—maybe she discovered the liqueur first and saw the recipe on the label. Anyway, she became very attached to the word, though, as you see, she changed it a little."

"That story's all over the place," I said.

"Maybe."

"What's the point?"

"How about romance?"

On Saturday of that same weekend that I didn't go to Silesia, I put on my new blue suit and went to Old Town, to see Chris Płatek get married. I went to three churches and saw three weddings in progress, but none was Chris'. I walked around for a while among the strolling couples. I ate an ice cream cone. When the stars came out I went back to the Victoria.

Irena hadn't arrived yet, so I sat on the sofa across from the elevator on my floor to wait. I felt warm in the suit. It was wool, with a vest. A tailor who had survived the Uprising and Auschwitz made it for me, a man who had only two words in English, "hello" and "good." I'd gone to his shop thinking I might have a sportcoat made; I pointed to a picture of one in an old copy of *Der Spiegel* on his cutting table. He shook his head no and made me this navy blue suit and pronounced it good.

Irena stepped out of the elevator. Her blonde hair fell to her shoulders, her blue eyes, rimmed by green liner, brightened briefly when she saw me, then assumed their usual expectation of defeat. She wore a blue polka dot dress and black mesh nylons. She walked straight to the sofa, sank down beside me, sighed, crossed her legs, and began to appraise her red nails.

"Hello," I said.

"You again," she said, still looking at her nails.

"You used to ask me, 'This time maybe?'"

"I know you better now. A cold man."

"I was hoping you would have dinner with me," I said.

She sighed heavily, and recrossed her legs. Still not looking at me, she said, "You are dressed like a diplomat tonight. Very pretty."

"Thank you," I said. "You look pretty too."

"Why are you dressed this way?"

I told her about Chris' wedding and not being able to find it.

Slowly she looked at me. "I see," she said. Then, returning to her nails, "Maybe you will find a wedding in America. Or a, you know, when someone dies. You are dressed for that too in your pretty American suit."

"As a matter of fact," I said, "this pretty suit was made by a Polish tailor." I told her about my neighbor in Żoliborz who had been in the Uprising and who told me about a friend of his, a tailor, and what he had been through. "He's a master, an artist," I said. "That's why I had the suit made. He's the last of a kind."

After a long moment, Irena shrugged and said, "Politics."

"Well, maybe," I said.

"But a beautiful suit just the same."

"How about dinner?"

"Go, please."

I went to my room, drank a beer, and came back. A short dark man with red jowls and a big nose was standing before her, rocking on his toes. I moved next to his ear. "I can have your thumbs broken," I said, wiggling my thumbs in his face. "Do you understand?"

He looked at Irena. She closed her eyes. Then all puffed up, as if he'd been greatly insulted, he disappeared around a corner.

"Let's go eat," I said.

"I do not need a manager," she said, "from America."

"Open your eyes."

"Go away."

"No."

Tuesday afternoon I was not eager for practice. On one side I felt guilty for not going down to Silesia for the tournament, and on the other I figured, hell, since our next game wasn't until October 2—two weeks from then—probably only a few guys would be there anyway. But mainly I felt guilty and not eager to face Dariusz.

I took a bus to Łazienki Park and walked under the leaves beginning to turn. I went down to the pavilion where you could see pictures of Warsaw before, during, and after the war. The horse-drawn, parasoled elegance turned to piles of brick and stone, the bricks and stones picked up, one by one, and put back, as close as possible, to where they were before. I thought of Christina standing at my door in her two pairs of lips, of Irena making a perfect impression of her lips on a napkin, of Zbyszek stealing home and coming up from his belly-slide smiling. I thought of him trying to catch the moon, of all of us trying to catch the moon.

At Skra, I learned from Pete and Mark, who arrived early, that Italy, Czechoslovakia, Sweden, and Austria had not appeared for the tournament, only a team from the Netherlands was there. I also learned that the "B" team—coached by Juan Echevarría in my absence—played four games and that Juan used Kutno guys almost exclusively. He put Mariusz, Mark, and Adam in two games, for two innings each, and did not play Pete, Froggy, or Norbert at all.

I said I was sorry to hear that.

Pete shrugged. Mark said, "It's only normal."

When Dariusz arrived, he came over to me and said, "Gary, you listen. Big no good plan with Kutno. Fuck Walter Szymański!" Then he shook my hand and beamed, "I am happy to see you."

"Same here."

"Same, yes. We are OK now."

After Irena and I left the Victoria we walked over to Old Town. If she didn't mind, I said, I wanted to look in a church there; maybe, earlier, I'd been wrong about the time of Chris' wedding; maybe it was now, I said.

"Why not," she sighed, "I am already a fool."

We came to the Cathedral of St. John the Baptist, Warsaw's oldest church. We stood in the cobblestone street looking at the dark portal, the half dozen teenagers milling on the steps eating ice cream cones, wrapped in their youth.

"This is where I was told," I said.

"Then go look," Irena said.

I took her hand and we went up the steps. Inside, up at the front, the main altar was lit but not for business—the rosy light there came mainly from votive candles—and off to the side at a crypt of some sort, illuminated by a spotlight, a few tiny women swathed in black knelt on the stone floor with their heads bowed. Among the odors of candle wax and old wood I could smell Irena's perfume—a scent like cherry brandy. She pulled her hand from my grasp, genuflected toward the tabernacle, and left.

I caught up with her in the street.

"You can walk fast on these stones," I said.

"So—no marriage."

"So let's eat."

"I am not hungry."

I led her to a restaurant just up ahead called Kamienne Schodki. It served only roast duck and red wine, and only candles were used to light the place. When the wine came, I raised my glass.

"Here's to your pretty eyes—but not to your sour expression."

"Why do you mock me?"

"I'm not mocking you, Irena."

"There was no marriage."

"I was told there was."

"I don't believe you."

She looked at the ceiling as if something threatening were about to fall down.

"I'm beginning to feel stiff holding my glass like this," I said. "Won't you join me in a toast?"

"What do you want of me?"

"A toast first, discussion later."

Sighing, she picked up her glass and I touched it with mine.

"*Na zdrowie,*" I said.

"*Na zdrowie.*"

Then she blotted her lips, and said, "So discuss."

"Unless I've lost my eye," I said, "I'd say you were about twenty-four. That's how old my daughter is. She has a smile I love to see. But she is not here and I'm hoping I can get you to smile in her place. That's it. That's what I want of you."

Irena's face softened; a little smile appeared, as if she couldn't help it. She was suddenly a very pretty young woman with blue eyes and hair bright as wheat, and all the rouge, eye liner, lipstick, and powder seemed only so much useless camouflage. Her own color and candlelight would be enough, would be plenty, to make most men feel weak and happy.

"Thank you," I said.

"For what?"

"For quite a lot."

"I don't understand," she said. "Does this mean, yes, you want to be with me tonight, or no?"

I missed Chris' wedding because it was on Friday, not Saturday. It was July's wedding that took place on Saturday—the following weekend.

Jacek D. picked me up at the Victoria in a taxi. With him were July's younger brother, Jacek L., and Jacek L.'s wife, Barbara.

"Too many Jaceks in Poland, Gary," said Jacek D. "We will call this one Jack. He speaks English too, but Barbara says she does not. I think she lies."

"It's a question of confidence," said Jack.

I got in back with Jack and Barbara. Jacek sat in front. I shook hands with Barbara, a petite blonde who could have been Irena's happy sister.

"Jack is my best friend," said Jacek. "We went to school together."

"That's true," said Jack.

As we passed the main Milicja station, Jacek said to Jack, "Maybe you would be kind to us and explain about that place."

Jack turned to me. "This is a joke that I am ashamed to tell," he said. "But I can tell it if you like."

"It's up to you," I said.

We arrived at the building where, at two o'clock, July's and Agnieszka's civil wedding would take place. On the sidewalk out front we met Froggy, who carried a bouquet of flowers. Jacek said, "My god, I don't have flowers. I must go buy some." The rest of us waited in front of the building, a gray boxy structure similar to all the others on that street. The sky everywhere was blue. Froggy, indicating my suit, said, "*Bardzo.*"

Jack said, "I will tell the joke now. You see, I had a choice—to serve my country in the Army or be in the Milicja. You know about the Milicja of course. Everyone hates them." He paused, and smiled at his wife. She knew what he was talking about. She reached up and affectionately fussed a moment with his hair. Like July, Jack had thinning blond hair and combed it forward to cover a high forehead. Also like his brother he had a relaxed manner that suggested he hadn't quite wakened from a nap.

"I was nineteen," he went on. "I didn't want to be a soldier, so I joined the Milicja. For one year I walked on the street in that uniform carrying a stick. Then for two years I was in Milicja school. Then I left them."

"How?"

"I failed my exams."

Barbara was smiling at Froggy who, his nose in his flowers, was smiling back.

"They just let you go?" I said.

"Oh no. After I failed my exams, I had to write letters to my chief, and letters to another chief. They fought me. I fought too. Believe me, it was very difficult."

"Do many Milicja feel as you did? Do they hate being policemen?"

Jack gave this thought. Then, slowly, he said, "I must tell you no. They have fear, yes, but they do not hate it. Many are from the villages, you understand. They would be farmers, poor farmers. In the Milicja they have a nice place to live, money, they can go about, maybe, and see things."

Jacek came across the street with a single rose. He said, "I found this on the ground. It's all I can find."

"Maybe later I will tell you more," Jack said to me. "Now we must go inside."

We climbed two flights of stairs. It was like any other office building in Warsaw—long hallways with official windows to line up in front of, grimy windows to look out of.

On the second floor I saw Dariusz and Henry. They stood among a small group of people waiting in front of an open door. Through the door I could see another group belonging to another wedding party. In Poland you line up to get married too.

Dariusz and Henry shook hands with us, Henry rolling his eyes at my suit, feeling the lapel, and Dariusz saying yes, yes, very nice, then unzipping his shoulder bag and taking out two Polish newspapers. Excited, he read to me the baseball scores from the Olympics in Seoul: Puerto Rico vs. Japan, the U.S. vs. Holland.

"For you," he said.

I thanked him for the papers, wishing I had worn cooler clothes. I was sweating.

Indicating the woman he was with, Dariusz said, "This is my friend Barbara, from Lublin. A very good woman."

Like Jack's Barbara, who stood beside her, this Barbara was also blonde, though not so petite. She was blushing.

"Are you a baseball fan?" I asked her.

"No English," Dariusz said, "but a very fine woman." He too was blushing. Everyone in our little circle seemed to be—Henry, Froggy, the other Barbara, even Jacek and his best friend Jack, whose joke was on hold. And there we stood in an office building, waiting for a Polish wedding. A Polish wedding, to me, meant a big hall, tables of food, kegs of beer, and a floor full of dancers whooping it up to a polka. It meant toot and stomp and the bride in the middle feeding her husband the first piece of cake, everyone kissing, dancing with aunts and uncles and cousins, shots of whiskey waiting on the bar, and the bridesmaids kicking their shoes off, the men untying their ties, going all afternoon. Going outside later and smelling the boutonniere on your chest, the grass under your feet, and if someone had a ball and a couple of gloves and you weren't too drunk—or even if you were, what the hell—throwing a few pitches, showing your stuff.

Of course that was the reception. Too warm in my suit, I was rushing things.

In the room where July's and Agnieszka's wedding took place, they sat side by side in separate chairs facing a man behind a desk. He wore a black robe like a judge. The rest of us sat or stood behind the bride and groom. July wore an oatmeal-colored suit, Agnieszka a light blue suit. The official asked them, "Are you satisfied?" They said yes. He asked a few more questions—I don't know what they were, but the answers were yes—and then Dariusz whispered, "Complete."

An organist and a violinist in the back of the room played something that sounded classical, allegro. In a line we went up to congratulate the newlyweds. Agnieszka—who attended the Sports Academy, where she played basketball—stood an inch or two taller than July; she had red hair and full, ruddy cheeks. Everyone kissed her hand and then, three times, her cheeks, and everyone kissed July three times on his cheeks. After that we were handed a glass of champagne by a clerk; we all sang the Polish song wishing them one hundred years of health and happiness—and Dariusz nudged me, "Only one hundred?"

That was it. We left to let the next wedding in.

Outside, July, laid back as always, said he planned to have a party tomorrow, at his place, but for now he must attend a family dinner at his in-laws' apartment. He and Agnieszka drove off, taking Jack and Barbara with them.

Froggy, Jacek, Henry, Dariusz, Barbara from Lublin, and I stood on the sidewalk. Jacek laughed, and immediately said, "I don't know what's so funny." Henry said we must go have a drink. Dariusz took out a piece of paper; on it, in a column, were written Kolejarz, Górnik, Kutno, Silesia Rybnik, and Cyprzanów. He said, "For sure three wins. And maybe—maybe—two more." He looked at me for a confirmation of his opinion.

As things turned out, the Sparks lost to Kolejarz and Kutno— the two away games—but defeated Górnik, Silesia Rybnik, and Cyprzanów. The victory over Rybnik—and Jan Cnota—was especially satisfying. Trailing 14–5 in the seventh, the Sparks scored 10 runs in the last 3 innings to defeat, on grass, without tricks, the heretofore perennial league champions. But Warsaw deposed them, 15–14. And the following Sunday—All Souls Eve—knocked off Cyprzanów and its fine pitcher, Janusz Rzytki, 16–6. So the Sparks won their last two games of the season in style against the two teams that previously, and for years, were ranked first and second; and they did it after being knocked down—humiliated—by Kutno, 25–2. They didn't quit. I know how they did it—I have all the score sheets from those games— but I can only imagine how they looked because when Dariusz turned to me for a confirmation of his opinion of how the Sparks might fare in their last five games, I told him I was going home.

He said he—and the others—would walk with me there; it was a fine day and maybe we would have a drink.

"Not the Victoria, Dariusz, the U.S.A."

"A shock," he said.

I tried to say why I was leaving, but Dariusz stopped me.

"I know," he said. "You must."

My last week in Poland—which was the last week of September—the hardwoods in Łazienki Park were red and gold, the seal pups at the Warsaw Zoo had lost their white fur and were gray as their mothers, and the city's buses were packed as usual— with the usual *babcia* or two on board keeping their eyes on standards. I could have used their strength—or patience—on the day I left. The team had come to the airport to see me off, Anna and Jacek Mydlarski were there too, all of them standing in line with me. When my turn came to enter the inspection aisle, where they could not go, I kissed Anna and shook everyone's hand again and made the promises you make and plan to keep.

I showed my papers to the Milicja in his booth. He said I needed my Polish visa application. I pointed out to him, as I had pointed out to another cop when I flew to Rome at Christmas, that all the information on my visa application form had been transferred by Polish authorities, as per government regulation, to my passport. *Dobrze*, that cop had said, and let me through. But this cop wanted the application form. OK, I said, give me one and I'll fill it out. He said he didn't have one. Well, where could I get one? He said he didn't know. He said to get out of the way so others could pass. I was standing with my bags in the narrow aisle; jammed behind me were a dozen or more Poles, with their belongings, and behind them were my friends, waving and smiling and calling out final good wishes. I was sweating.

Look, I told the cop, I can't move. He shrugged. Too bad, his face said. All the heat in my body shot to my head. I started swearing. I called him and his system everything I could think of—if I was thinking—but there were the words, I could hear them, and what was worse I could see myself carrying on like a madman, could see Dariusz too, and all the others, and how helpless they felt. I wanted to reach in the booth and grab the cop, and I might have, but there was Anna suddenly beside me—how she managed to squeeze past the crowd, I don't know—asking what the problem was. Then she was gone. I continued to rage—at the pointlessness, at the God damn this and the God damn that. "*Spokojnie*, Gary. *Spokojnie*." It was Dariusz, crooning to me across the distance; and he kept it up, like a songbird, until Anna, that magician, came back with the paper I needed.

*The Sparks sent me home with a sabre. Crouched in front are Norbert
(left) and Krzysztof Jurek. Standing (from left) are Paweł Płatek,
Fleetfoot, Adam, Mariusz, Froggy, George, Dariusz, Henry, and
Jacek D. George is holding another gift: a copper plate bearing an
embossed mermaid.*

      On my next-to-last day in Poland I had gone to practice
as usual. All of the Sparks were there—plus a new guy named
Krzysztof (Chris) Jurek who had a very good arm and could run
and who wore a cap that said "U.S.A." on it. Dariusz said that
Chris looked American, not Polish.

"Why?" I said.

"He is always smiling, like you. Happy boy."

We both laughed.

I gave my Tigers cap to Pete, my duffel bag to Froggy, and
copies of my books to the readers. I offered my jockstrap as well,
but the Sparks said I must keep that for next time.

Their gift to me was a sword with my name on it.

BOOKS BY GARY GILDNER

POETRY
Blue Like the Heavens: New & Selected Poems 1984
The Runner 1978
Nails 1975
Digging for Indians 1971
First Practice 1969

LIMITED EDITIONS
Jabón 1981
Letters from Vicksburg 1976
Eight Poems 1973

FICTION
The Second Bridge 1987
A Week in South Dakota 1987
The Crush 1983

MEMOIR
The Warsaw Sparks 1990

ANTHOLOGY
Out of This World: Poems from the Hawkeye State 1975